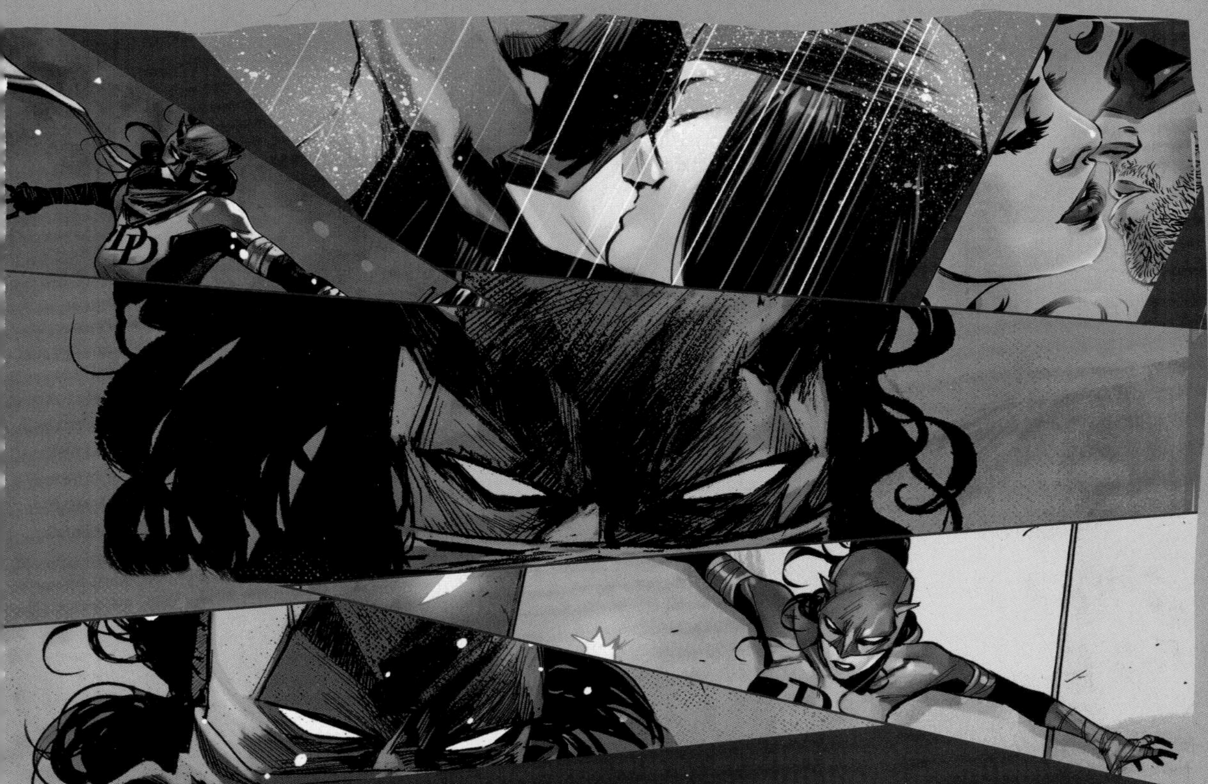

DAREDEVIL
WOMAN WITHOUT FEAR

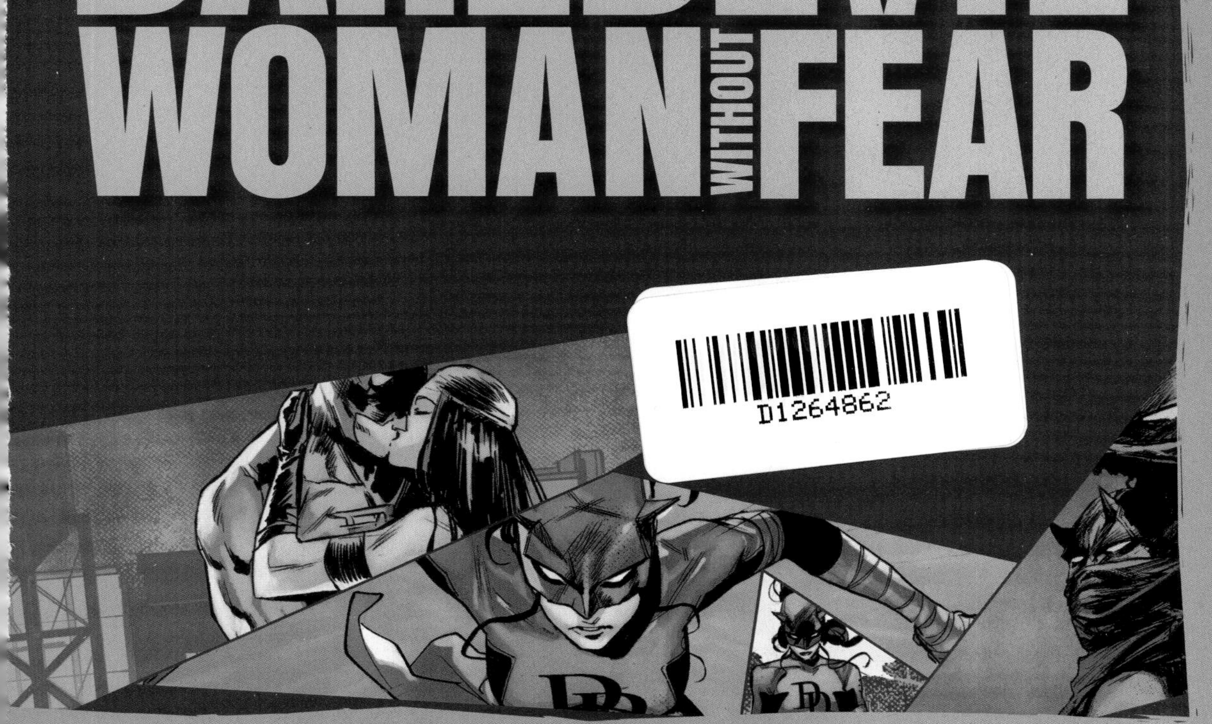

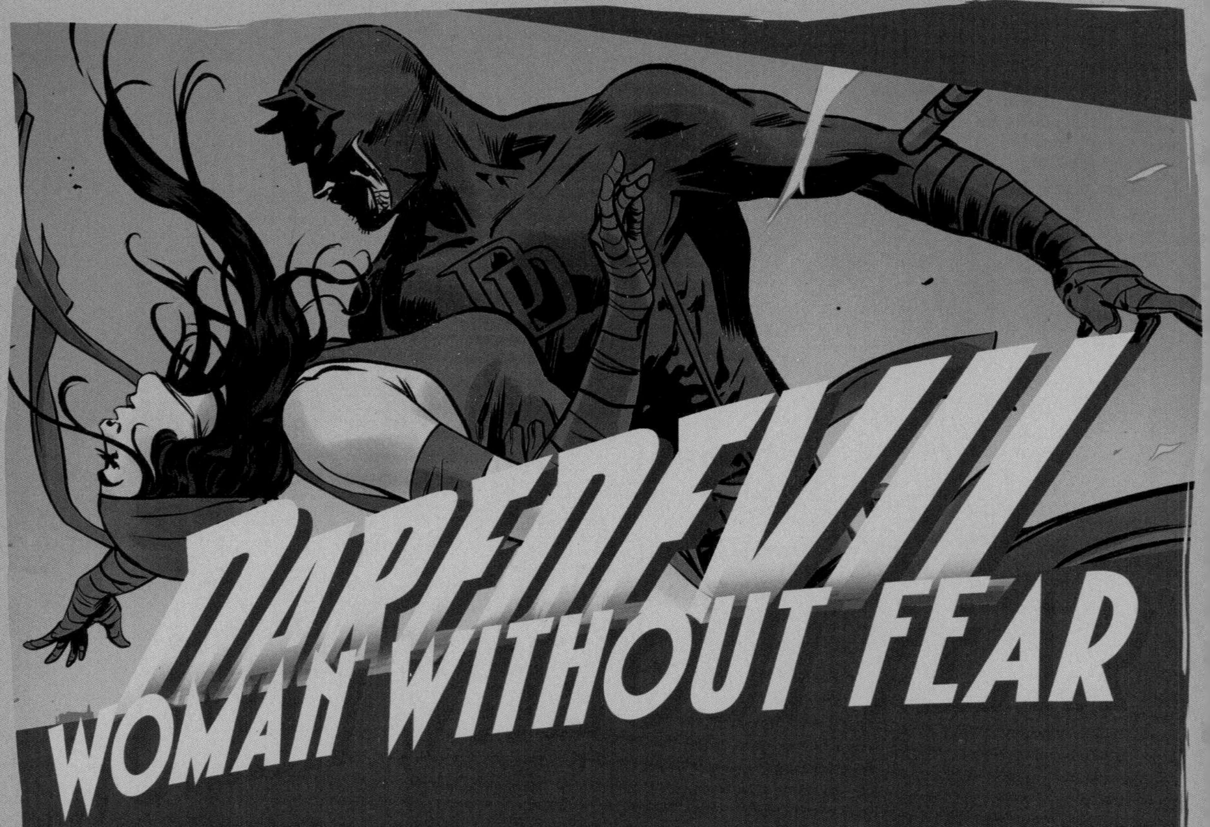
DAREDEVIL
WOMAN WITHOUT FEAR

***Daredevil: Woman Without Fear* #1-3**

Chip Zdarsky
WRITER

Rafael De Latorre
ARTIST

Federico Blee
COLOR ARTIST

VC's Clayton Cowles
LETTERER

Chris Bachalo
COVER ART

***Elektra* #100**

Ann Nocenti
WRITER

Sid Kotian
ARTIST

Edgar Delgado
COLOR ARTIST

VC's Clayton Cowles
LETTERER

Dan Panosian
COVER ART

"Waltz"

Declan Shalvey
WRITER

Stefano Raffaele
ARTIST

Rachelle Rosenberg
COLOR ARTIST

VC's Clayton Cowles
LETTERER

***Daily Bugle* Funny Pages**

By Ty Templeton

"Mini Marvels"

By Chris Giarrusso

Tom Groneman
ASSOCIATE EDITOR

Devin Lewis
EDITOR

COLLECTION EDITOR — DANIEL KIRCHHOFFER
ASSISTANT MANAGING EDITOR — MAIA LOY
ASSOCIATE MANAGER, TALENT RELATIONS — LISA MONTALBANO
DIRECTOR, PRODUCTION & SPECIAL PROJECTS — JENNIFER GRÜNWALD
VP PRODUCTION & SPECIAL PROJECTS — JEFF YOUNGQUIST

BOOK DESIGNER — SARAH SPADACCINI
SENIOR DESIGNER — JAY BOWEN
SVP PRINT, SALES & MARKETING — DAVID GABRIEL
EDITOR IN CHIEF — C.B. CEBULSKI

DAREDEVIL: WOMAN WITHOUT FEAR. Contains material originally published in magazine form as DAREDEVIL: WOMAN WITHOUT FEAR (2022) #1-3 and ELEKTRA (2022) #100. First printing 2022. ISBN 978-1-302-93493-4. Published by MARVEL WORLDWIDE, INC., a subsidiary of MARVEL ENTERTAINMENT, LLC. OFFICE OF PUBLICATION: 1290 Avenue of the Americas, New York, NY 10104. **Printed in Canada.** KEVIN FEIGE, Chief Creative Officer; DAN BUCKLEY, President, Marvel Entertainment; JOE QUESADA, EVP & Creative Director; DAVID BOGART, Associate Publisher & SVP of Talent Affairs; TOM BREVOORT, VP, Executive Editor; NICK LOWE, Executive Editor, VP of Content, Digital Publishing; DAVID GABRIEL, VP of Print & Digital Publishing; MARK ANNUNZIATO, VP of Planning & Forecasting; JEFF YOUNGQUIST, VP of Production & Special Projects; ALEX MORALES, Director of Publishing Operations; DAN EDINGTON, Director of Editorial Operations; RICKEY PURDIN, Director of Talent Relations; JENNIFER GRÜNWALD, Director of Production & Special Projects; SUSAN CRESPI, Production Manager; STAN LEE, Chairman Emeritus. For information regarding advertising in Marvel Comics or on Marvel.com, please contact Vit DeBellis, Custom Solutions & Integrated Advertising Manager, at vdebellis@marvel.com. For Marvel subscription inquiries, please call 888-511-5480. **Manufactured between 5/6/2022 and 6/7/2022 by SOLISCO PRINTERS, SCOTT, QC, CANADA.**

10 9 8 7 6 5 4 3 2 1

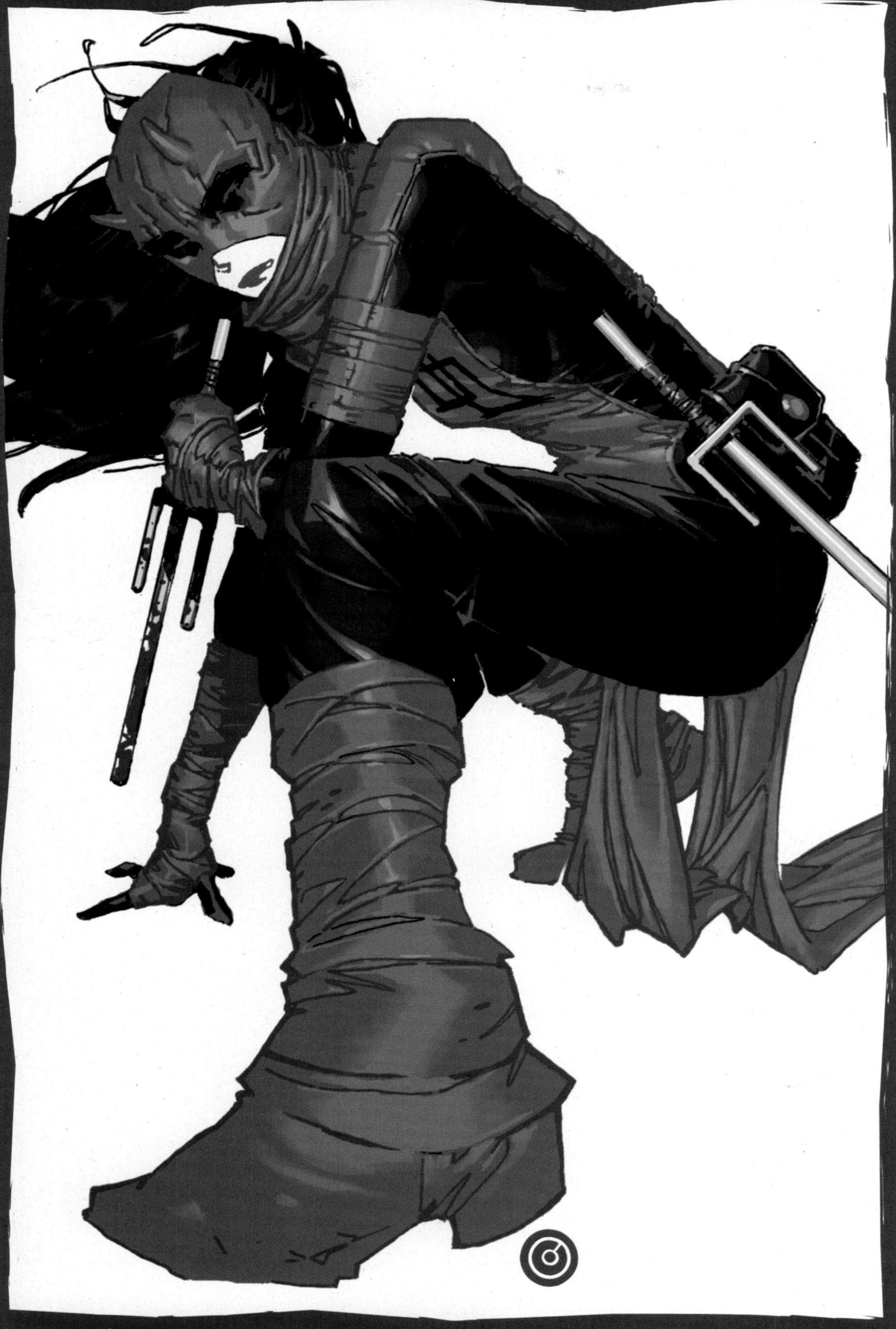

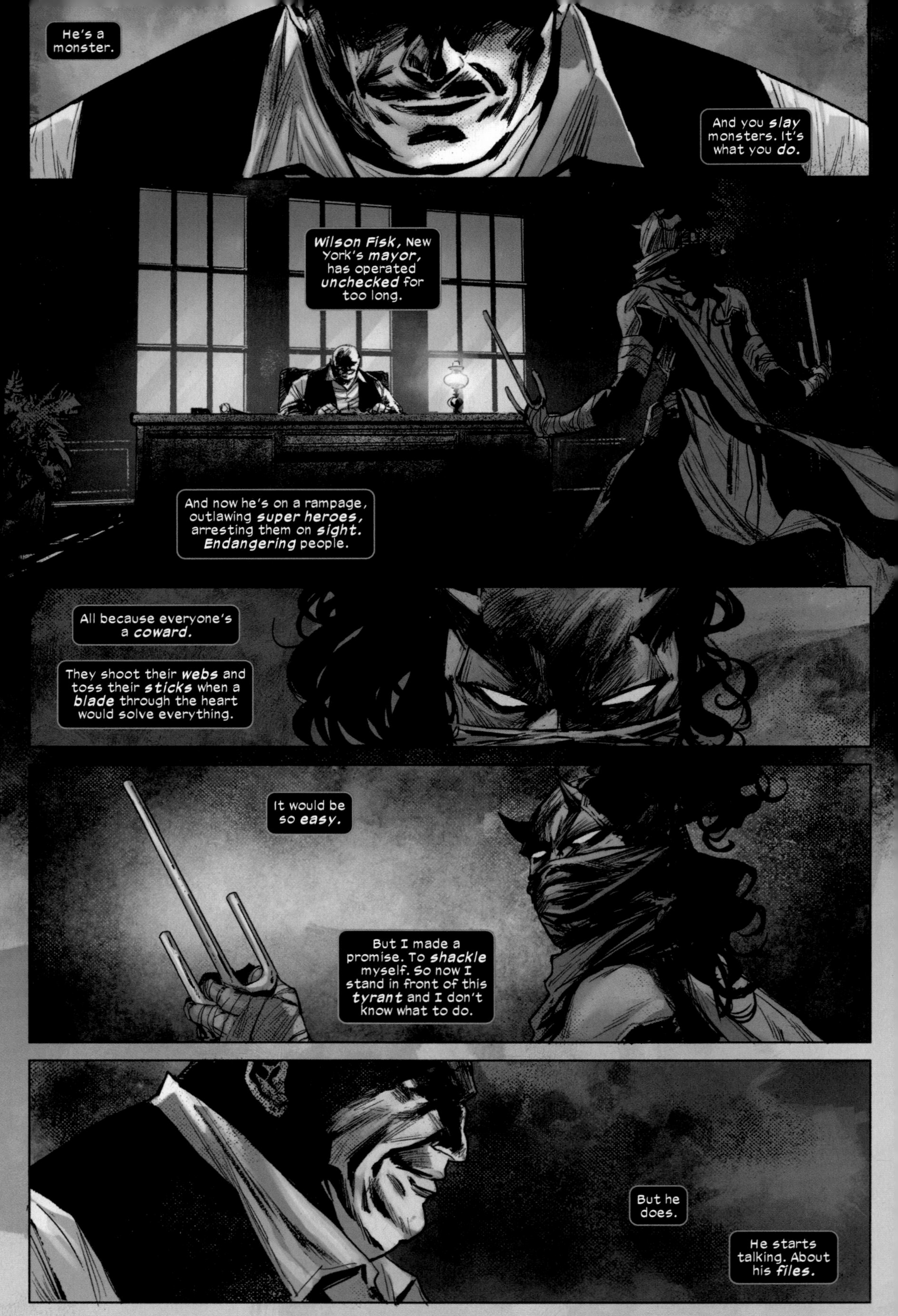
He's a monster.
And you slay monsters. It's what you do.
Wilson Fisk, New York's mayor, has operated unchecked for too long.
And now he's on a rampage, outlawing super heroes, arresting them on sight. Endangering people.
All because everyone's a coward.
They shoot their webs and toss their sticks when a blade through the heart would solve everything.
It would be so easy.
But I made a promise. To shackle myself. So now I stand in front of this tyrant and I don't know what to do.
But he does.
He starts talking. About his files.

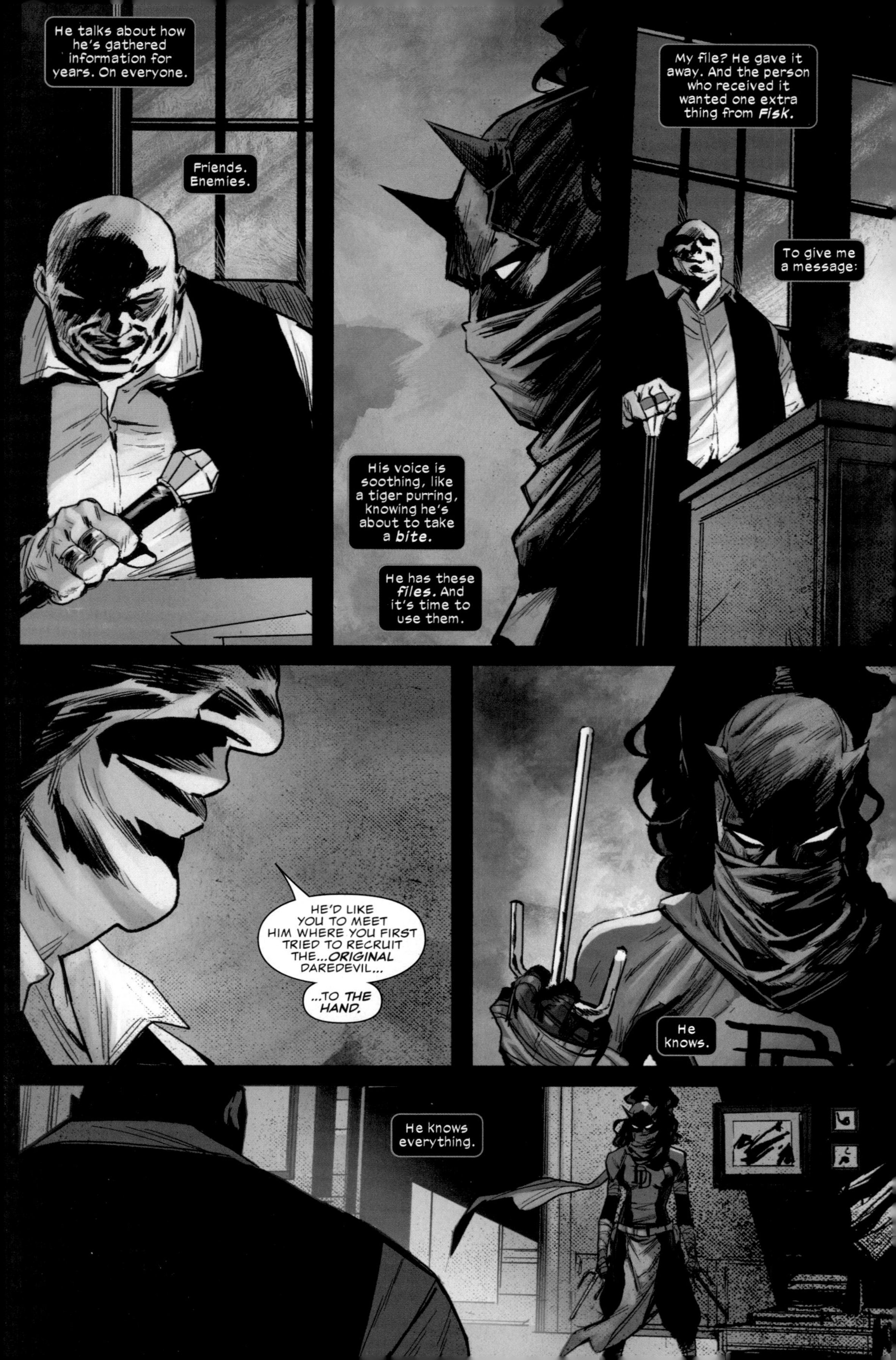
He talks about how he's gathered information for years. On everyone.
Friends. Enemies.
His voice is soothing, like a tiger purring, knowing he's about to take a *bite.*
He has these *files.* And it's time to use them.
My file? He gave it away. And the person who received it wanted one extra thing from *Fisk.*
To give me a message:
HE'D LIKE YOU TO MEET HIM WHERE YOU FIRST TRIED TO RECRUIT THE...*ORIGINAL* DAREDEVIL...
...TO *THE HAND.*
He knows.
He knows everything.

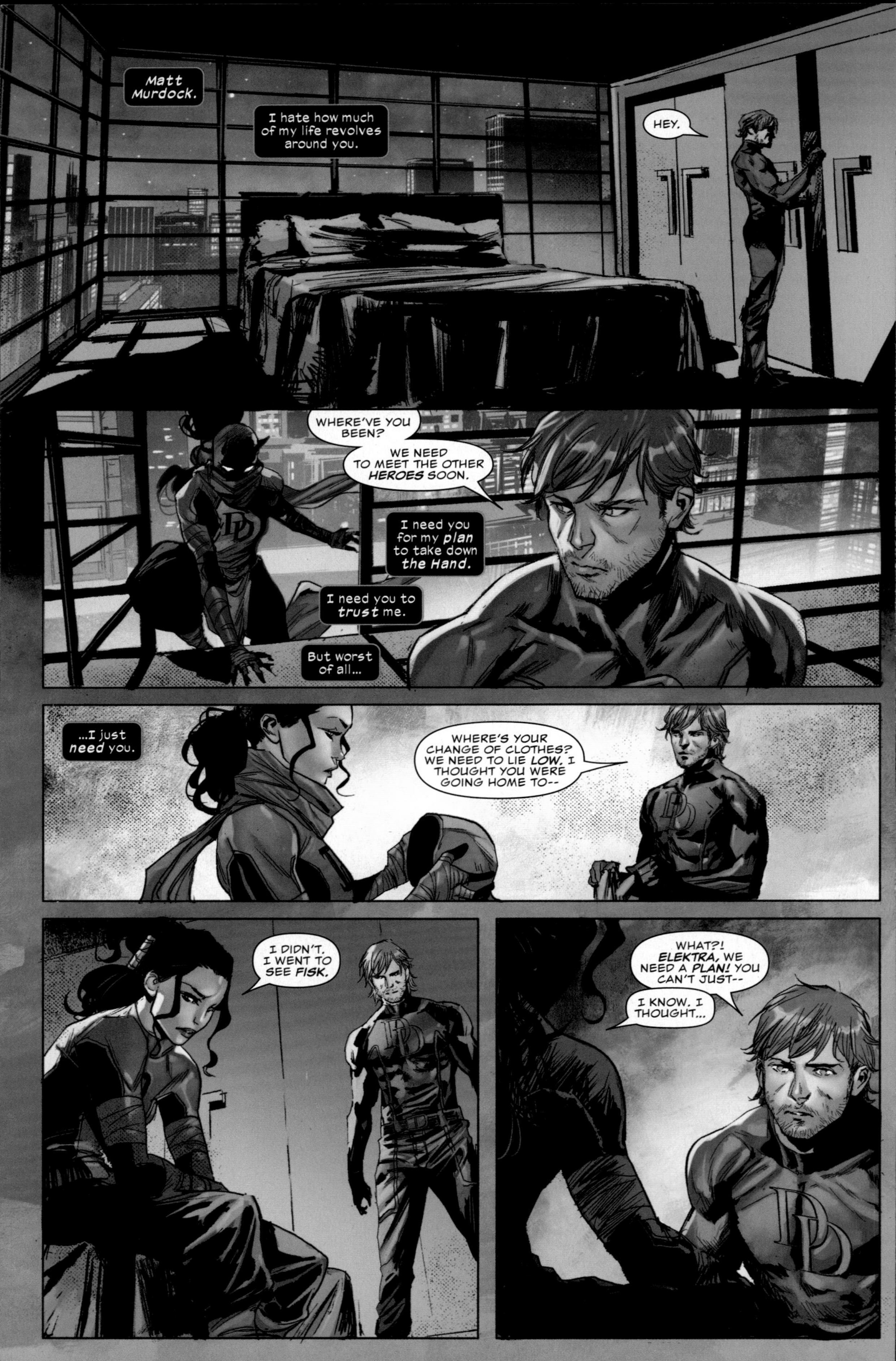
Matt Murdock.
I hate how much of my life revolves around you.
HEY.
WHERE'VE YOU BEEN?
WE NEED TO MEET THE OTHER HEROES SOON.
I need you for my plan to take down the Hand.
I need you to trust me.
But worst of all...
...I just need you.
WHERE'S YOUR CHANGE OF CLOTHES? WE NEED TO LIE LOW. I THOUGHT YOU WERE GOING HOME TO--
I DIDN'T. I WENT TO SEE FISK.
WHAT?! ELEKTRA, WE NEED A PLAN! YOU CAN'T JUST--
I KNOW. I THOUGHT...

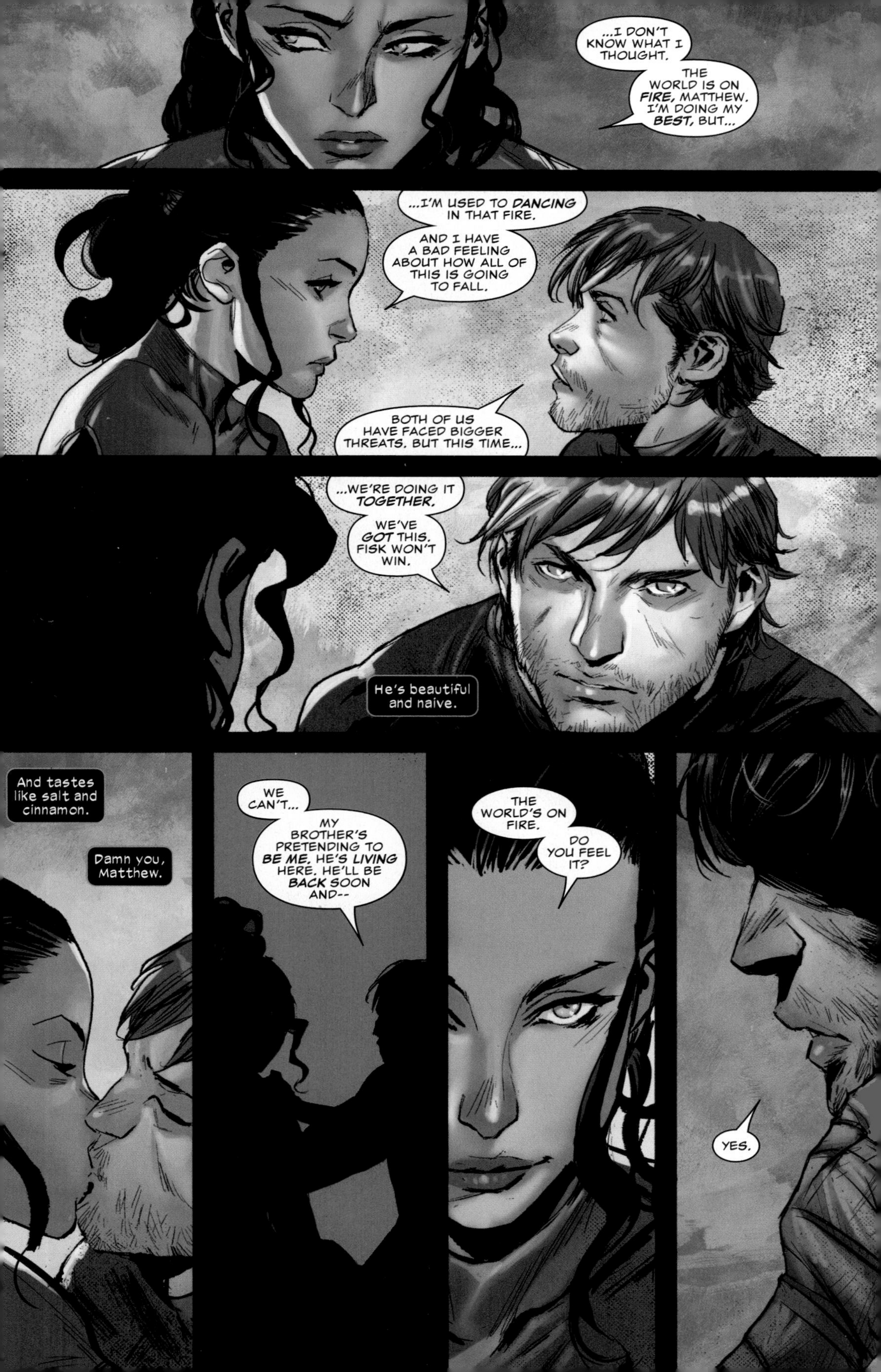
...I DON'T KNOW WHAT I THOUGHT.
THE WORLD IS ON FIRE, MATTHEW. I'M DOING MY BEST, BUT...
...I'M USED TO DANCING IN THAT FIRE.
AND I HAVE A BAD FEELING ABOUT HOW ALL OF THIS IS GOING TO FALL.
BOTH OF US HAVE FACED BIGGER THREATS. BUT THIS TIME...
...WE'RE DOING IT TOGETHER.
WE'VE GOT THIS. FISK WON'T WIN.
He's beautiful and naive.
And tastes like salt and cinnamon.
Damn you, Matthew.
WE CAN'T...
MY BROTHER'S PRETENDING TO BE ME. HE'S LIVING HERE. HE'LL BE BACK SOON AND--
THE WORLD'S ON FIRE.
DO YOU FEEL IT?
YES.

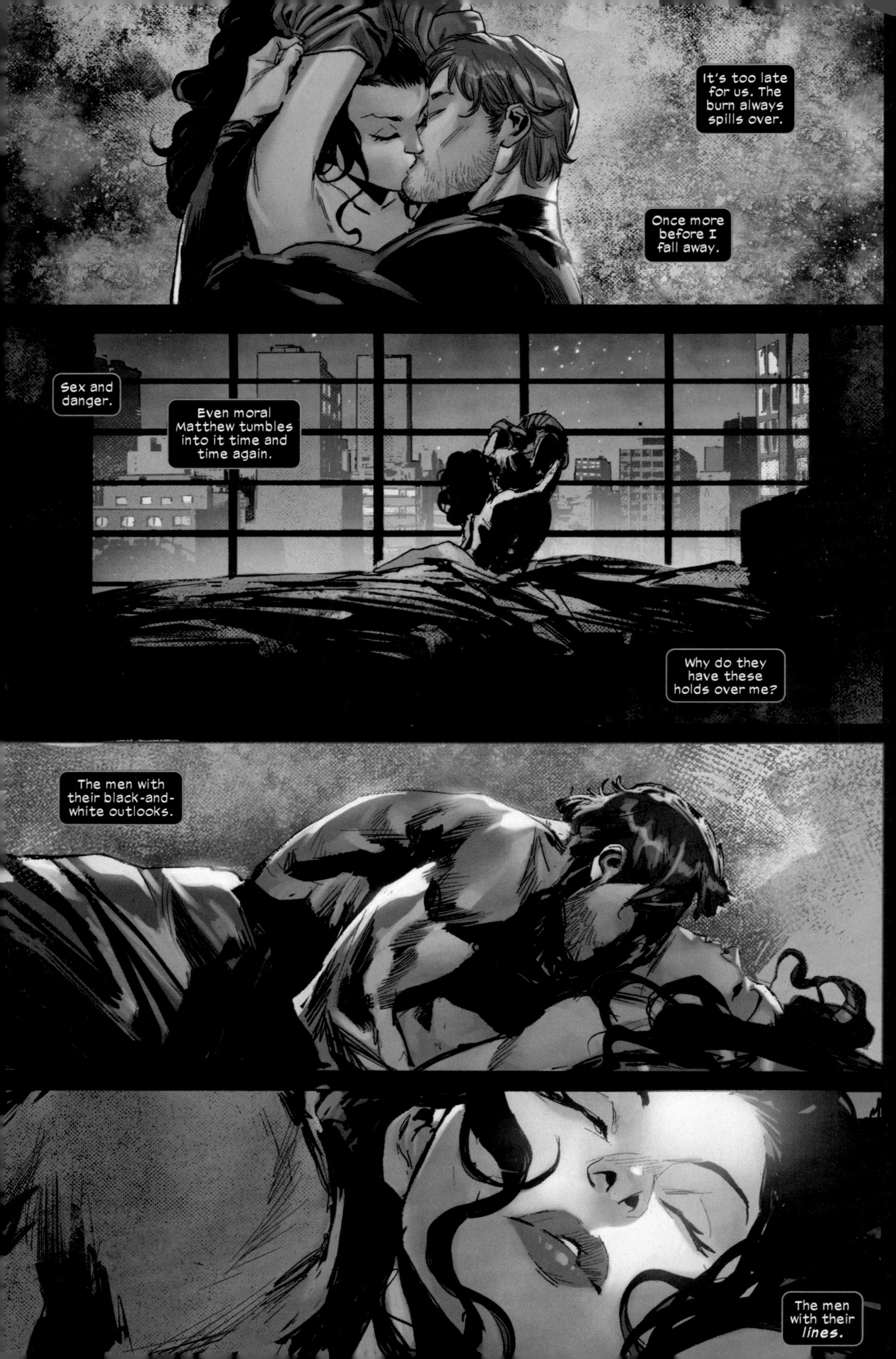
It's too late for us. The burn always spills over.
Once more before I fall away.
Sex and danger.
Even moral Matthew tumbles into it time and time again.
Why do they have these holds over me?
The men with their black-and-white outlooks.
The men with their *lines.*

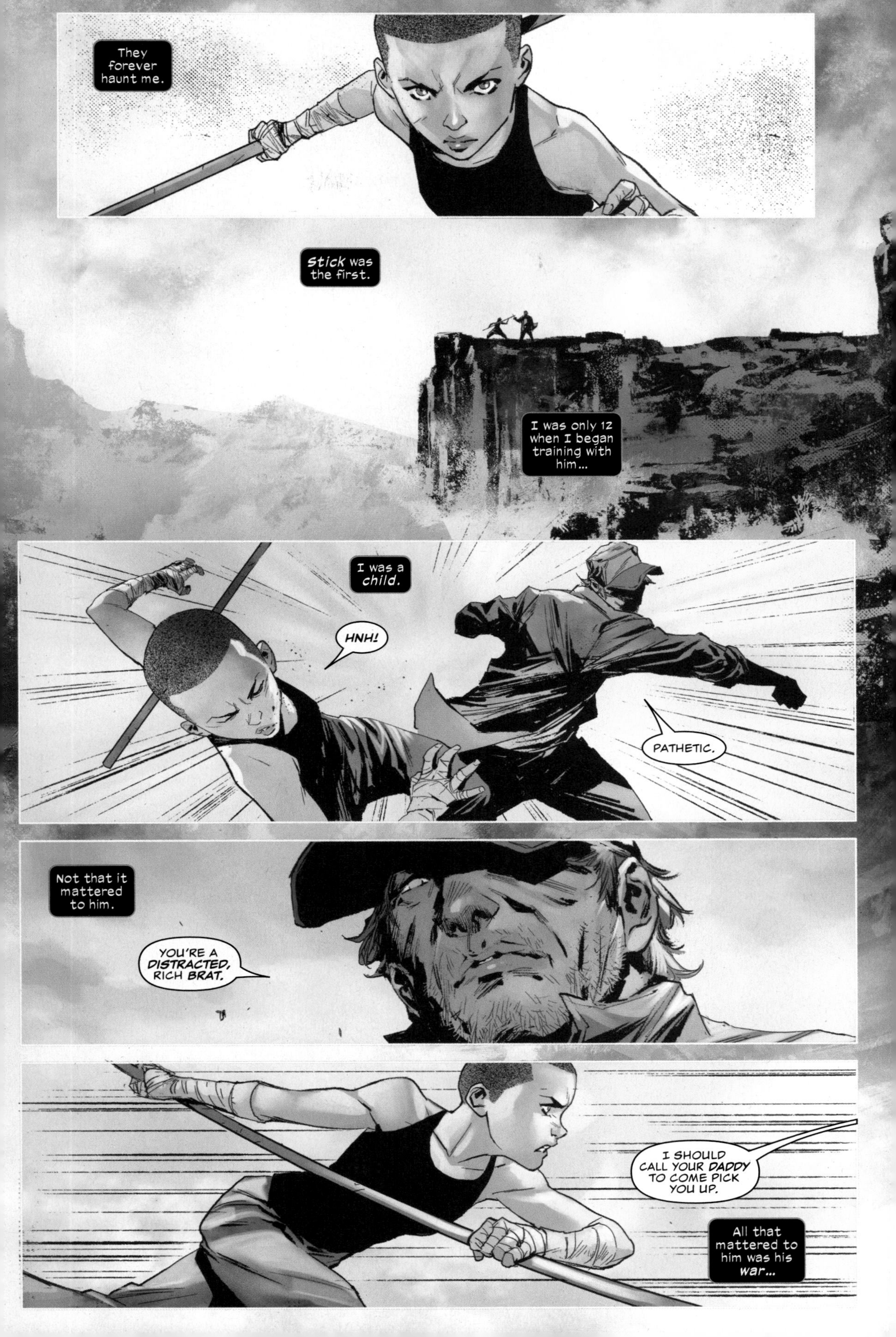
They forever haunt me.
Stick was the first.
I was only 12 when I began training with him...
I was a child.
HNH!
PATHETIC.
Not that it mattered to him.
YOU'RE A DISTRACTED, RICH BRAT.
I SHOULD CALL YOUR DADDY TO COME PICK YOU UP.
All that mattered to him was his war...

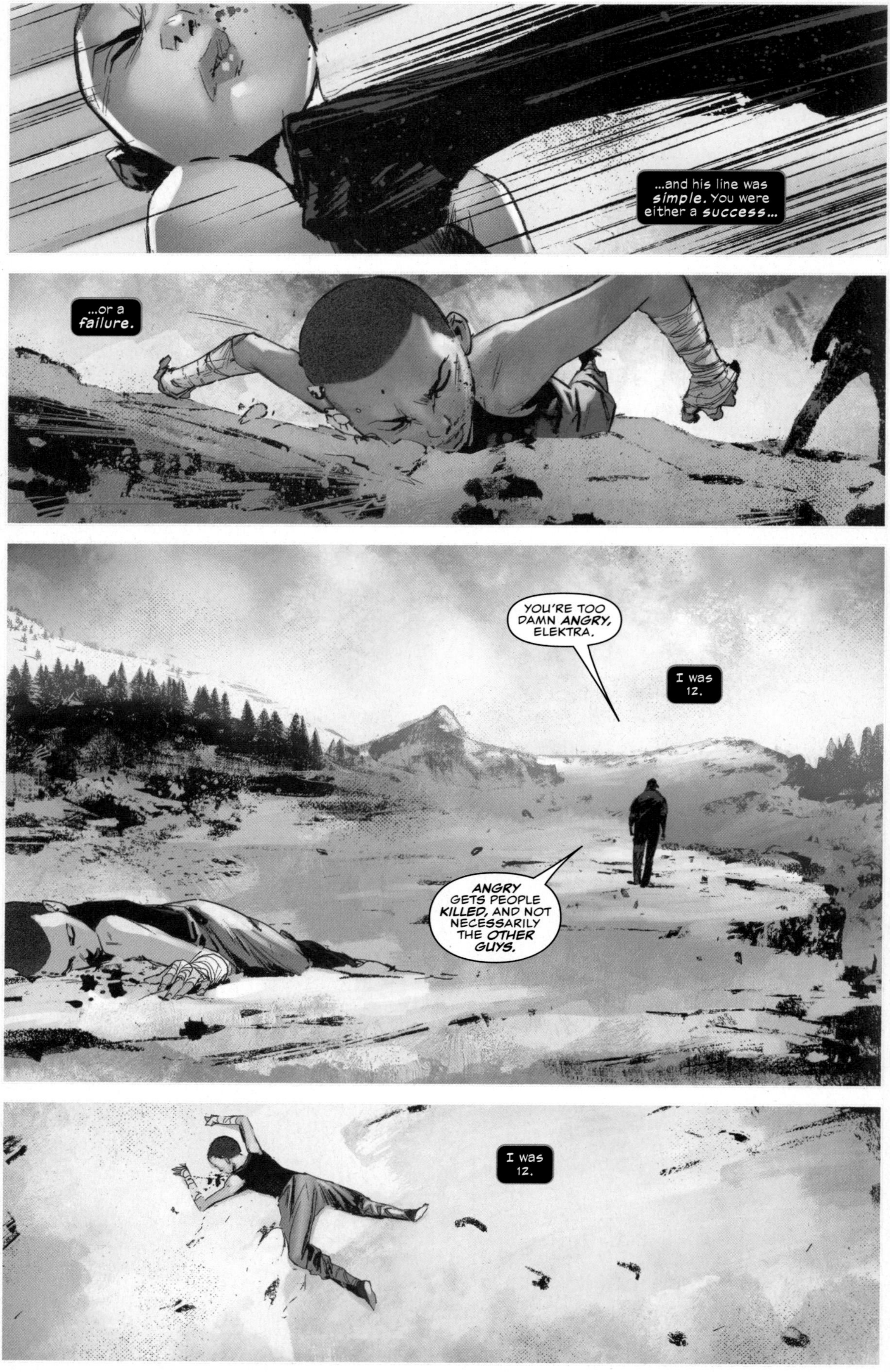

...and his line was *simple.* You were either a *success...*
...or a *failure.*
YOU'RE TOO DAMN **ANGRY,** ELEKTRA.
I was 12.
ANGRY GETS PEOPLE **KILLED,** AND NOT NECESSARILY THE **OTHER GUYS.**
I was 12.

I went back again when I was older. Back to *stick*. After this place, after...

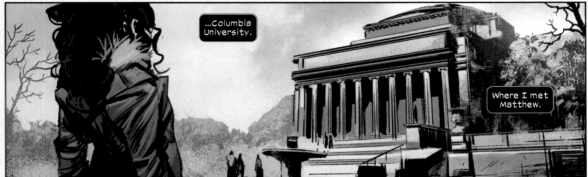

...Columbia University.

Where I met Matthew.

Where I fell in love with him.

And betrayed him.

I don't know who has the file or what else is *in* it.

There's no plan here. I'm a walking target, hoping to draw them out.

It was foolish coming here.

But I need to *know*. Need to know who--

ELEKTRA...?

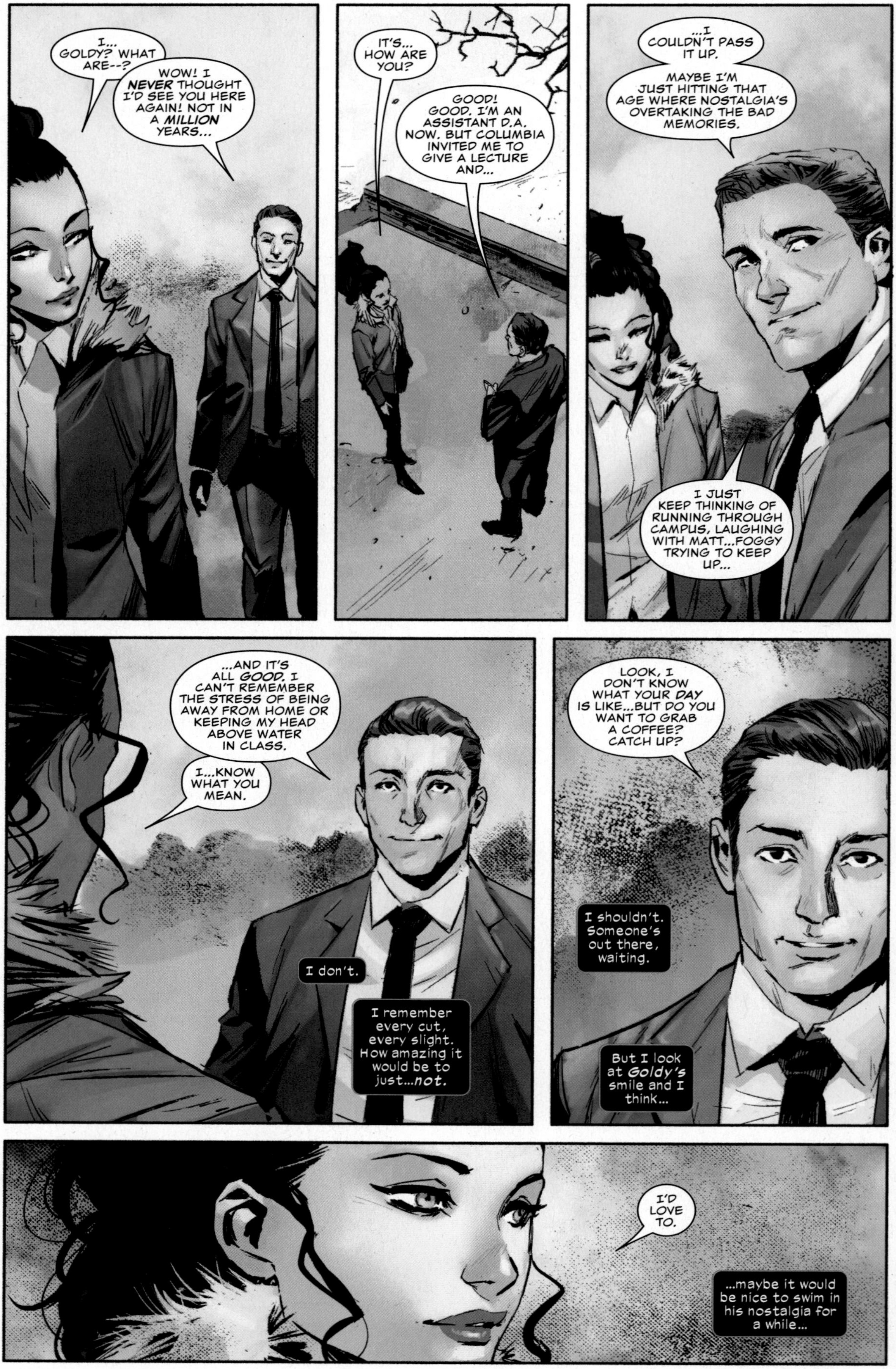

I... GOLDY? WHAT ARE--?
WOW! I NEVER THOUGHT I'D SEE YOU HERE AGAIN! NOT IN A MILLION YEARS...
IT'S... HOW ARE YOU?
GOOD! GOOD. I'M AN ASSISTANT D.A. NOW. BUT COLUMBIA INVITED ME TO GIVE A LECTURE AND...
...I COULDN'T PASS IT UP.
MAYBE I'M JUST HITTING THAT AGE WHERE NOSTALGIA'S OVERTAKING THE BAD MEMORIES.
I JUST KEEP THINKING OF RUNNING THROUGH CAMPUS, LAUGHING WITH MATT...FOGGY TRYING TO KEEP UP...
...AND IT'S ALL GOOD. I CAN'T REMEMBER THE STRESS OF BEING AWAY FROM HOME OR KEEPING MY HEAD ABOVE WATER IN CLASS.
I...KNOW WHAT YOU MEAN.
I don't.
I remember every cut, every slight. How amazing it would be to just...not.
LOOK, I DON'T KNOW WHAT YOUR DAY IS LIKE...BUT DO YOU WANT TO GRAB A COFFEE? CATCH UP?
I shouldn't. Someone's out there, waiting.
But I look at Goldy's smile and I think...
I'D LOVE TO.
...maybe it would be nice to swim in his nostalgia for a while...

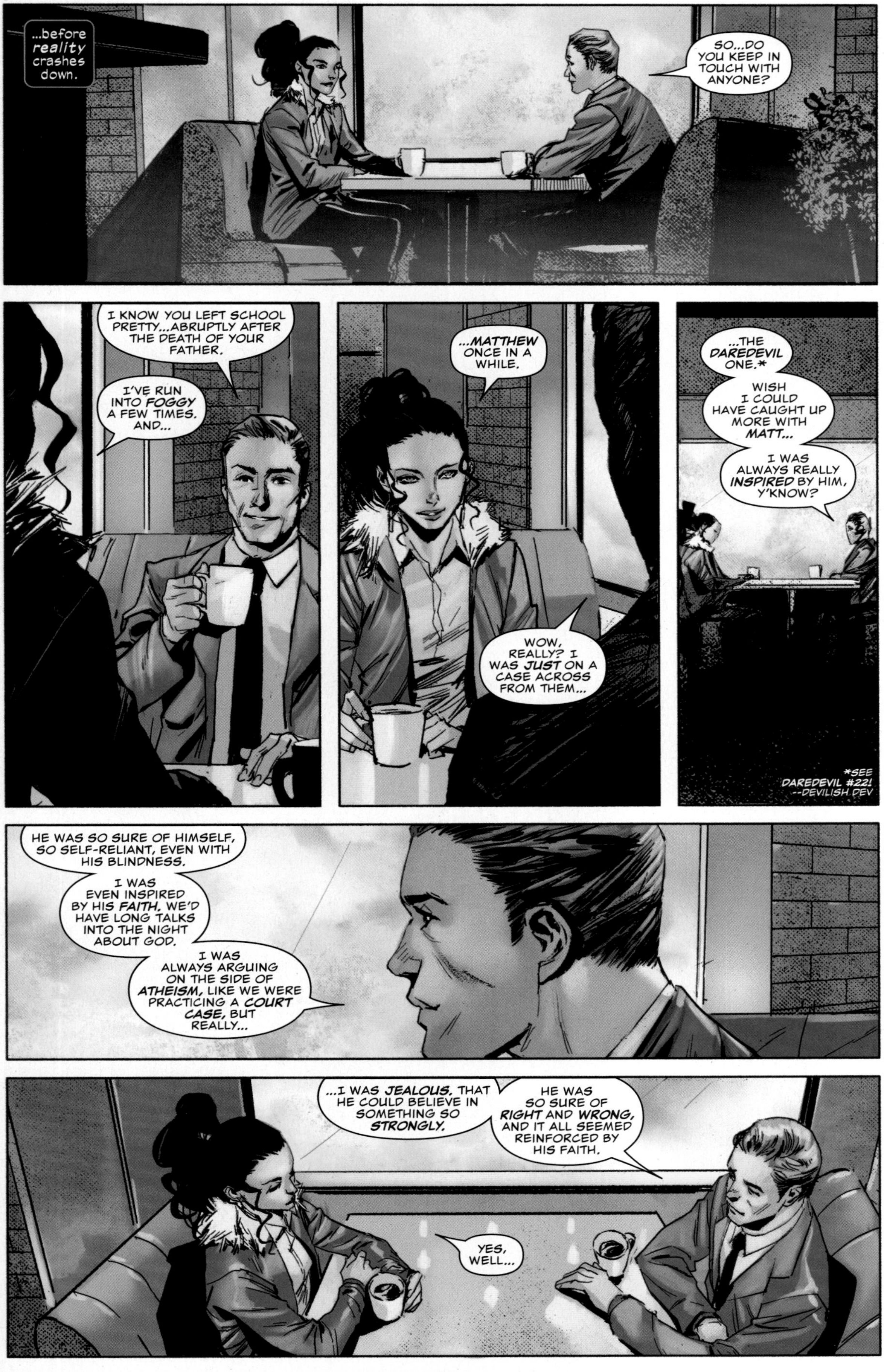
...before reality crashes down.
SO...DO YOU KEEP IN TOUCH WITH ANYONE?
I KNOW YOU LEFT SCHOOL PRETTY...ABRUPTLY AFTER THE DEATH OF YOUR FATHER.
I'VE RUN INTO FOGGY A FEW TIMES. AND...
...MATTHEW ONCE IN A WHILE.
WOW, REALLY? I WAS JUST ON A CASE ACROSS FROM THEM...
...THE DAREDEVIL ONE.*
WISH I COULD HAVE CAUGHT UP MORE WITH MATT...
I WAS ALWAYS REALLY INSPIRED BY HIM, Y'KNOW?
*SEE DAREDEVIL #22! --DEVILISH DEV
HE WAS SO SURE OF HIMSELF, SO SELF-RELIANT, EVEN WITH HIS BLINDNESS.
I WAS EVEN INSPIRED BY HIS FAITH. WE'D HAVE LONG TALKS INTO THE NIGHT ABOUT GOD.
I WAS ALWAYS ARGUING ON THE SIDE OF ATHEISM, LIKE WE WERE PRACTICING A COURT CASE, BUT REALLY...
...I WAS JEALOUS. THAT HE COULD BELIEVE IN SOMETHING SO STRONGLY.
HE WAS SO SURE OF RIGHT AND WRONG, AND IT ALL SEEMED REINFORCED BY HIS FAITH.
YES, WELL...

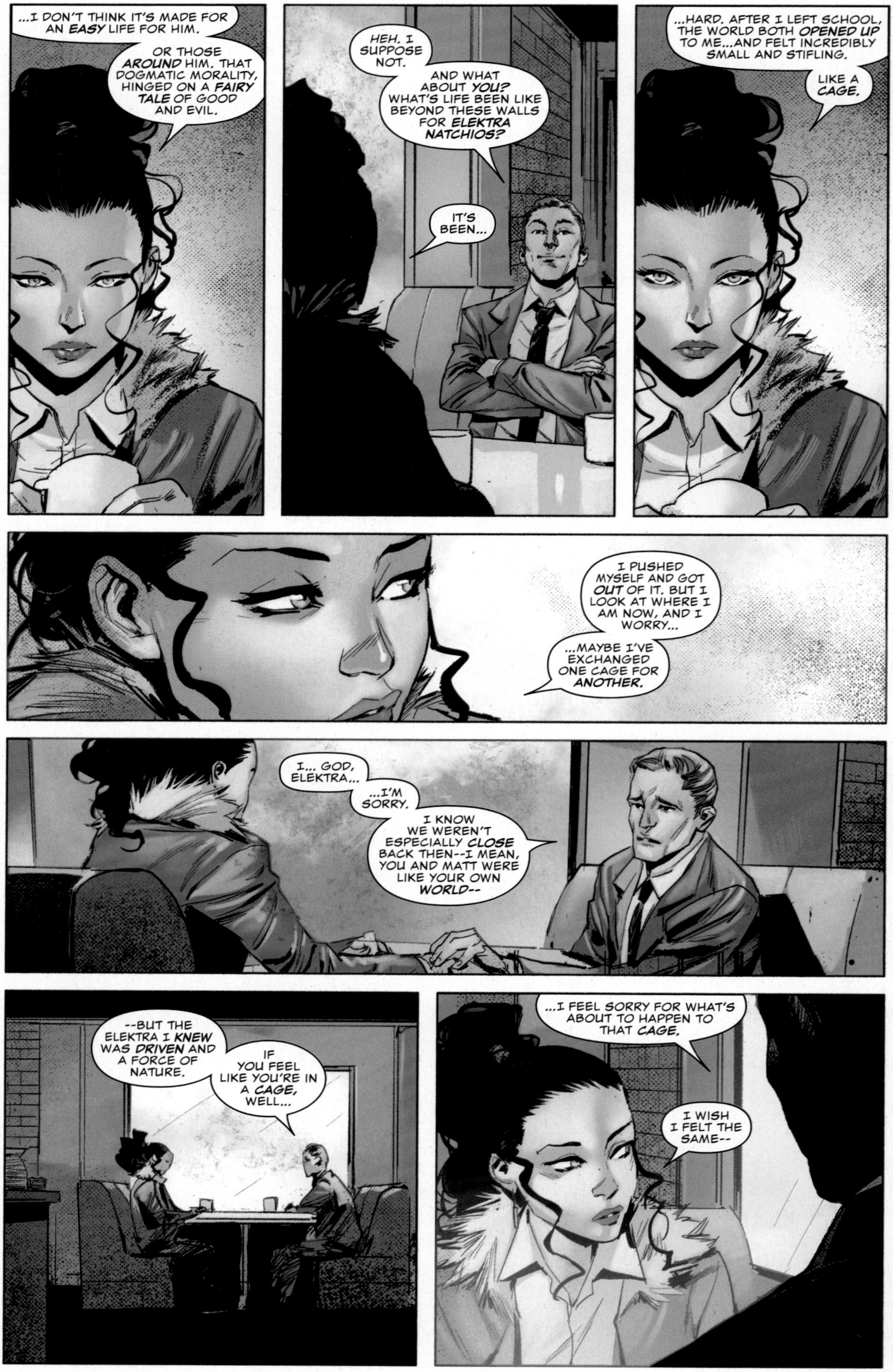
...I DON'T THINK IT'S MADE FOR AN EASY LIFE FOR HIM.
OR THOSE AROUND HIM. THAT DOGMATIC MORALITY, HINGED ON A FAIRY TALE OF GOOD AND EVIL.
HEH. I SUPPOSE NOT.
AND WHAT ABOUT YOU? WHAT'S LIFE BEEN LIKE BEYOND THESE WALLS FOR ELEKTRA NATCHIOS?
IT'S BEEN...
...HARD. AFTER I LEFT SCHOOL, THE WORLD BOTH OPENED UP TO ME...AND FELT INCREDIBLY SMALL AND STIFLING.
LIKE A CAGE.
I PUSHED MYSELF AND GOT OUT OF IT. BUT I LOOK AT WHERE I AM NOW, AND I WORRY...
...MAYBE I'VE EXCHANGED ONE CAGE FOR ANOTHER.
I... GOD, ELEKTRA...
...I'M SORRY.
I KNOW WE WEREN'T ESPECIALLY CLOSE BACK THEN--I MEAN, YOU AND MATT WERE LIKE YOUR OWN WORLD--
--BUT THE ELEKTRA I KNEW WAS DRIVEN AND A FORCE OF NATURE.
IF YOU FEEL LIKE YOU'RE IN A CAGE, WELL...
...I FEEL SORRY FOR WHAT'S ABOUT TO HAPPEN TO THAT CAGE.
I WISH I FELT THE SAME--

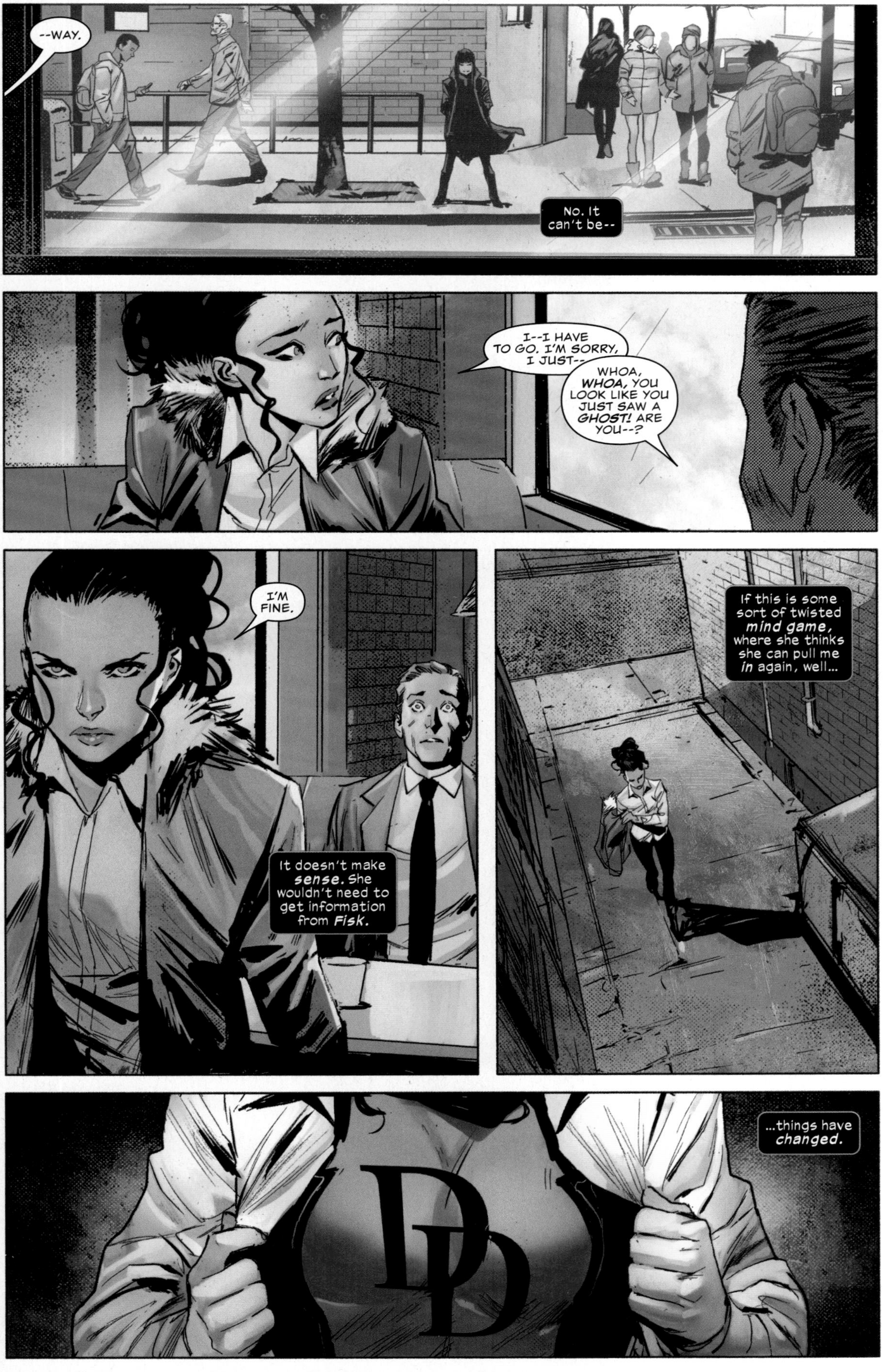
--WAY.
No. It can't be--
I--I HAVE TO GO. I'M SORRY, I JUST--
WHOA, WHOA, YOU LOOK LIKE YOU JUST SAW A GHOST! ARE YOU--?
I'M FINE.
It doesn't make sense. She wouldn't need to get information from Fisk.
If this is some sort of twisted mind game, where she thinks she can pull me in again, well...
...things have changed.
DD

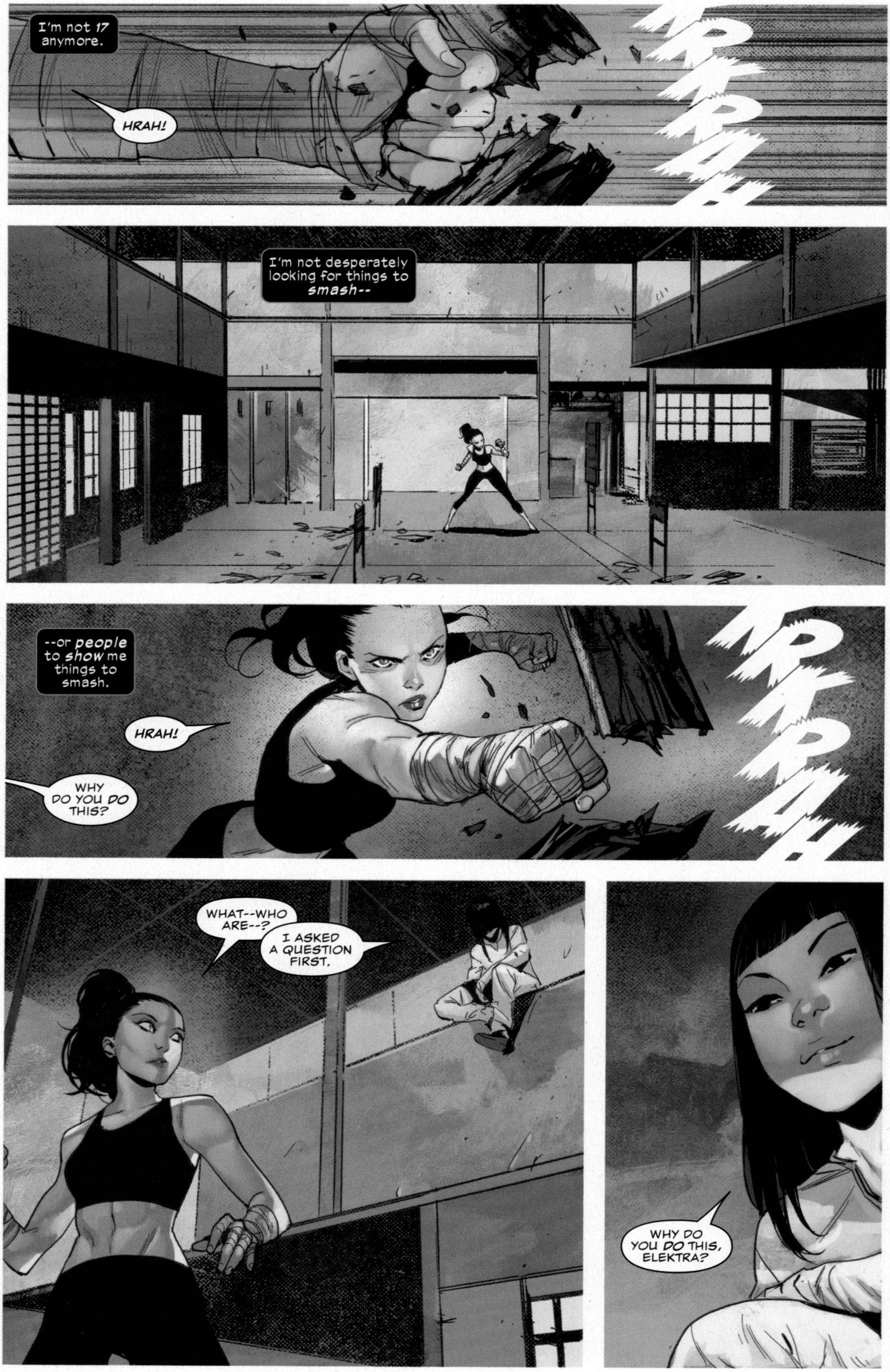

I'm not 17 anymore.
HRAH!
KRKRAH
I'm not desperately looking for things to smash--
--or people to show me things to smash.
HRAH!
WHY DO YOU DO THIS?
KRKRAH
WHAT--WHO ARE--?
I ASKED A QUESTION FIRST.
WHY DO YOU DO THIS, ELEKTRA?

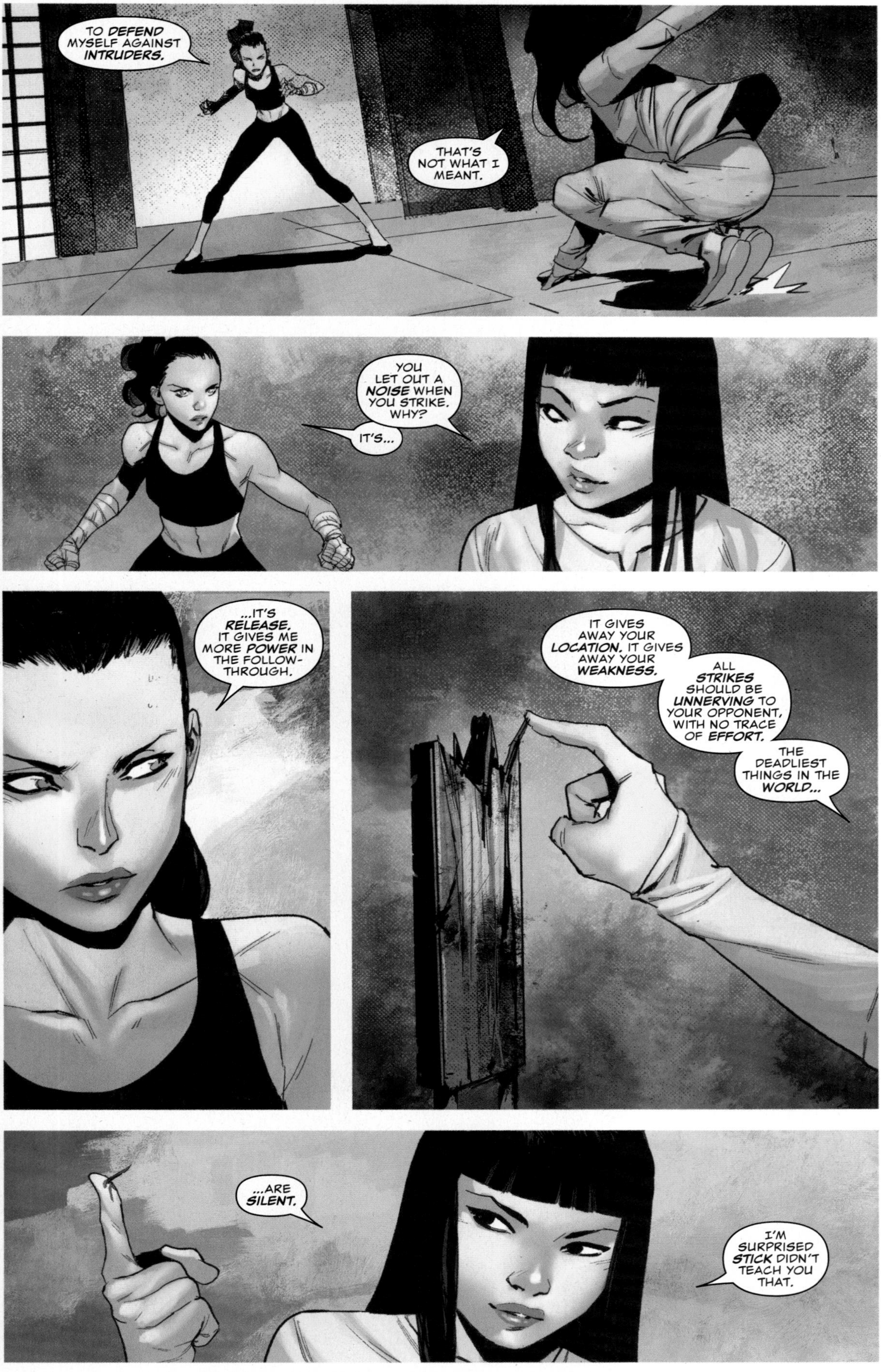
TO DEFEND MYSELF AGAINST INTRUDERS.
THAT'S NOT WHAT I MEANT.
YOU LET OUT A NOISE WHEN YOU STRIKE. WHY?
IT'S...
...IT'S RELEASE. IT GIVES ME MORE POWER IN THE FOLLOW-THROUGH.
IT GIVES AWAY YOUR LOCATION. IT GIVES AWAY YOUR WEAKNESS.
ALL STRIKES SHOULD BE UNNERVING TO YOUR OPPONENT, WITH NO TRACE OF EFFORT.
THE DEADLIEST THINGS IN THE WORLD...
...ARE SILENT.
I'M SURPRISED STICK DIDN'T TEACH YOU THAT.

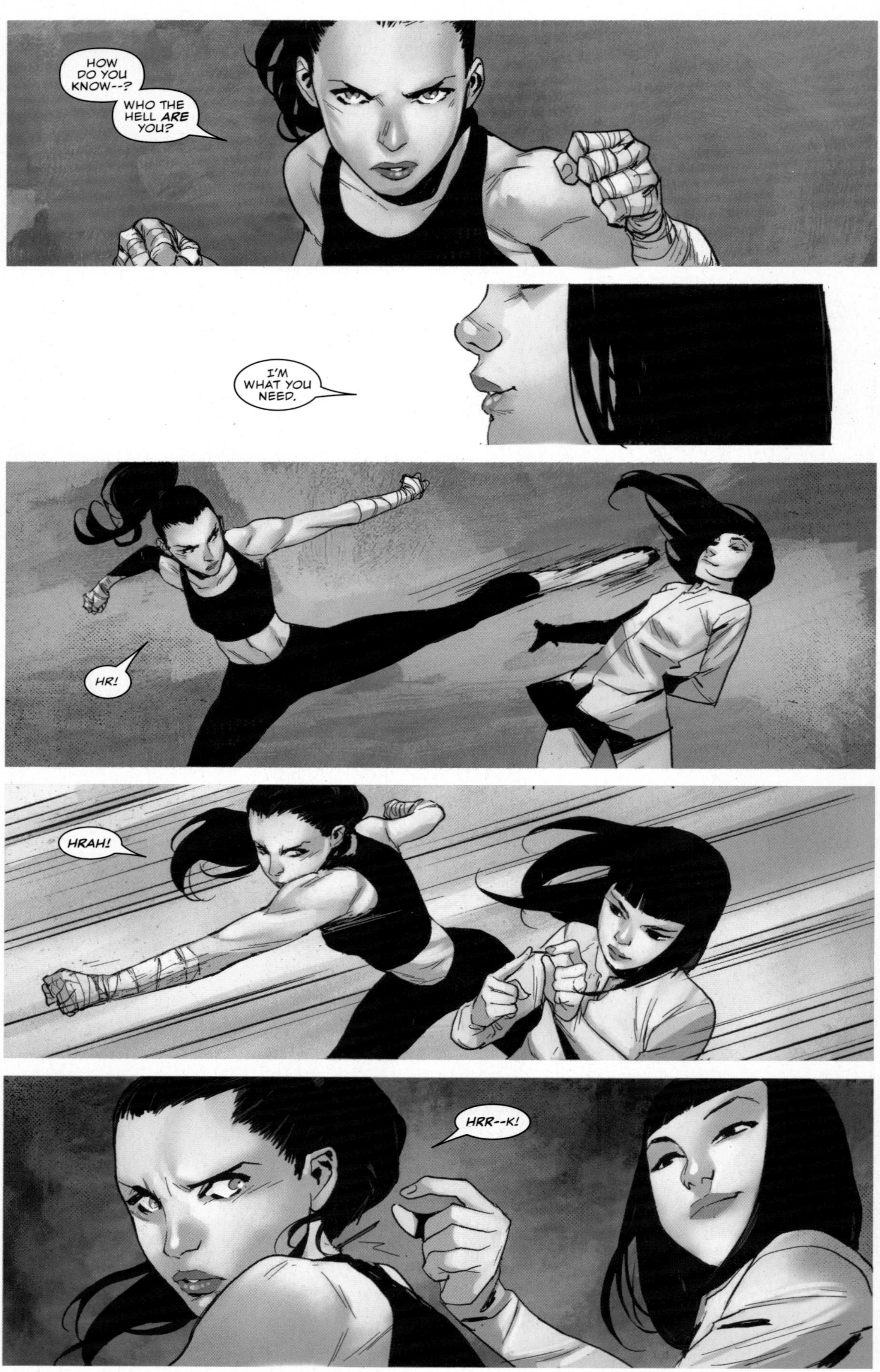
HOW DO YOU KNOW--?
WHO THE HELL **ARE** YOU?
I'M WHAT YOU NEED.
HR!
HRAH!
HRR--K!

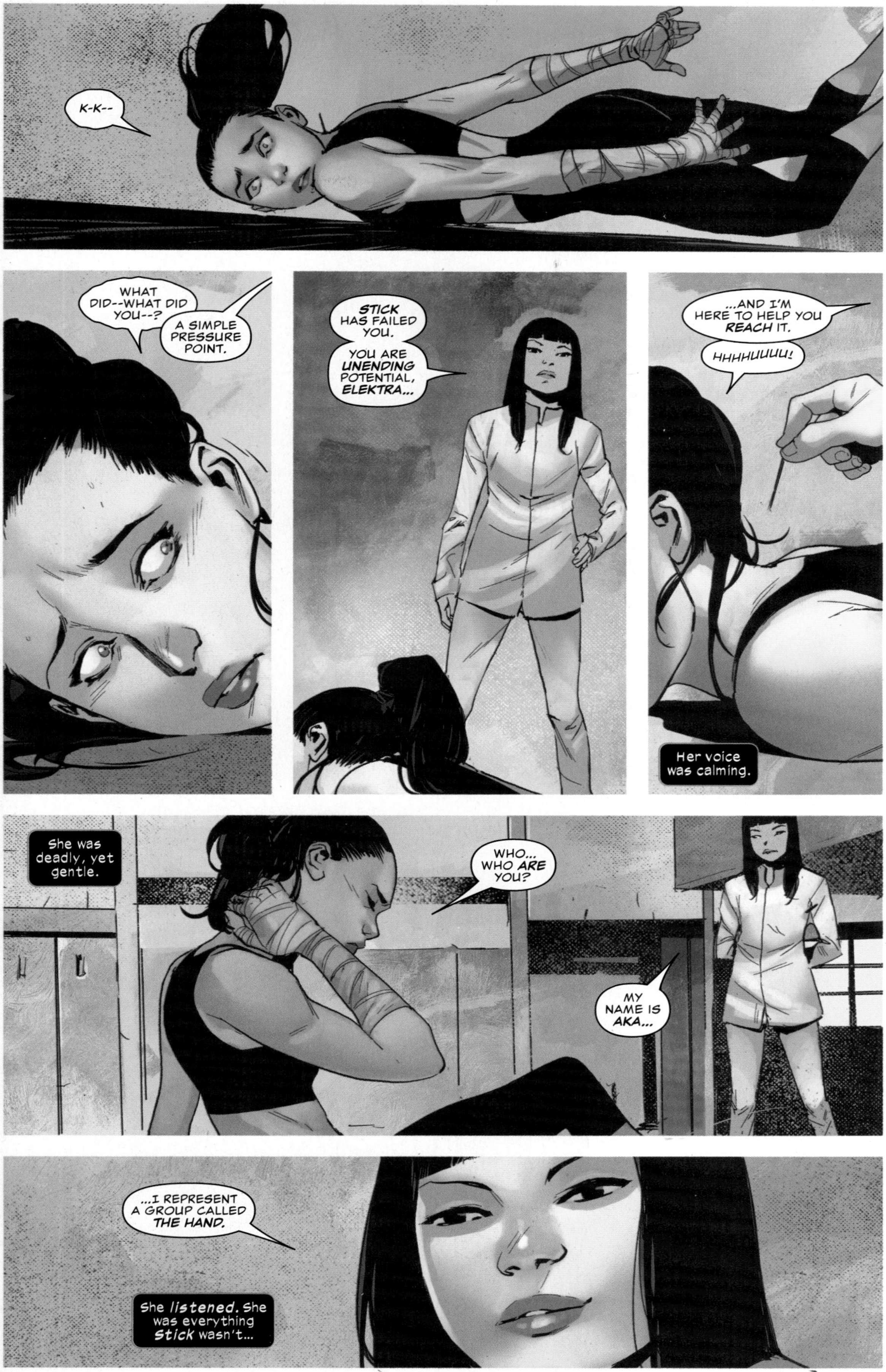

K-K--
WHAT DID--WHAT DID YOU--?
A SIMPLE PRESSURE POINT.
STICK HAS FAILED YOU.
YOU ARE UNENDING POTENTIAL, ELEKTRA...
...AND I'M HERE TO HELP YOU REACH IT.
HHHHUUUU!
Her voice was calming.
She was deadly, yet gentle.
WHO... WHO ARE YOU?
MY NAME IS AKA...
...I REPRESENT A GROUP CALLED THE HAND.
She listened. She was everything Stick wasn't...

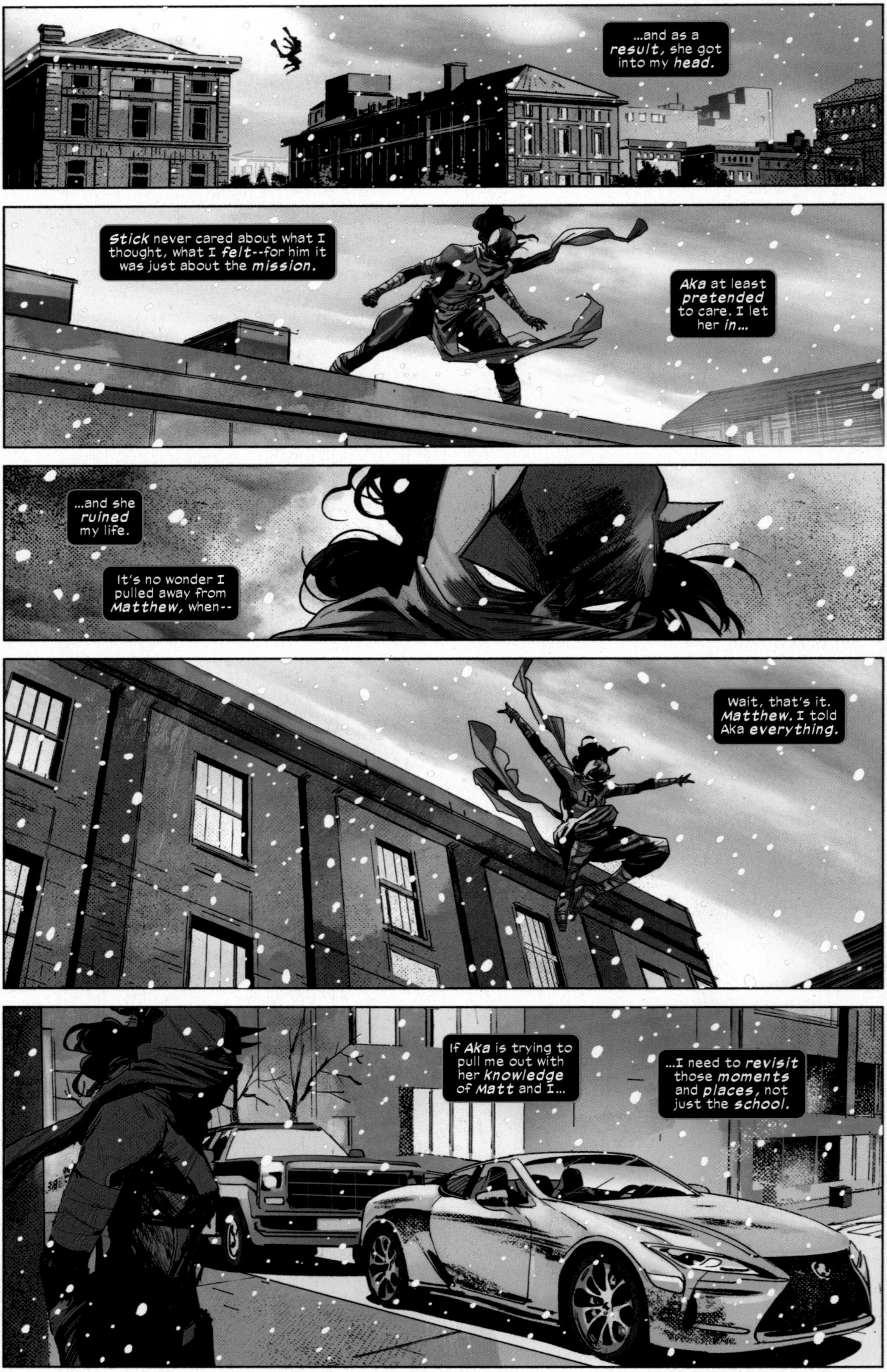
...and as a result, she got into my head.
Stick never cared about what I thought, what I felt--for him it was just about the mission.
Aka at least pretended to care. I let her in...
...and she ruined my life.
It's no wonder I pulled away from Matthew, when--
Wait, that's it. Matthew. I told Aka everything.
If Aka is trying to pull me out with her knowledge of Matt and I...
...I need to revisit those moments and places, not just the school.

Dammit, Matthew...

...it was all so out of control.

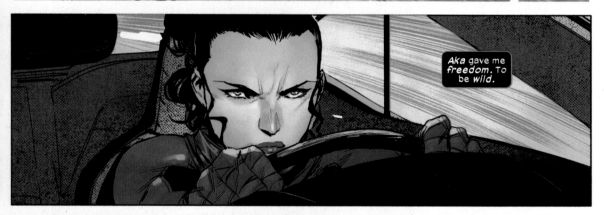

Aka gave me *freedom*. To be *wild*.

To be *dangerous*.

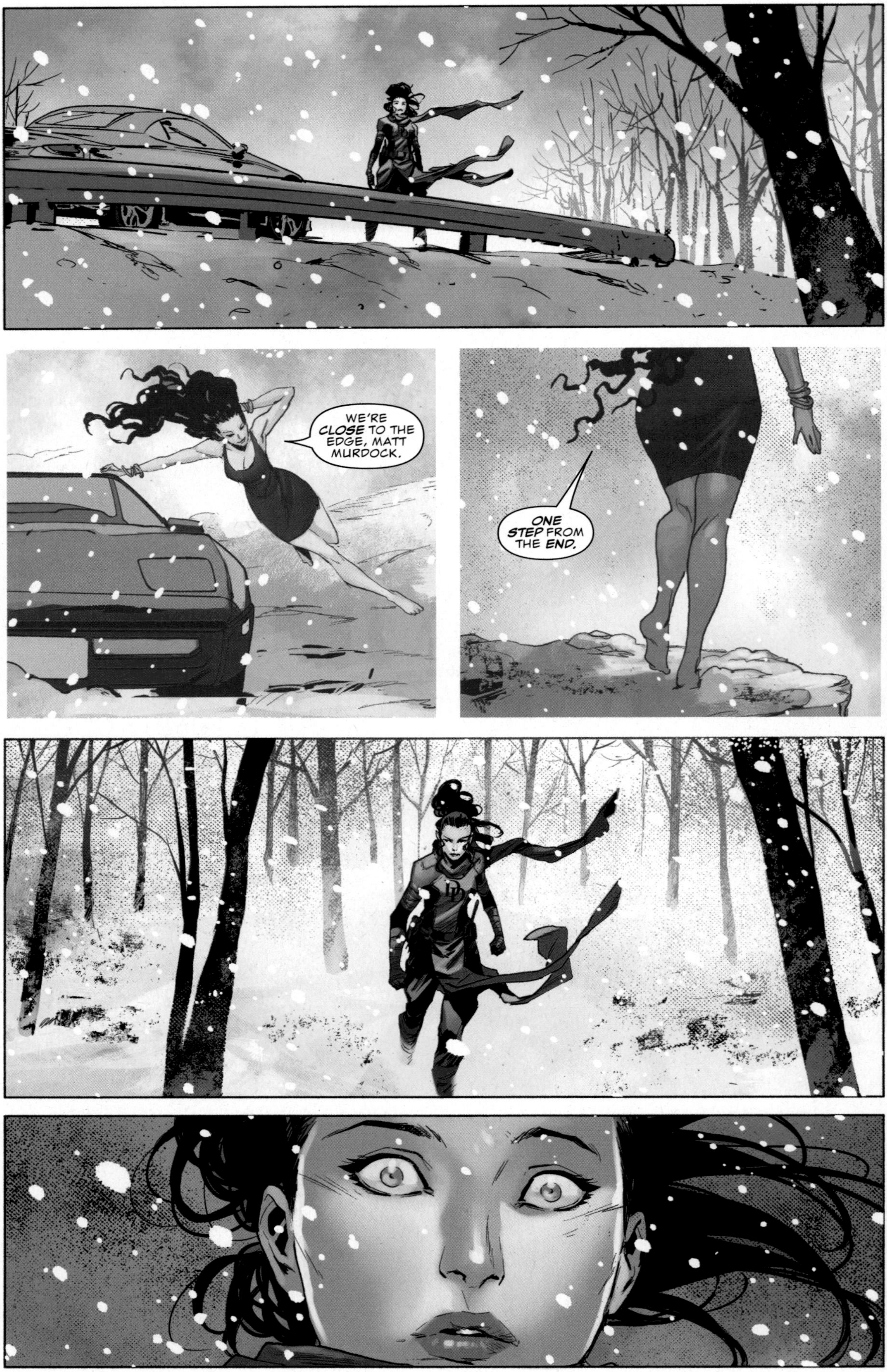
WE'RE CLOSE TO THE EDGE, MATT MURDOCK.
ONE STEP FROM THE END.

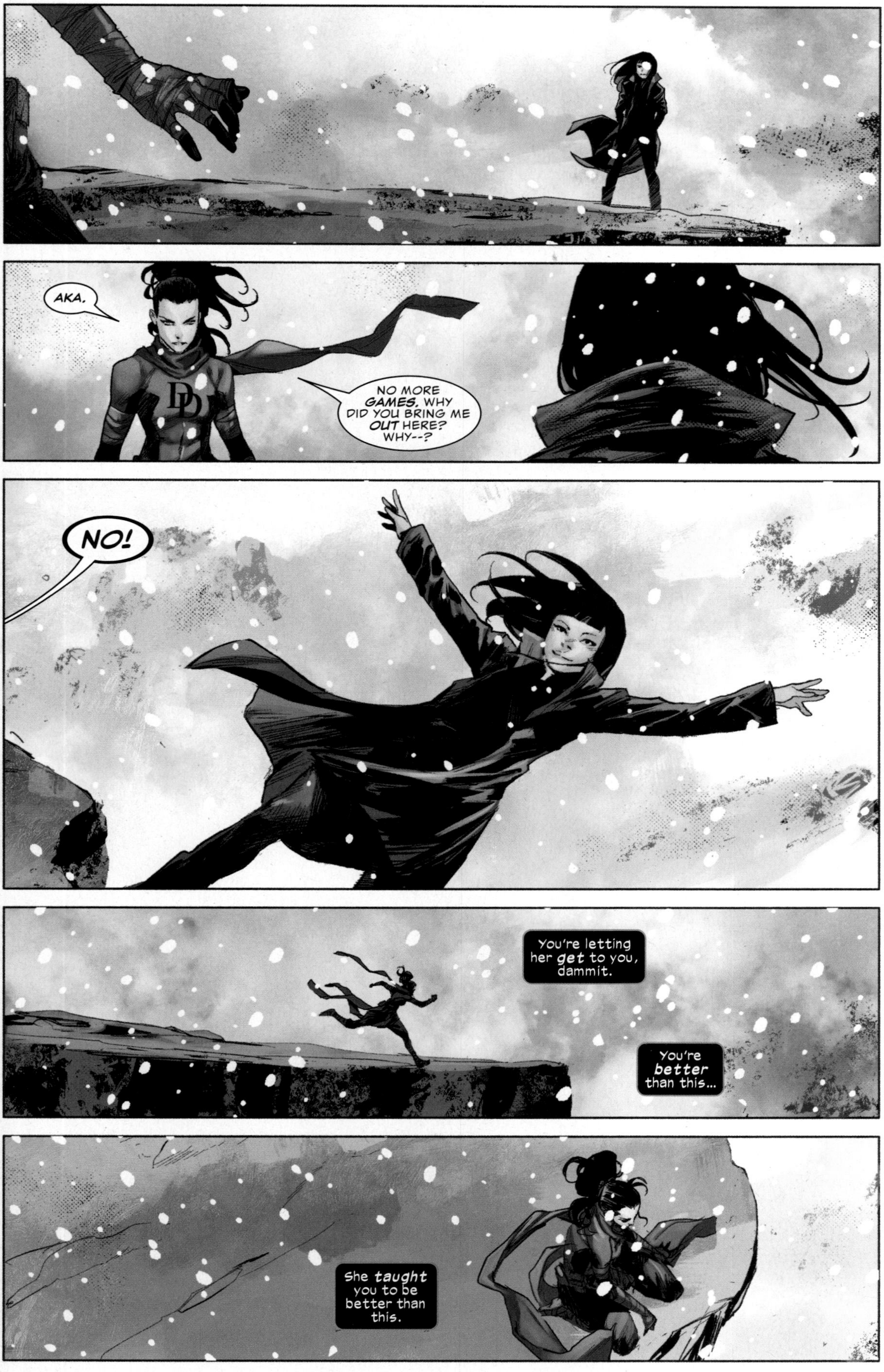

AKA.
NO MORE GAMES. WHY DID YOU BRING ME OUT HERE? WHY--?
NO!
You're letting her get to you, dammit.
You're better than this...
She taught you to be better than this.

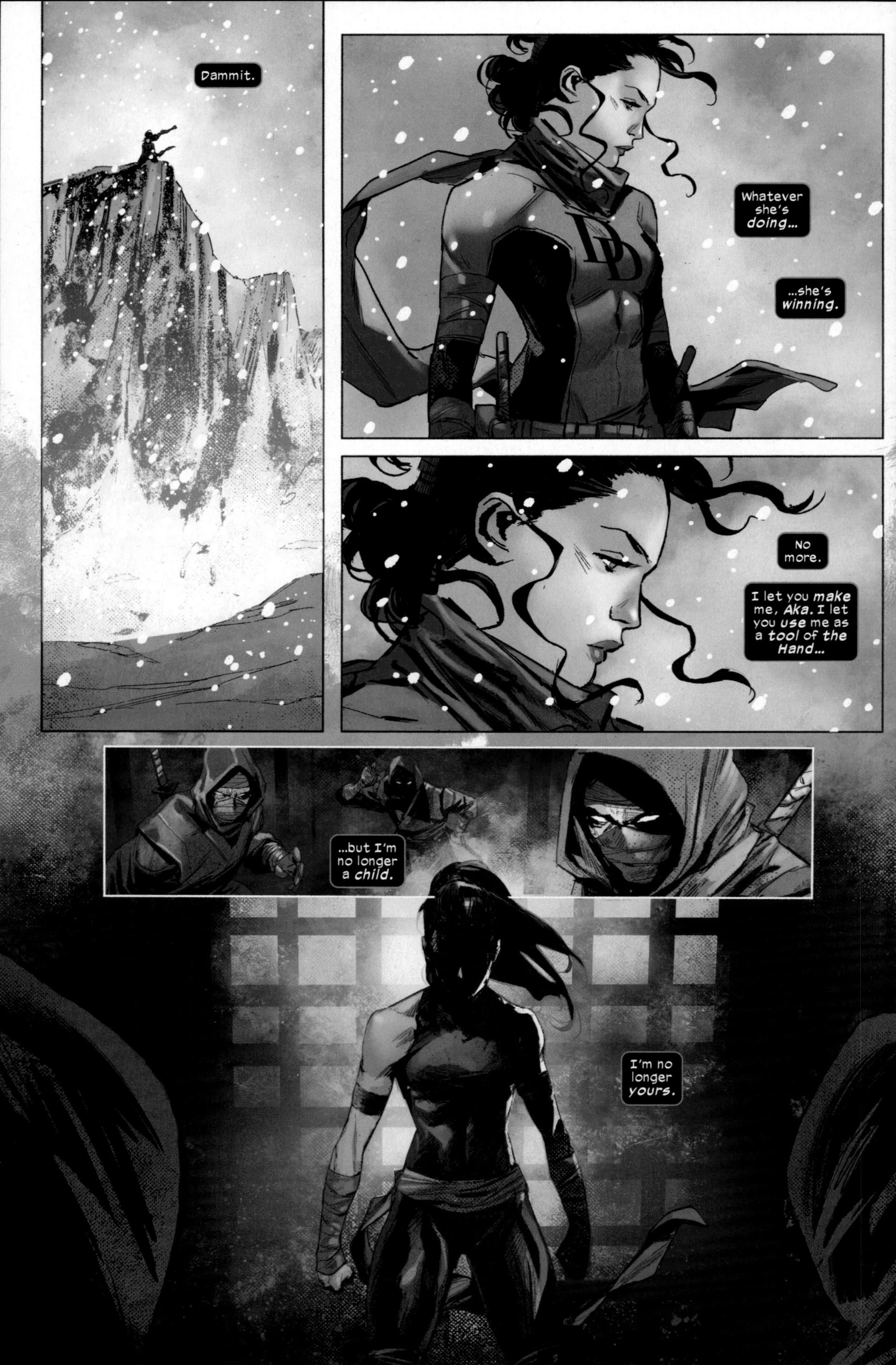
Dammit.
Whatever she's doing...
...she's winning.
No more.
I let you make me, Aka. I let you use me as a tool of the Hand...
...but I'm no longer a child.
I'm no longer yours.

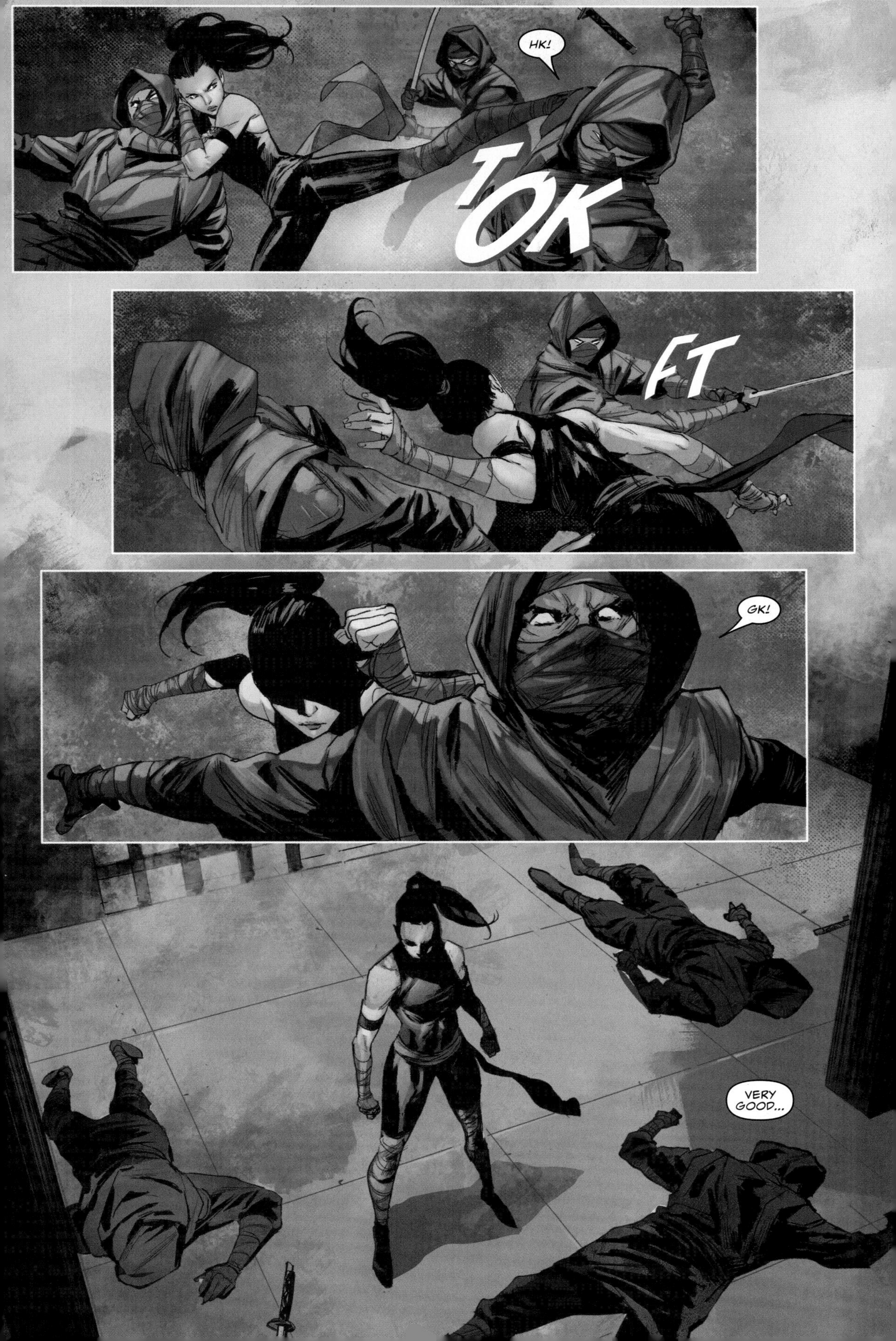
HK!
TOK
FT
GK!
VERY GOOD...

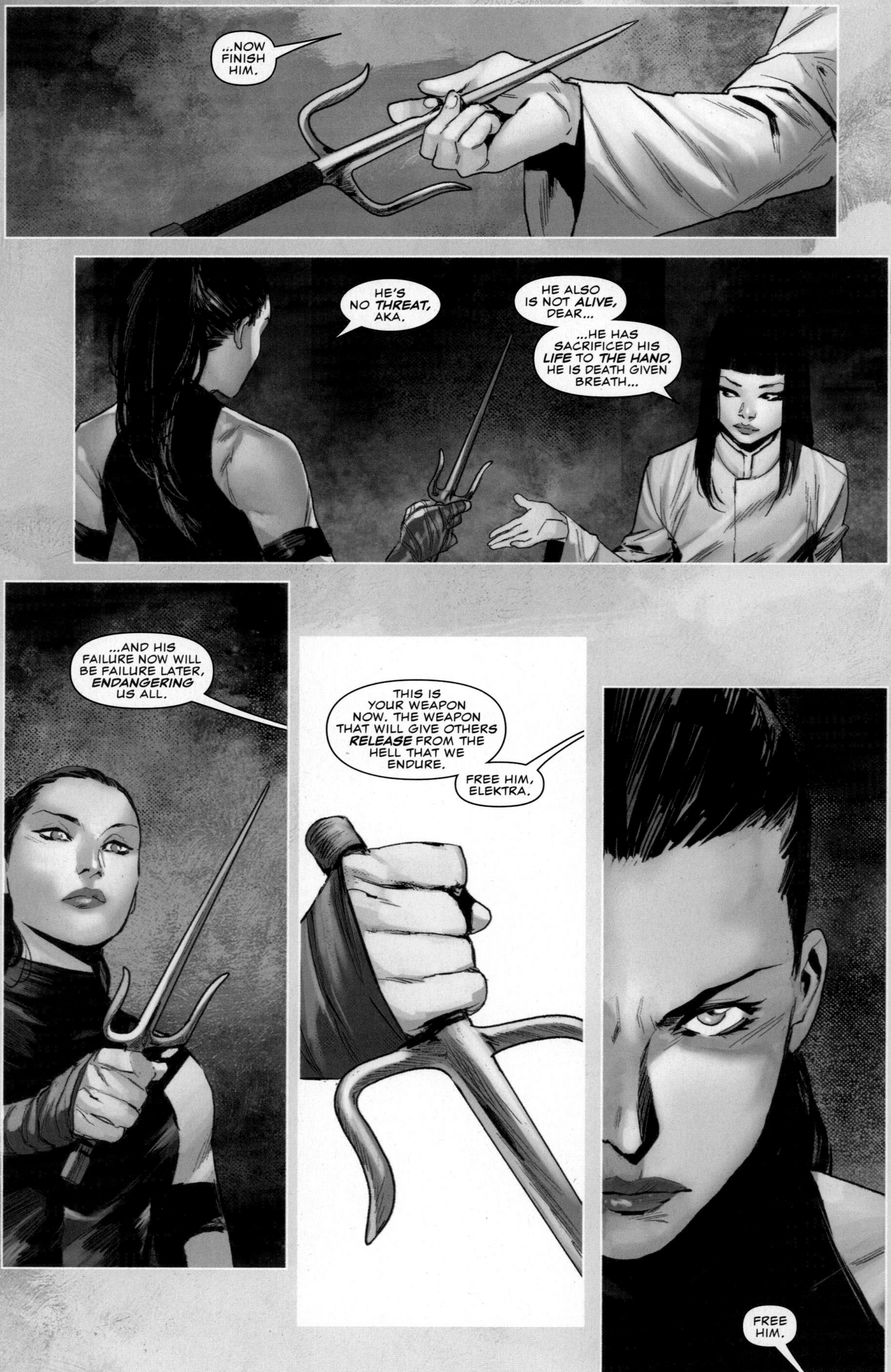
...NOW FINISH HIM.
HE'S NO THREAT, AKA.
HE ALSO IS NOT ALIVE, DEAR...
...HE HAS SACRIFICED HIS LIFE TO THE HAND. HE IS DEATH GIVEN BREATH...
...AND HIS FAILURE NOW WILL BE FAILURE LATER, ENDANGERING US ALL.
THIS IS YOUR WEAPON NOW. THE WEAPON THAT WILL GIVE OTHERS RELEASE FROM THE HELL THAT WE ENDURE.
FREE HIM, ELEKTRA.
FREE HIM.

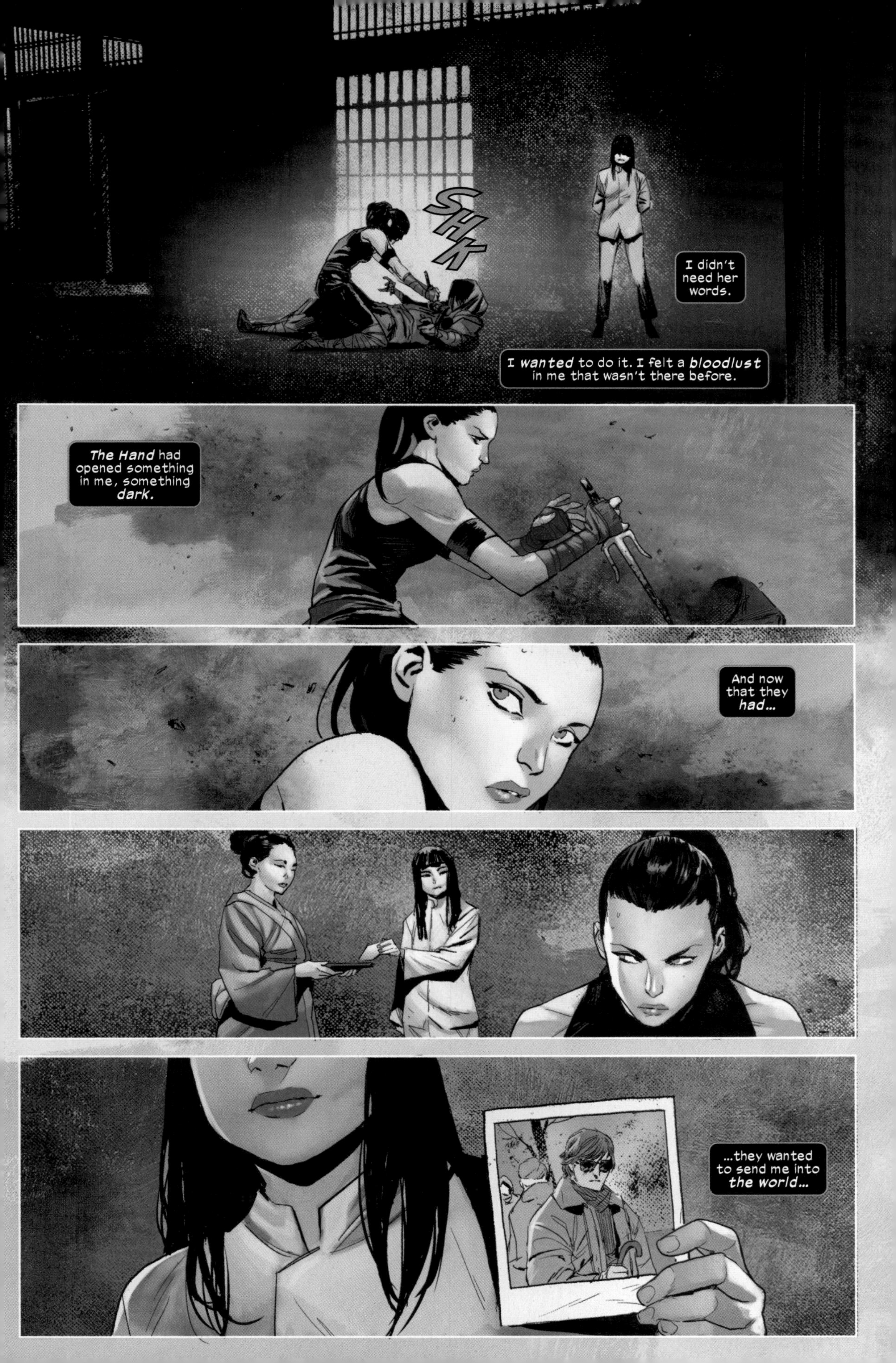
SHK
I didn't need her words.
I *wanted* to do it. I felt a *bloodlust* in me that wasn't there before.
The Hand had opened something in me, something *dark.*
And now that they *had...*
...they wanted to send me into *the world...*

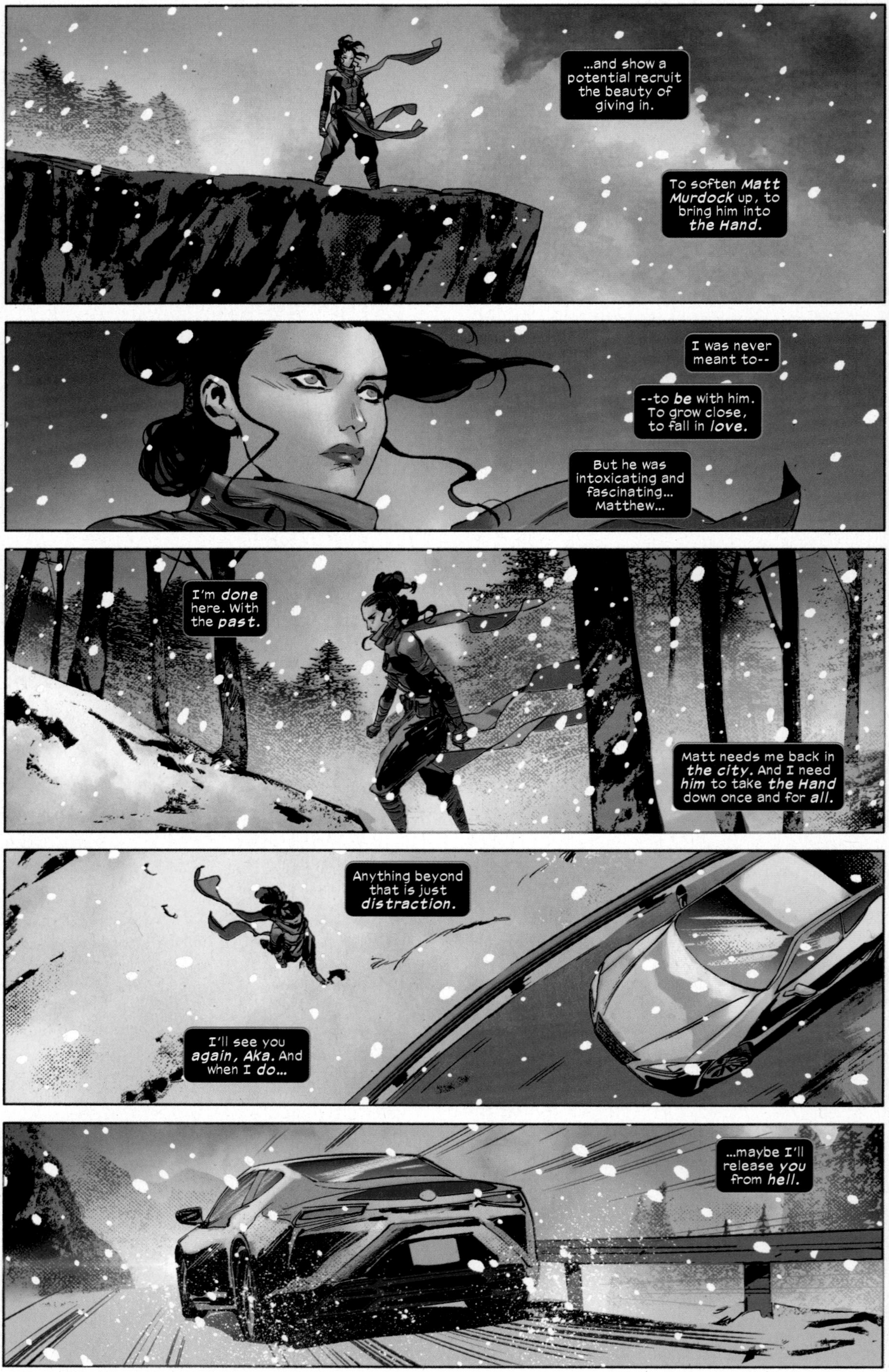
...and show a potential recruit the beauty of giving in.
To soften Matt Murdock up, to bring him into the Hand.
I was never meant to--
--to be with him. To grow close, to fall in love.
But he was intoxicating and fascinating... Matthew...
I'm done here. With the past.
Matt needs me back in the city. And I need him to take the Hand down once and for all.
Anything beyond that is just distraction.
I'll see you again, Aka. And when I do...
...maybe I'll release you from hell.

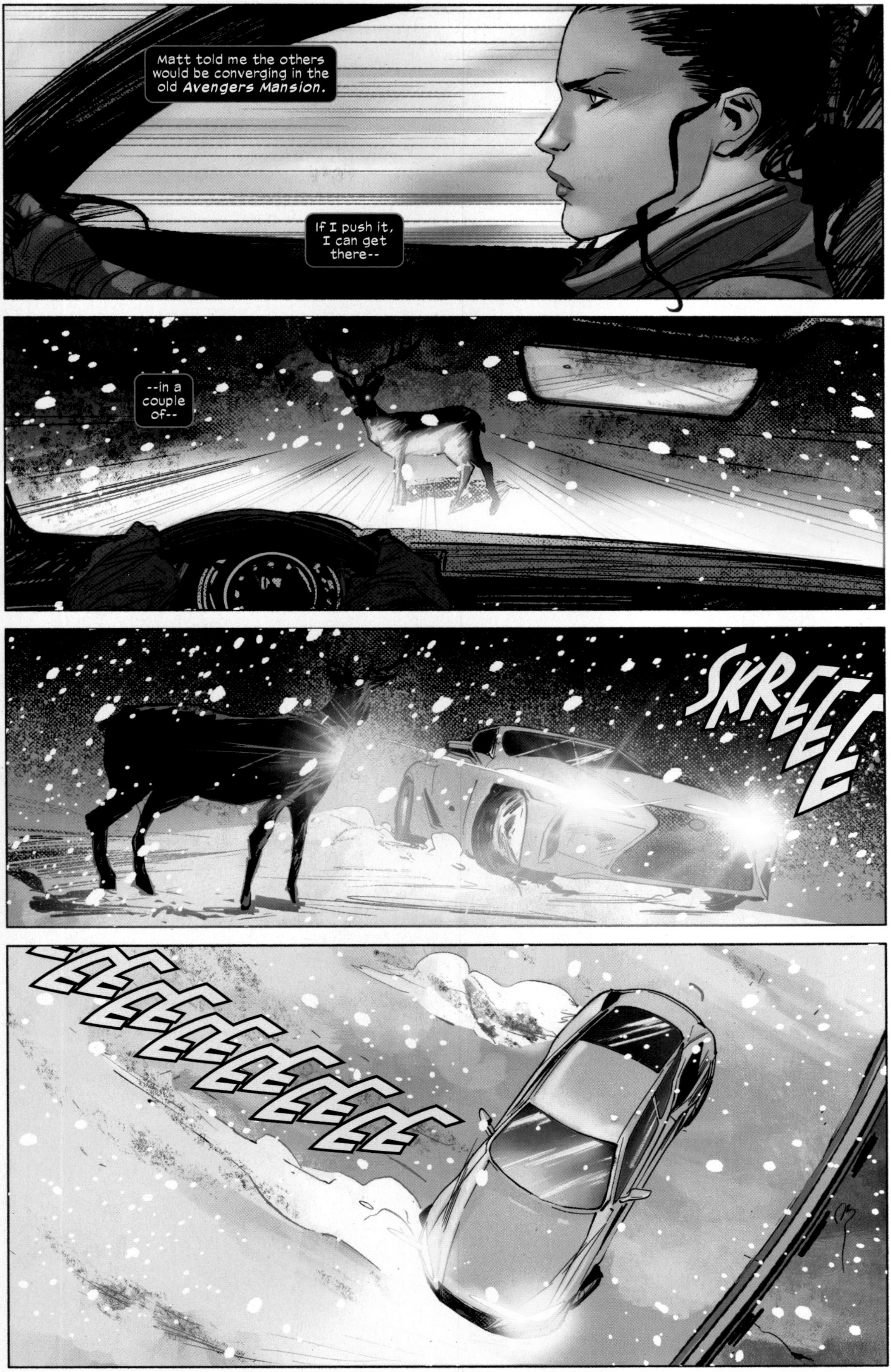

Matt told me the others would be converging in the old *Avengers Mansion.*
If I push it, I can get there--
--in a couple of--
SKREEEE
EEEEEEEEEEEEEEE

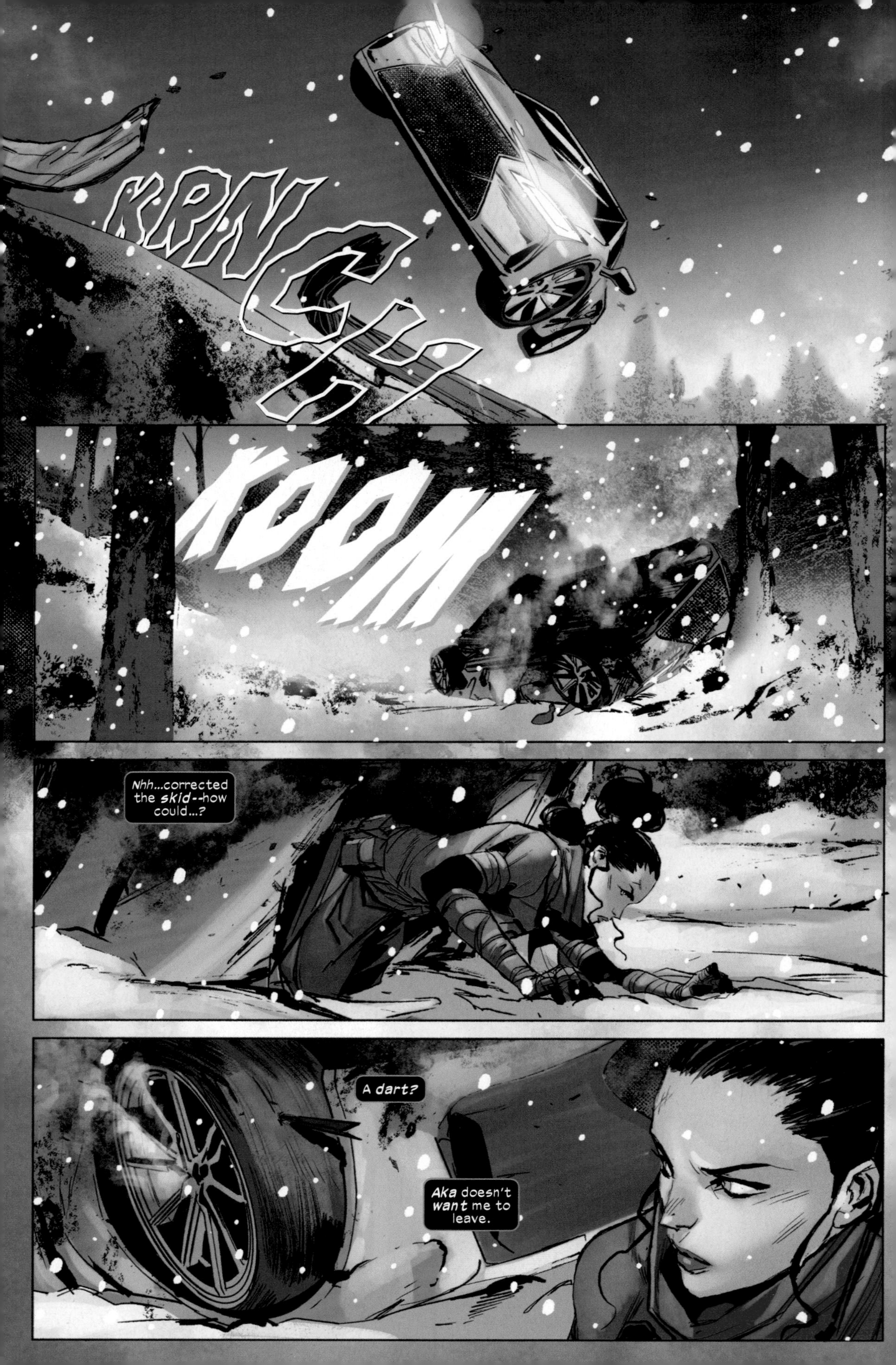
KRNCHH
KOOM
Nhh...corrected the skid--how could...?
A dart?
Aka doesn't want me to leave.

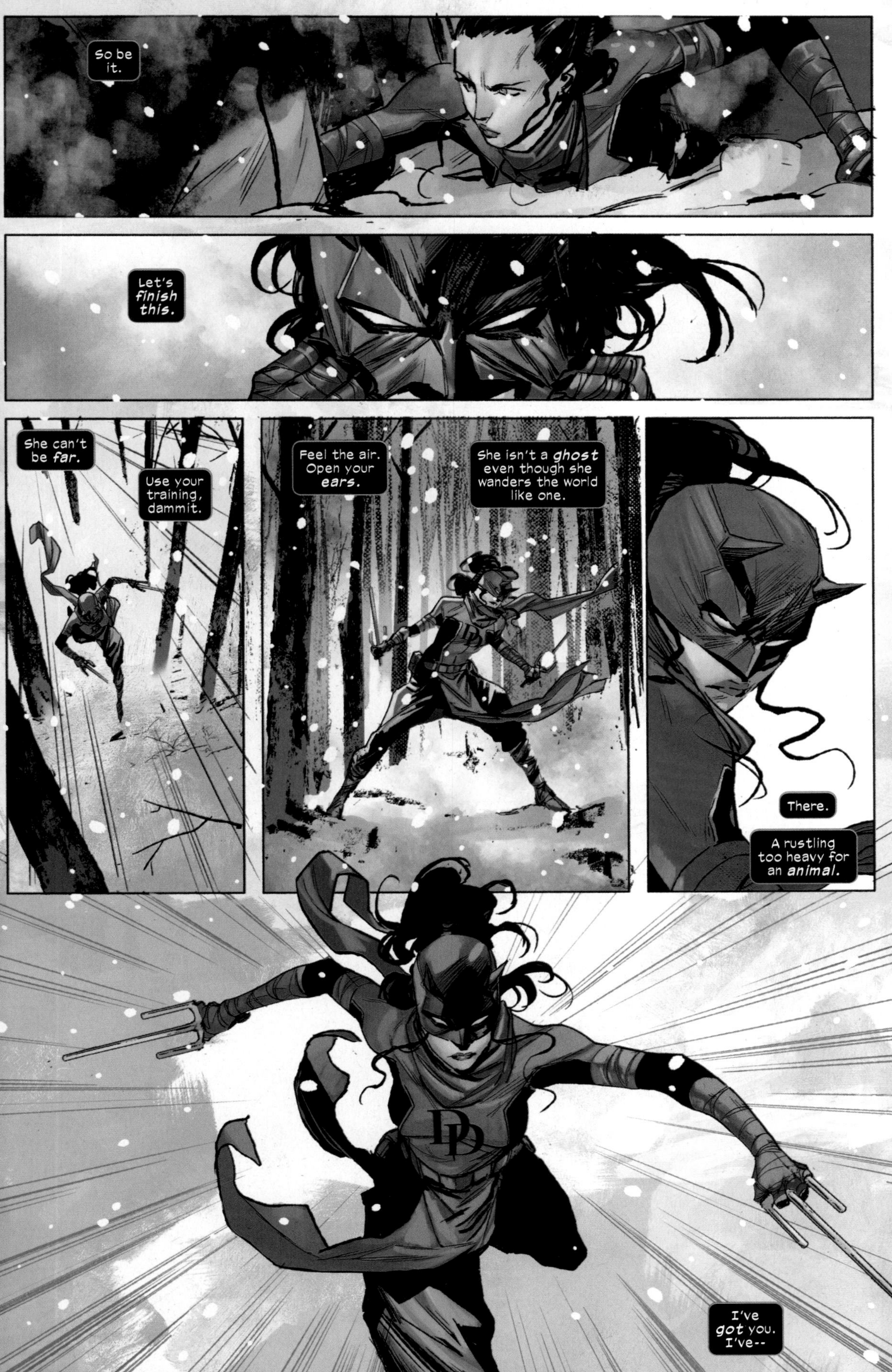
So be it.
Let's finish this.
She can't be far.
Use your training, dammit.
Feel the air. Open your ears.
She isn't a ghost even though she wanders the world like one.
There.
A rustling too heavy for an animal.
I've got you. I've--

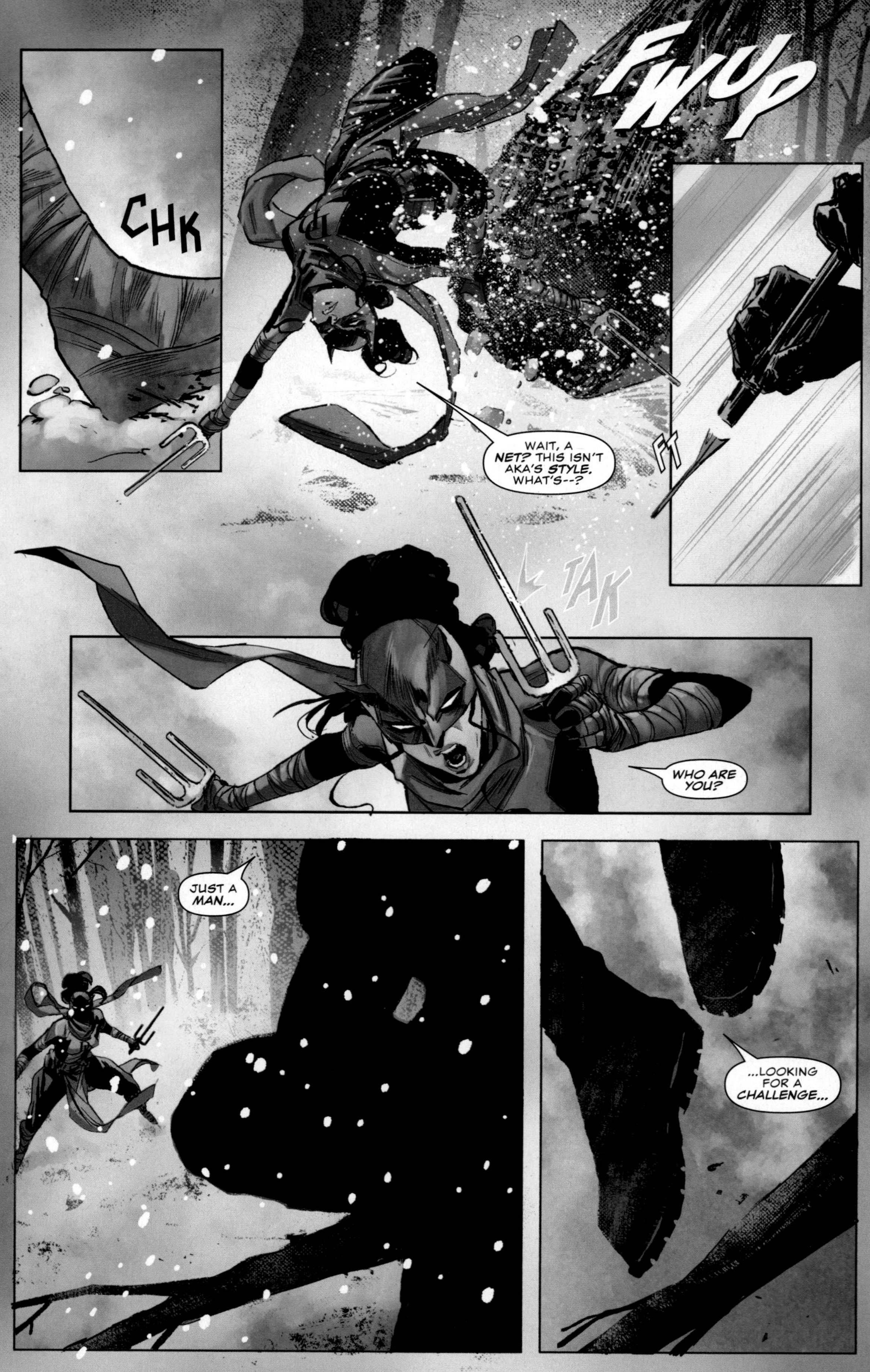
CHK
FWUP
WAIT, A NET? THIS ISN'T AKA'S STYLE. WHAT'S--?
FT
TAK
WHO ARE YOU?
JUST A MAN...
...LOOKING FOR A CHALLENGE...

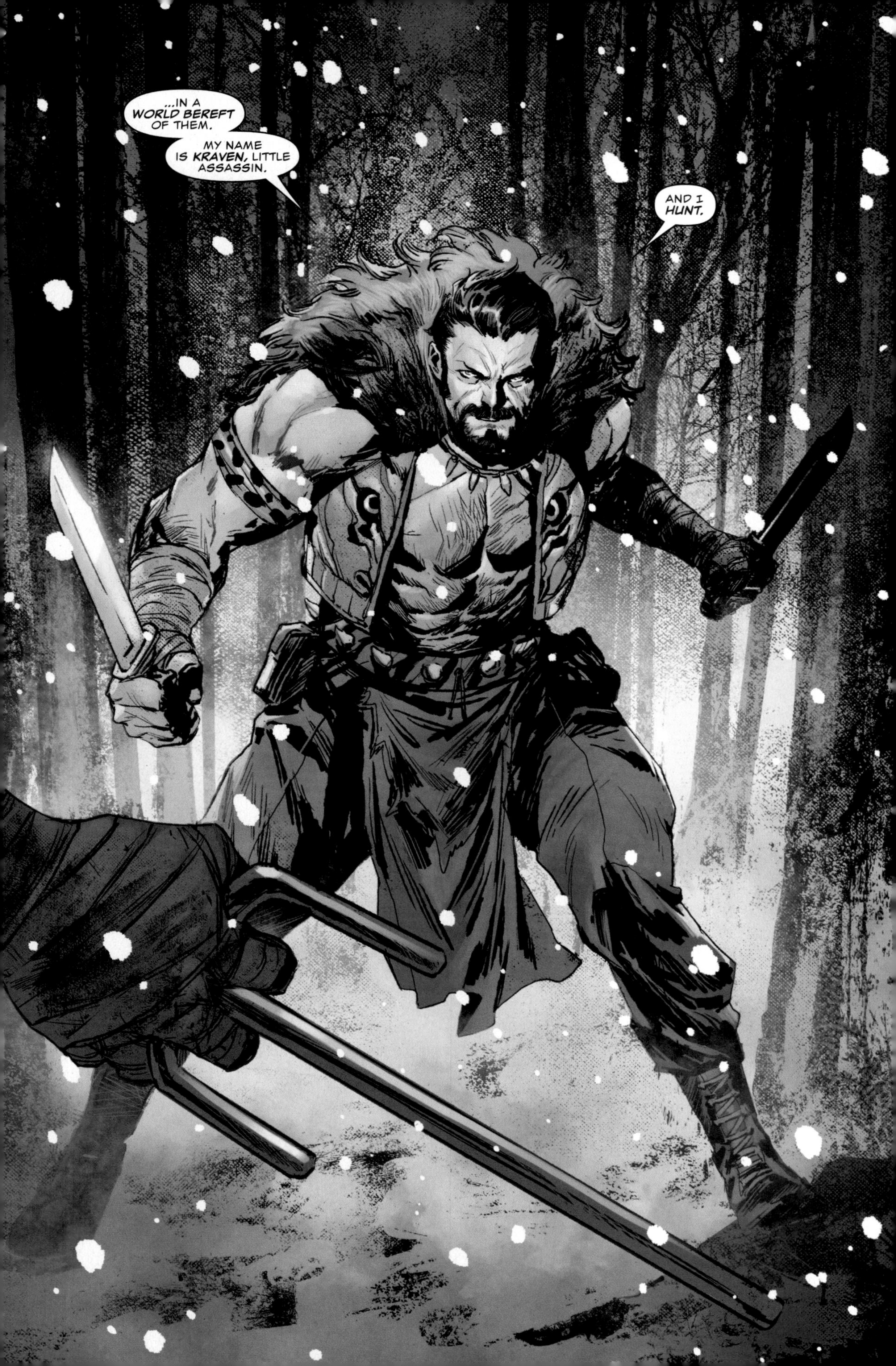
...IN A WORLD BEREFT OF THEM.
MY NAME IS KRAVEN, LITTLE ASSASSIN.
AND I HUNT.

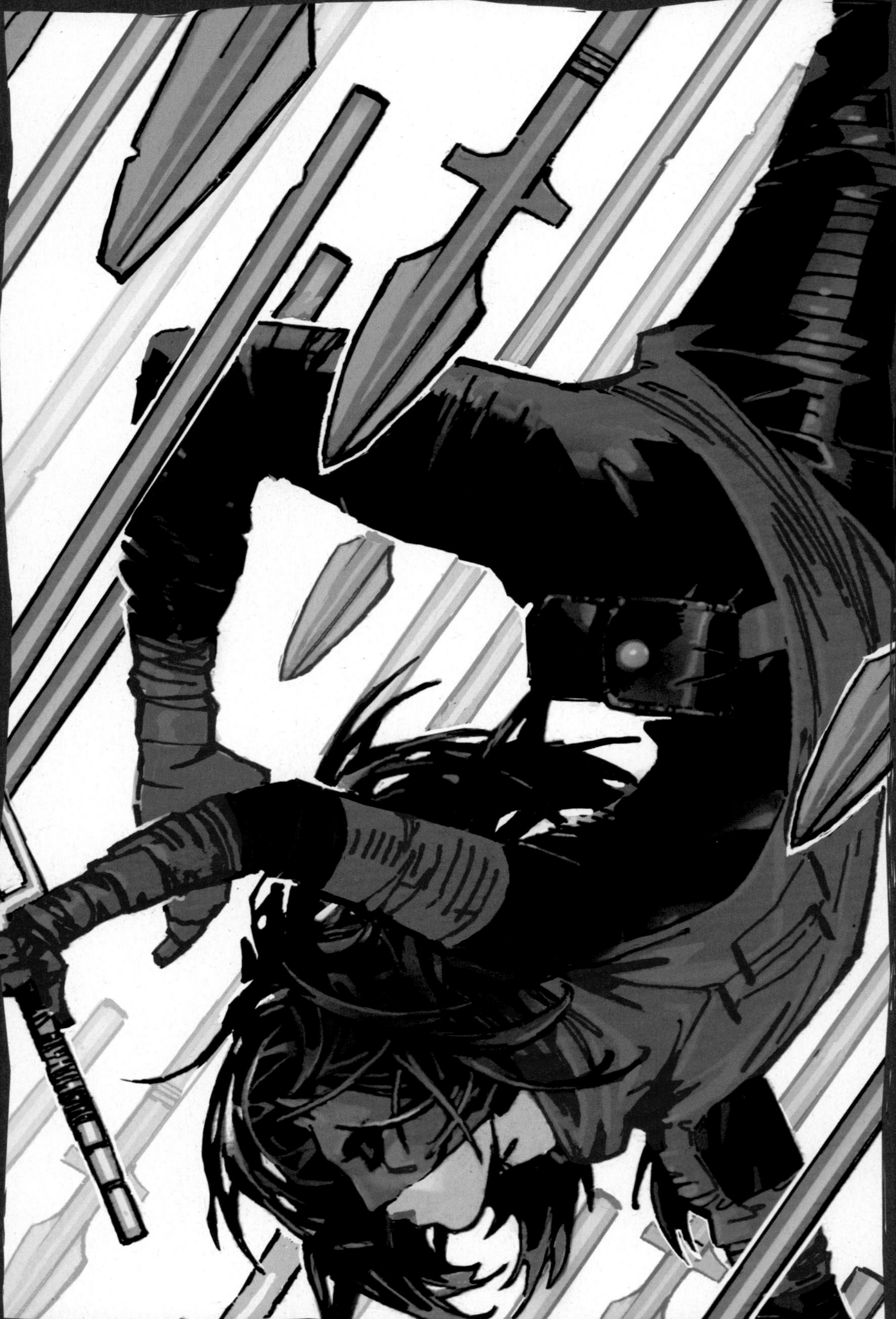

2

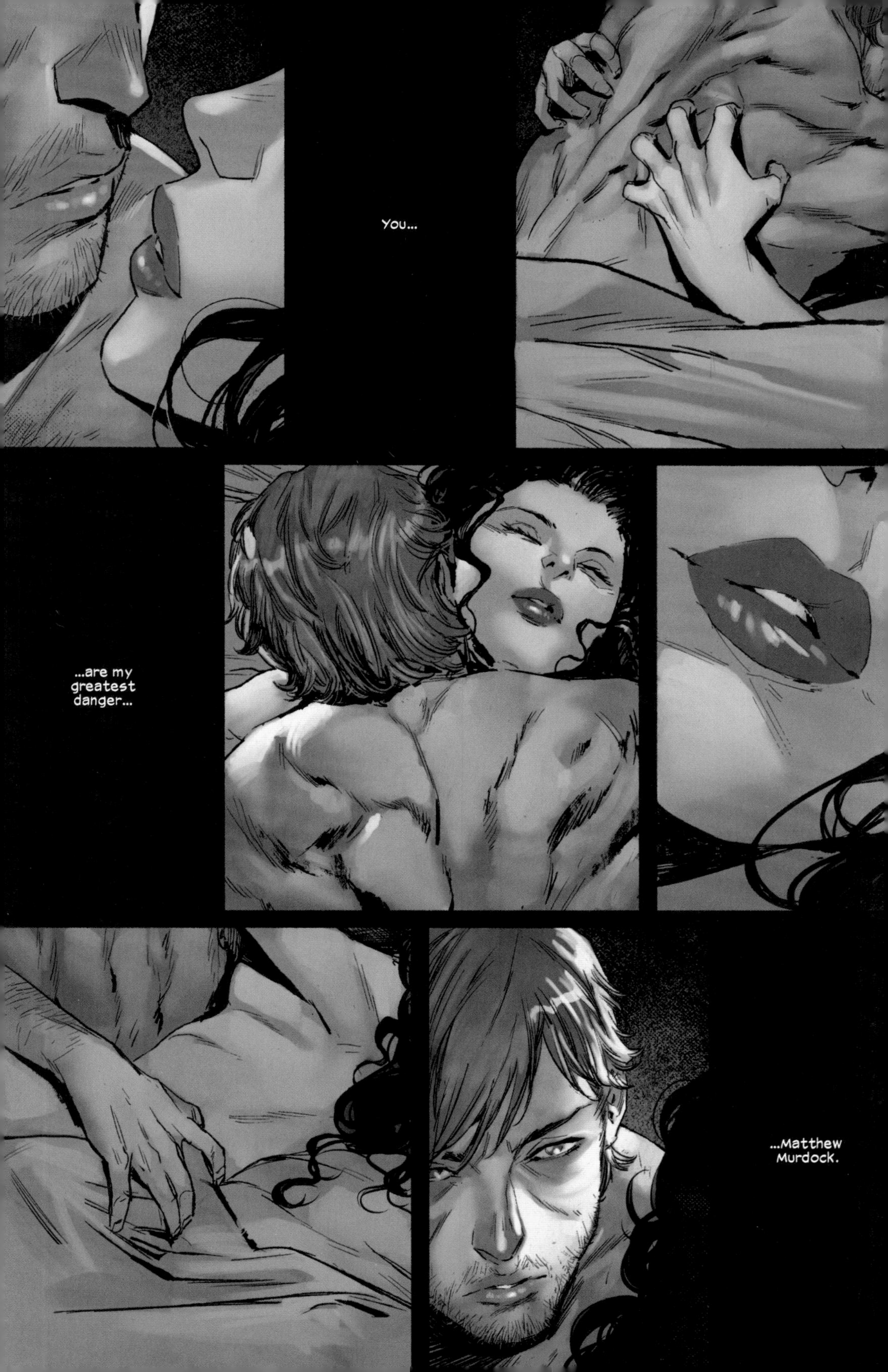
YOU...
...are my greatest danger...
...Matthew Murdock.

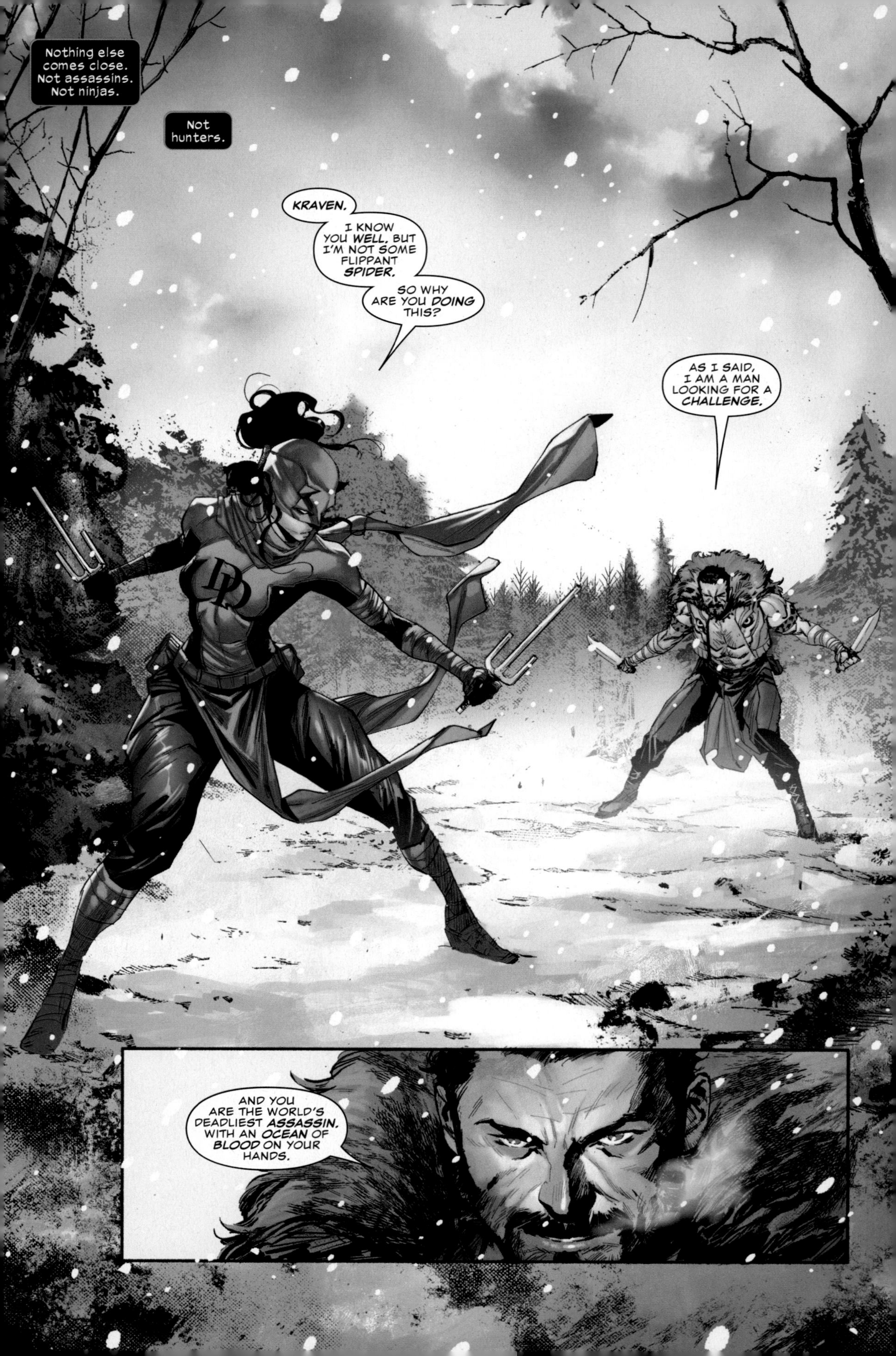
Nothing else comes close. Not assassins. Not ninjas.
Not hunters.
KRAVEN.
I KNOW YOU WELL, BUT I'M NOT SOME FLIPPANT SPIDER.
SO WHY ARE YOU DOING THIS?
AS I SAID, I AM A MAN LOOKING FOR A CHALLENGE.
AND YOU ARE THE WORLD'S DEADLIEST ASSASSIN, WITH AN OCEAN OF BLOOD ON YOUR HANDS.

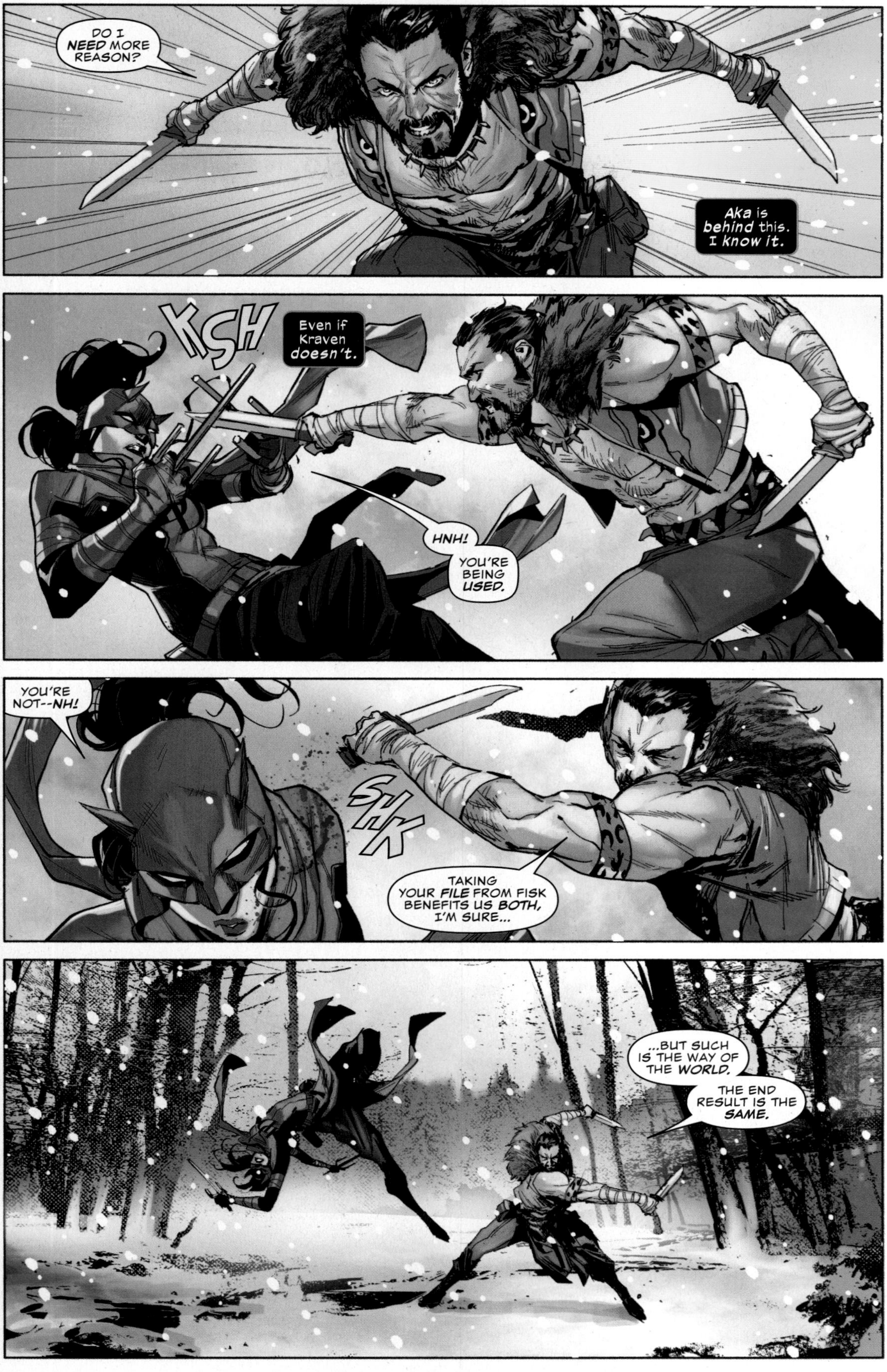
DO I NEED MORE REASON?
Aka is behind this. I know it.
KSH
Even if Kraven doesn't.
HNH!
YOU'RE BEING USED.
YOU'RE NOT--NH!
SHK
TAKING YOUR FILE FROM FISK BENEFITS US BOTH, I'M SURE...
...BUT SUCH IS THE WAY OF THE WORLD.
THE END RESULT IS THE SAME.

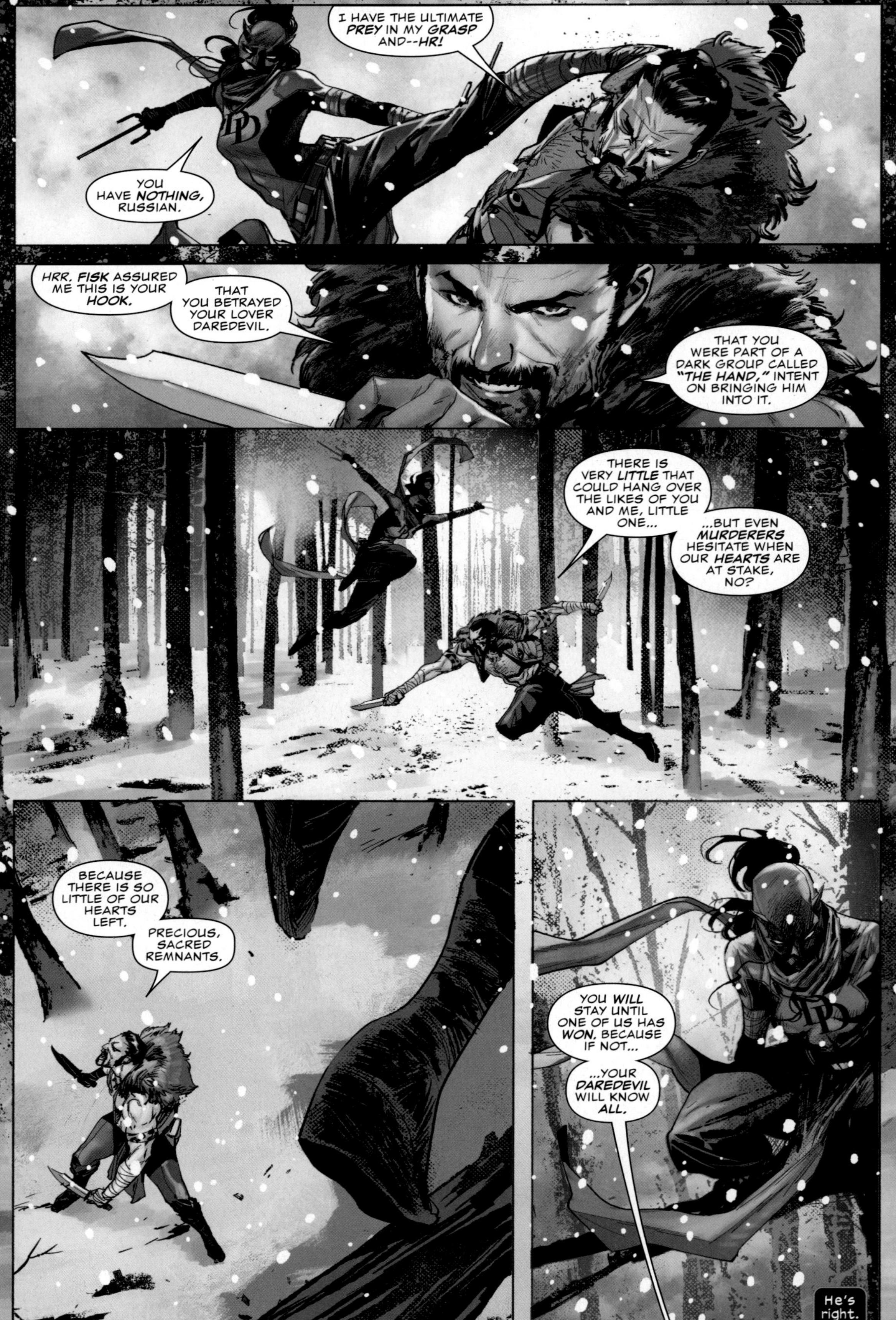
I HAVE THE ULTIMATE PREY IN MY GRASP AND--HR!
YOU HAVE NOTHING, RUSSIAN.
HRR. FISK ASSURED ME THIS IS YOUR HOOK.
THAT YOU BETRAYED YOUR LOVER DAREDEVIL.
THAT YOU WERE PART OF A DARK GROUP CALLED "THE HAND," INTENT ON BRINGING HIM INTO IT.
THERE IS VERY LITTLE THAT COULD HANG OVER THE LIKES OF YOU AND ME, LITTLE ONE...
...BUT EVEN MURDERERS HESITATE WHEN OUR HEARTS ARE AT STAKE, NO?
BECAUSE THERE IS SO LITTLE OF OUR HEARTS LEFT.
PRECIOUS, SACRED REMNANTS.
YOU WILL STAY UNTIL ONE OF US HAS WON, BECAUSE IF NOT...
...YOUR DAREDEVIL WILL KNOW ALL.
He's right.

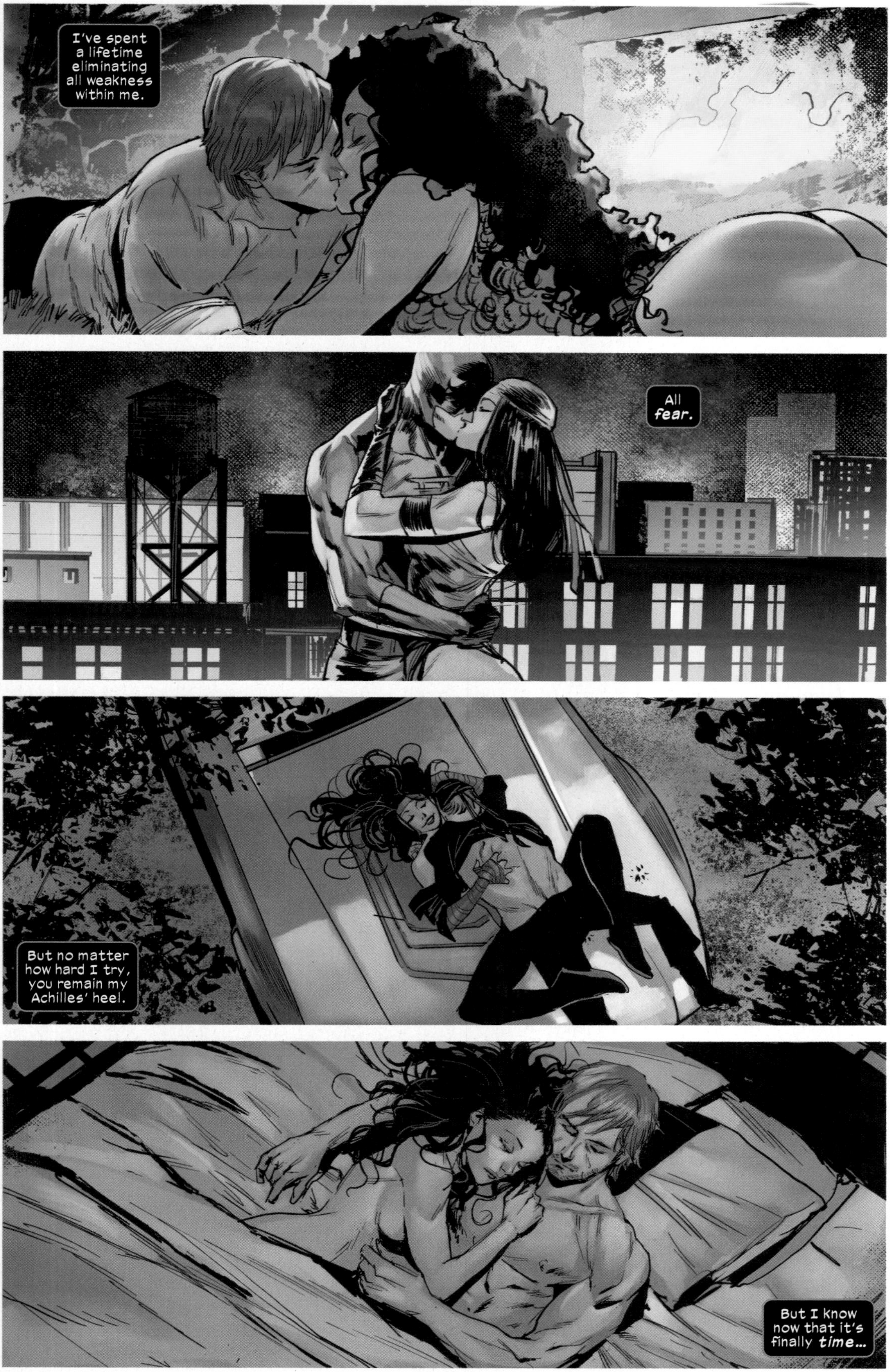
I've spent a lifetime eliminating all weakness within me.
All *fear.*
But no matter how hard I try, you remain my Achilles' heel.
But I know now that it's finally *time...*

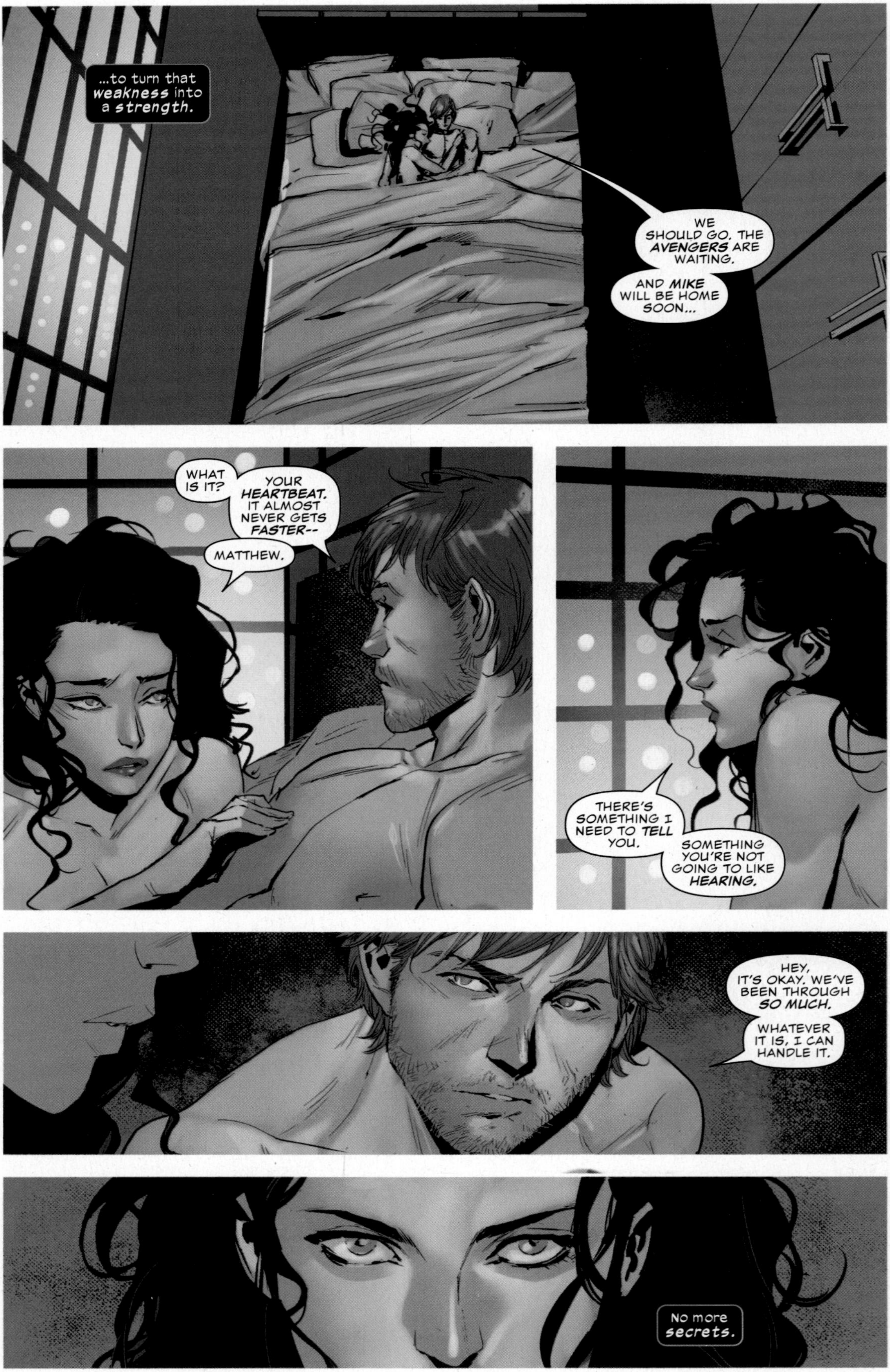
...to turn that weakness into a strength.
WE SHOULD GO. THE AVENGERS ARE WAITING.
AND MIKE WILL BE HOME SOON...
WHAT IS IT?
YOUR HEARTBEAT. IT ALMOST NEVER GETS FASTER--
MATTHEW.
THERE'S SOMETHING I NEED TO TELL YOU.
SOMETHING YOU'RE NOT GOING TO LIKE HEARING.
HEY, IT'S OKAY. WE'VE BEEN THROUGH SO MUCH.
WHATEVER IT IS, I CAN HANDLE IT.
No more secrets.

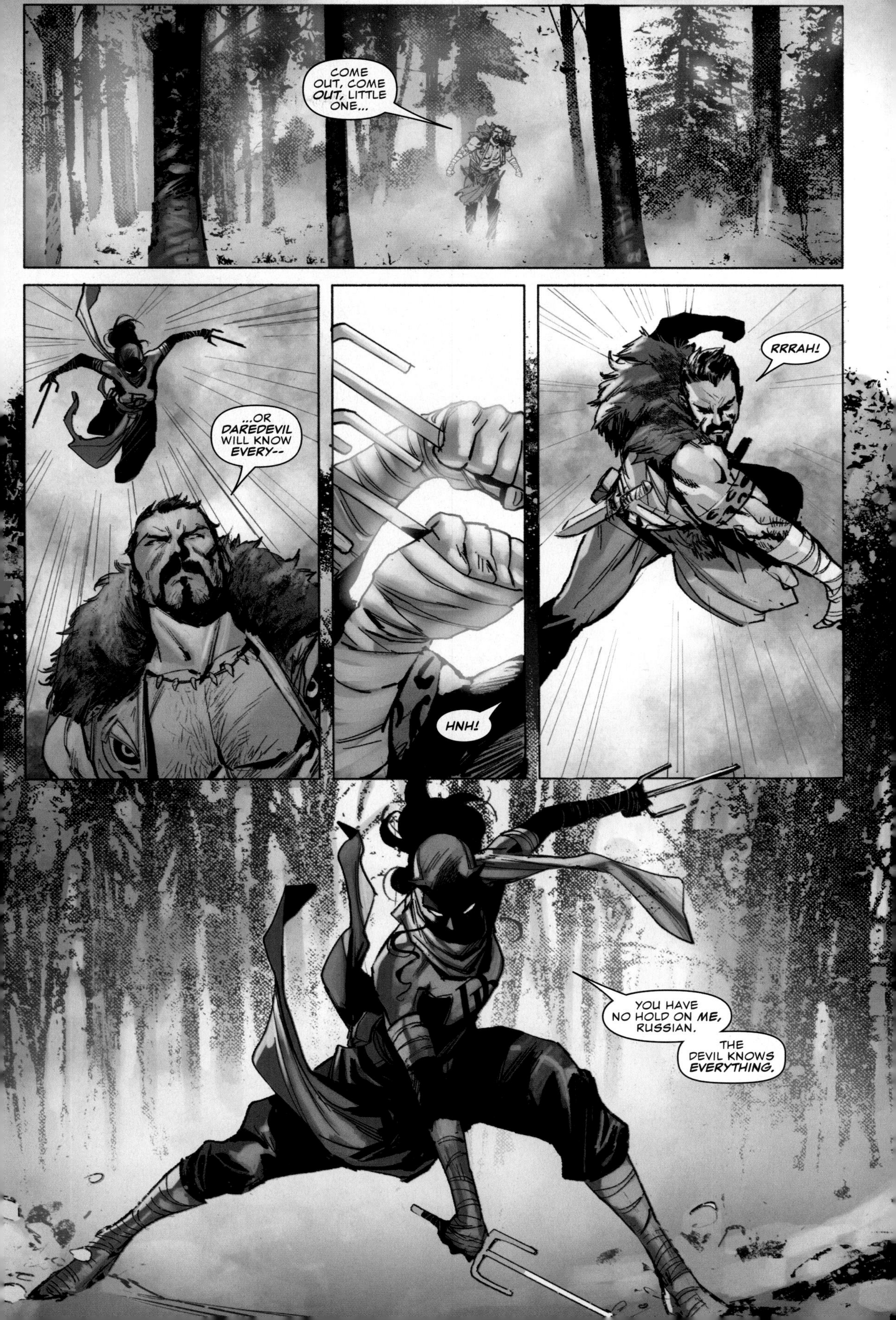
COME OUT, COME OUT, LITTLE ONE...
...OR DAREDEVIL WILL KNOW EVERY--
HNH!
RRRAH!
YOU HAVE NO HOLD ON ME, RUSSIAN.
THE DEVIL KNOWS EVERYTHING.

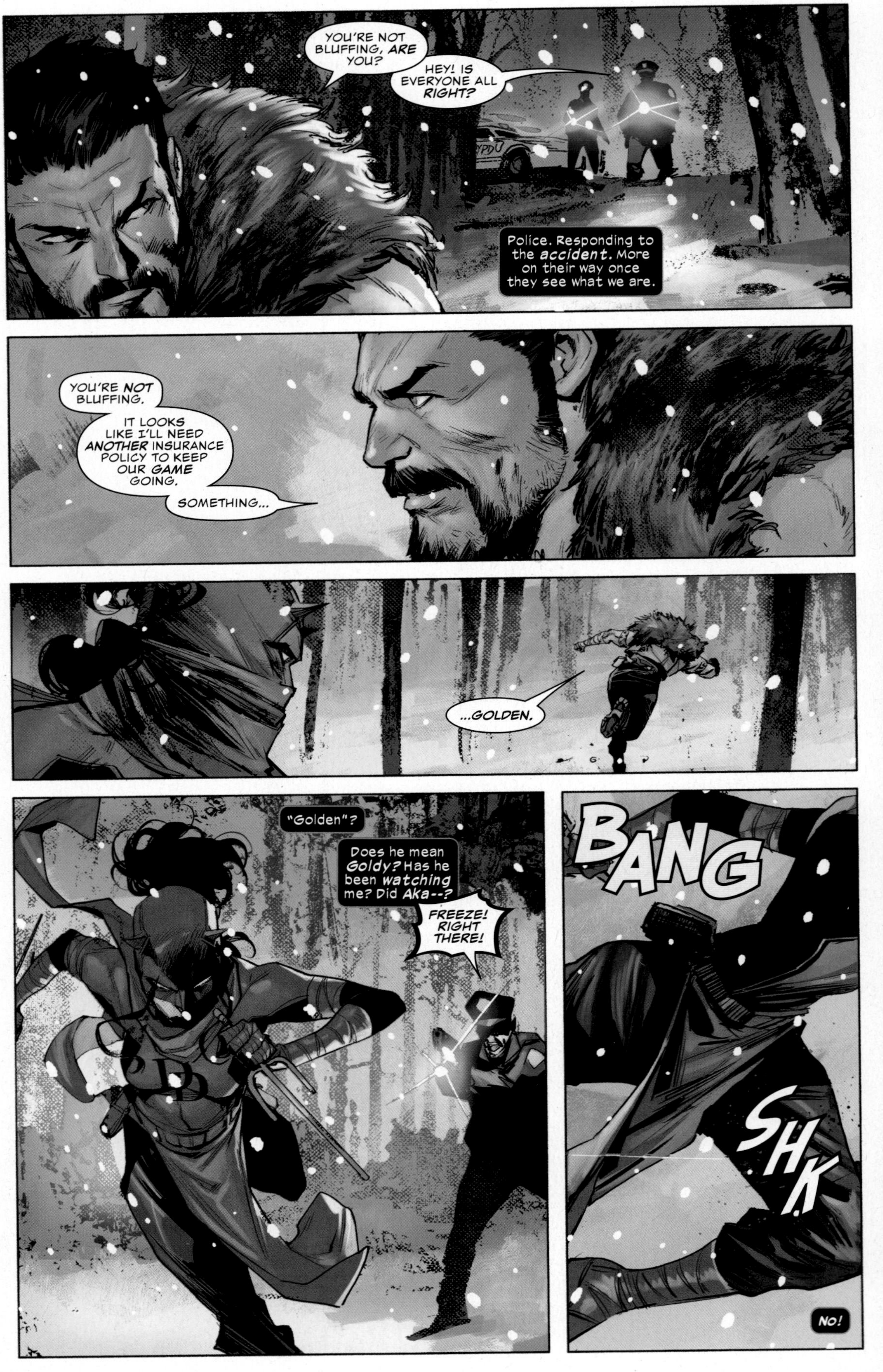
YOU'RE NOT BLUFFING, ARE YOU?
HEY! IS EVERYONE ALL RIGHT?
Police. Responding to the accident. More on their way once they see what we are.
YOU'RE NOT BLUFFING.
IT LOOKS LIKE I'LL NEED ANOTHER INSURANCE POLICY TO KEEP OUR GAME GOING.
SOMETHING...
...GOLDEN.
"Golden"?
Does he mean Goldy? Has he been watching me? Did Aka--?
FREEZE! RIGHT THERE!
BANG
SHK
NO!

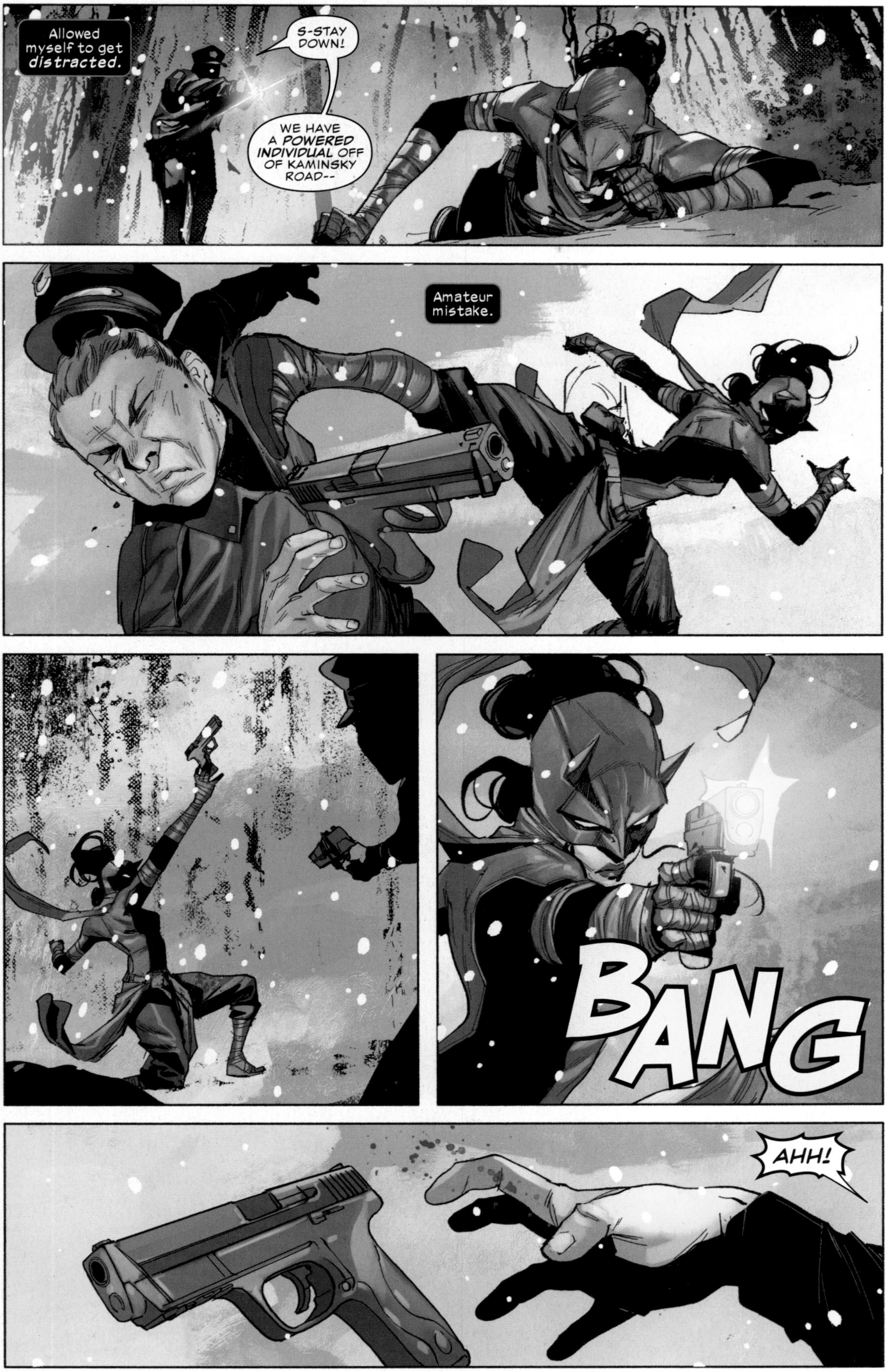
Allowed myself to get *distracted.*
S-STAY DOWN!
WE HAVE A ***POWERED INDIVIDUAL*** OFF OF KAMINSKY ROAD--
Amateur mistake.
BANG
AHH!

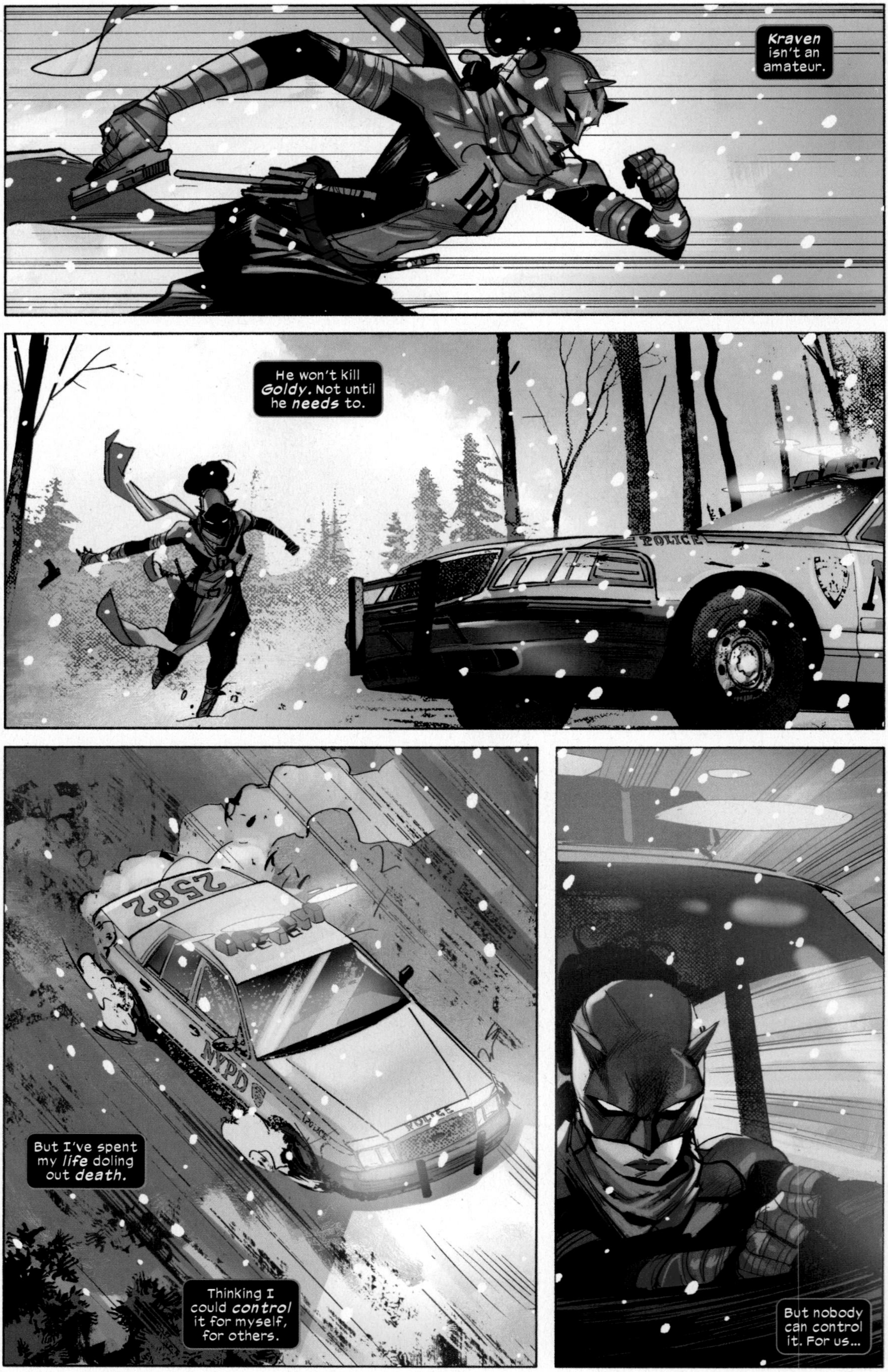
Kraven isn't an amateur.
He won't kill Goldy. Not until he needs to.
POLICE
2582
NYPD
POLICE
But I've spent my life doling out death.
Thinking I could control it for myself, for others.
But nobody can control it. For us...

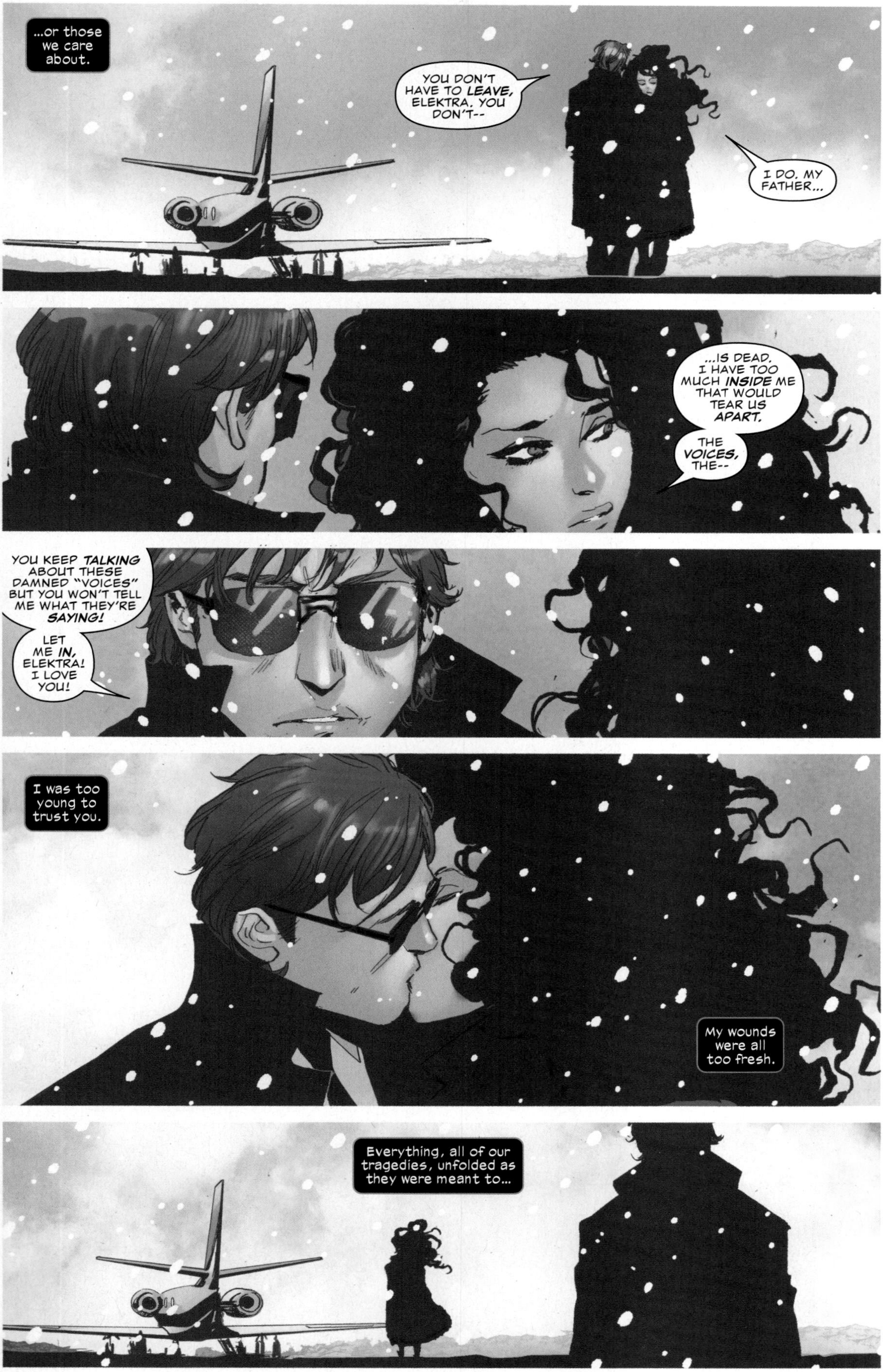
...or those we care about.
YOU DON'T HAVE TO LEAVE, ELEKTRA. YOU DON'T--
I DO. MY FATHER...
...IS DEAD. I HAVE TOO MUCH INSIDE ME THAT WOULD TEAR US APART.
THE VOICES, THE--
YOU KEEP TALKING ABOUT THESE DAMNED "VOICES" BUT YOU WON'T TELL ME WHAT THEY'RE SAYING!
LET ME IN, ELEKTRA! I LOVE YOU!
I was too young to trust you.
My wounds were all too fresh.
Everything, all of our tragedies, unfolded as they were meant to...

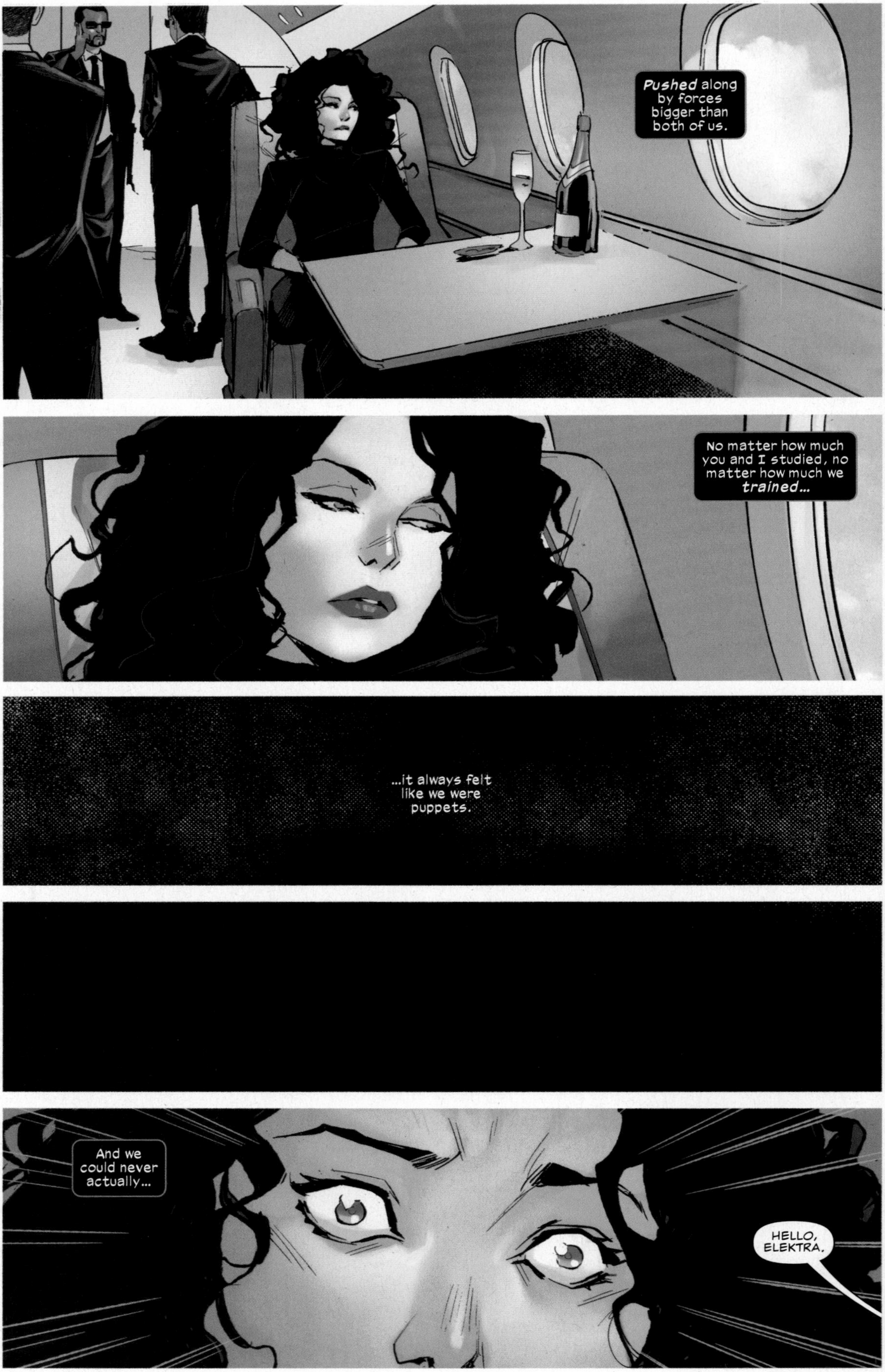
Pushed along by forces bigger than both of us.
No matter how much you and I studied, no matter how much we trained...
...it always felt like we were puppets.
And we could never actually...
HELLO, ELEKTRA.

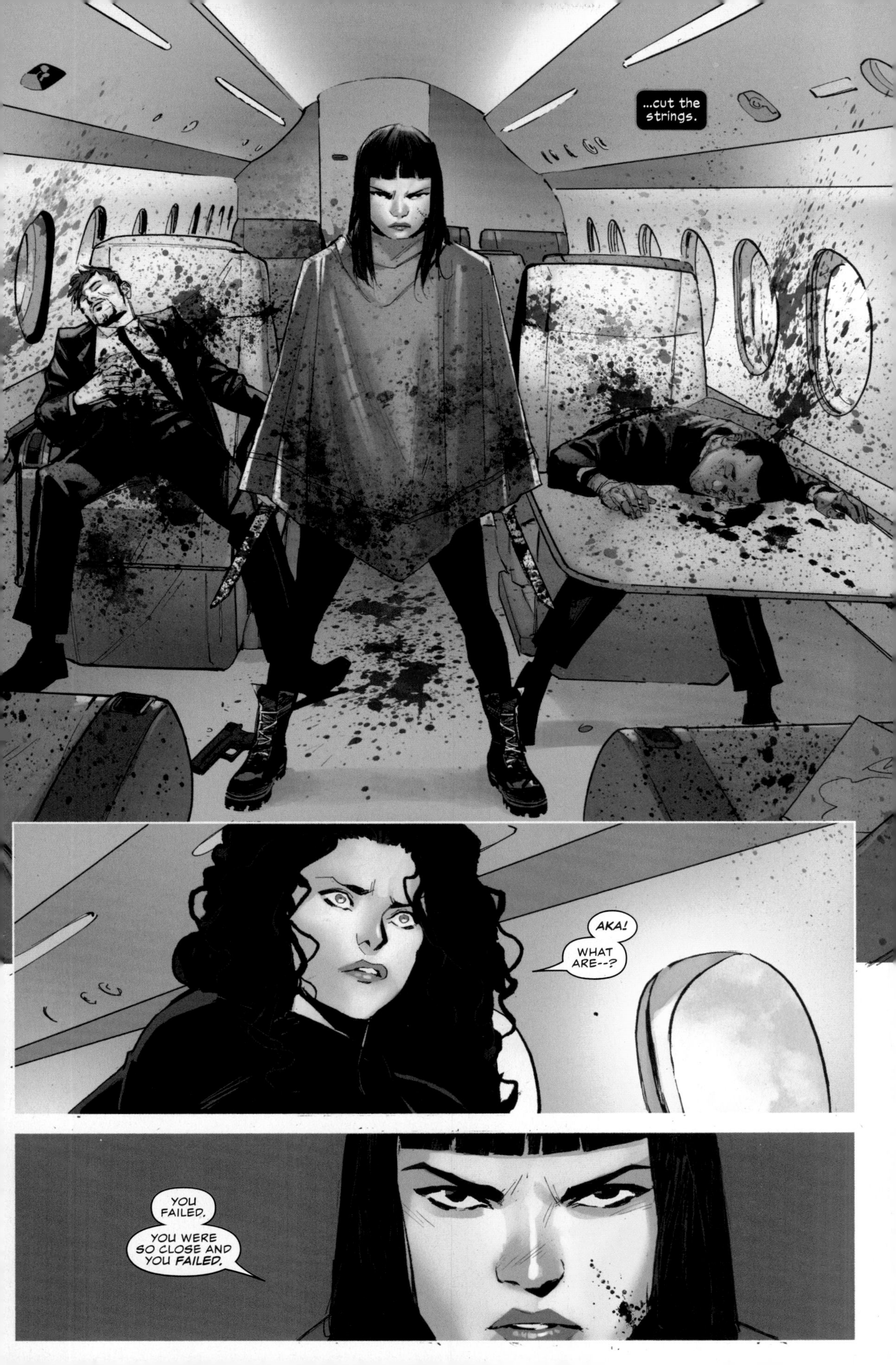
...cut the strings.
AKA!
WHAT ARE--?
YOU FAILED.
YOU WERE SO CLOSE AND YOU FAILED.

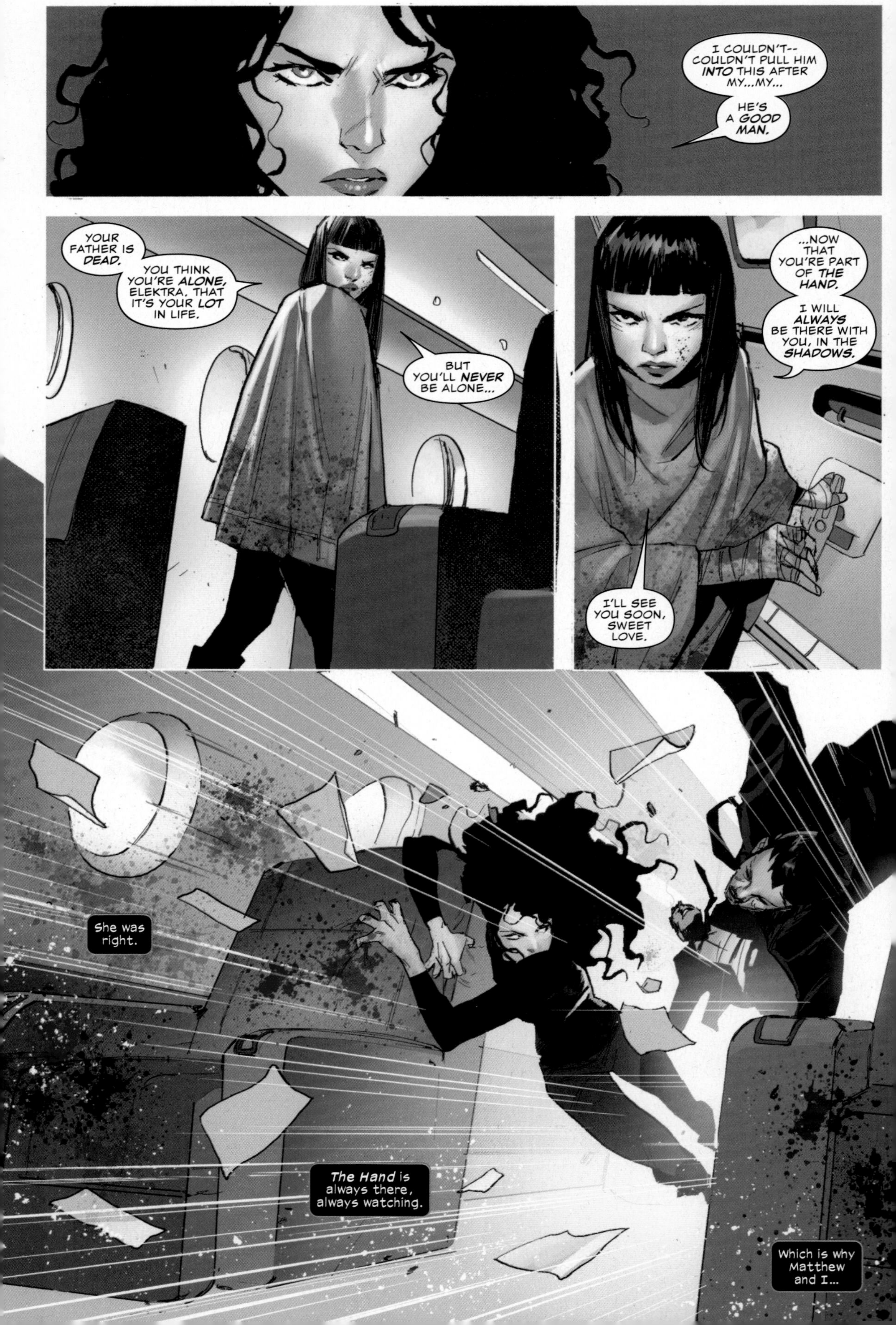
I COULDN'T--
COULDN'T PULL HIM INTO THIS AFTER MY...MY...
HE'S A GOOD MAN.
YOUR FATHER IS DEAD.
YOU THINK YOU'RE ALONE, ELEKTRA. THAT IT'S YOUR LOT IN LIFE.
BUT YOU'LL NEVER BE ALONE...
...NOW THAT YOU'RE PART OF THE HAND.
I WILL ALWAYS BE THERE WITH YOU, IN THE SHADOWS.
I'LL SEE YOU SOON, SWEET LOVE.
She was right.
The Hand is always there, always watching.
Which is why Matthew and I...

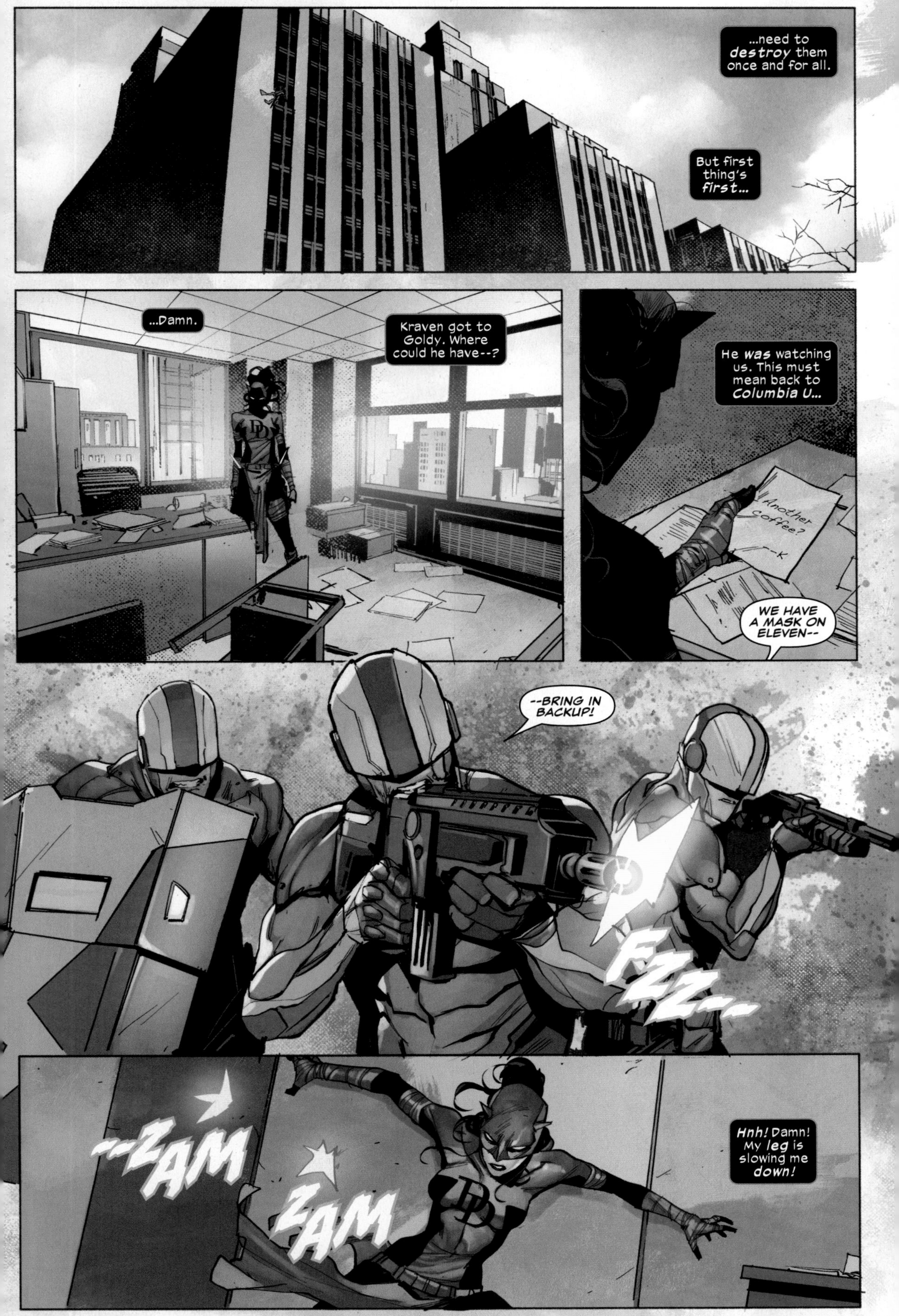

...need to destroy them once and for all.
But first thing's first...
...Damn.
Kraven got to Goldy. Where could he have--?
He was watching us. This must mean back to Columbia U...
Another coffee? --K
WE HAVE A MASK ON ELEVEN--
--BRING IN BACKUP!
FZZ...
--ZAM
ZAM
Hnh! Damn! My leg is slowing me down!

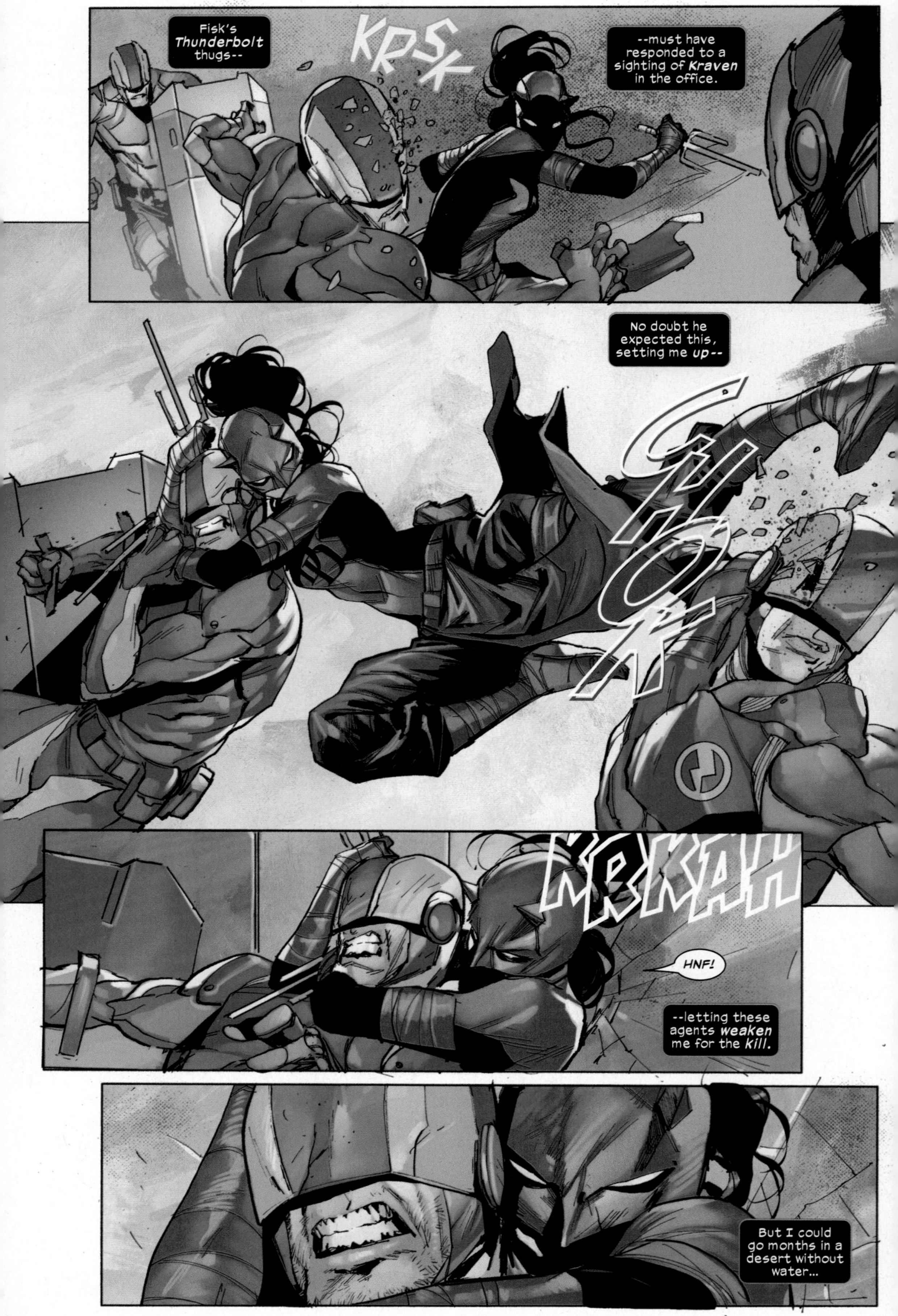

Fisk's *Thunderbolt* thugs--
KRSK
--must have responded to a sighting of *Kraven* in the office.
No doubt he expected this, setting me *up*--
CHOK
KRKAH
HNF!
--letting these agents *weaken* me for the *kill*.
But I could go months in a desert without water...

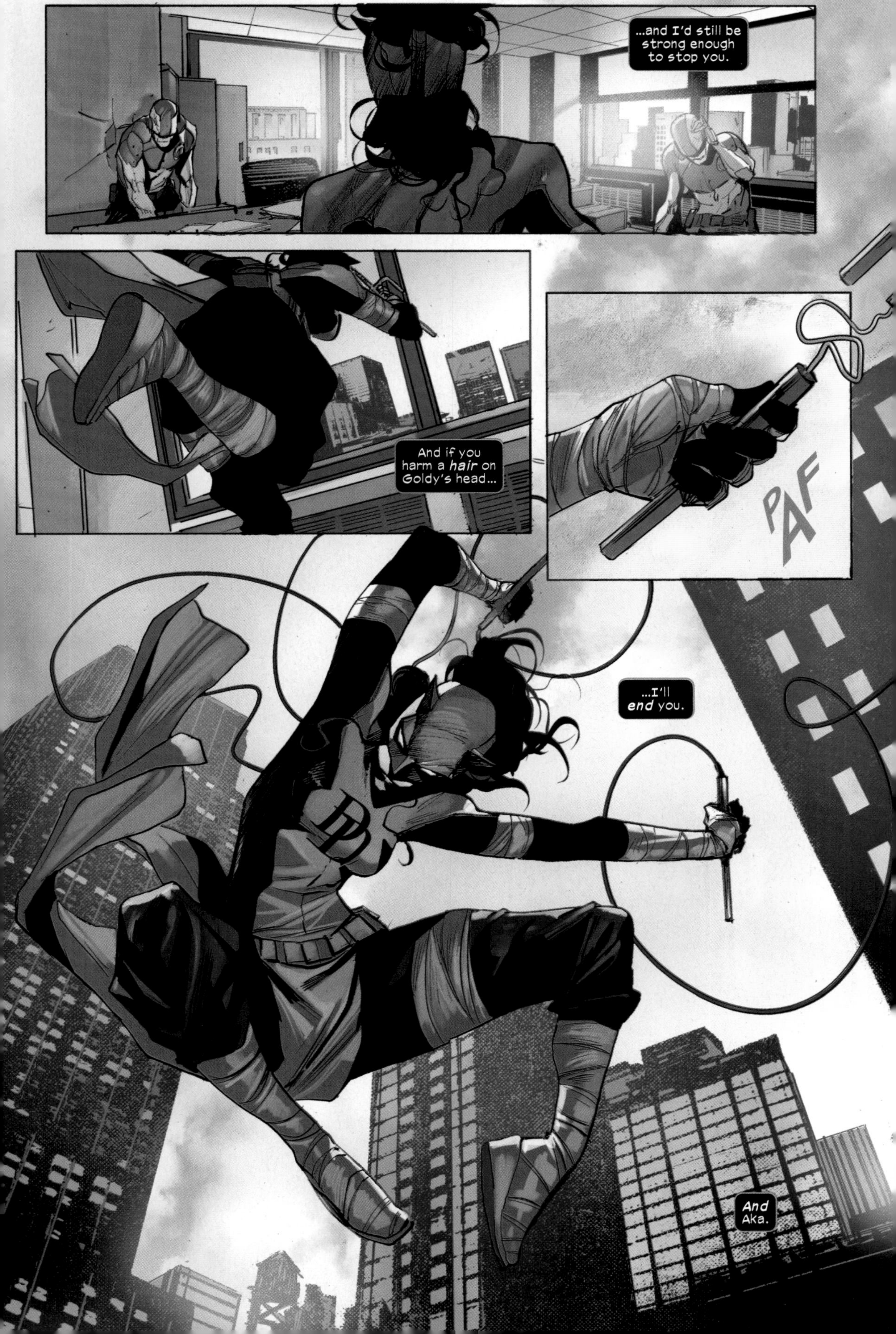
...and I'd still be strong enough to stop you.
And if you harm a *hair* on Goldy's head...
PAF
...I'll *end* you.
And Aka.

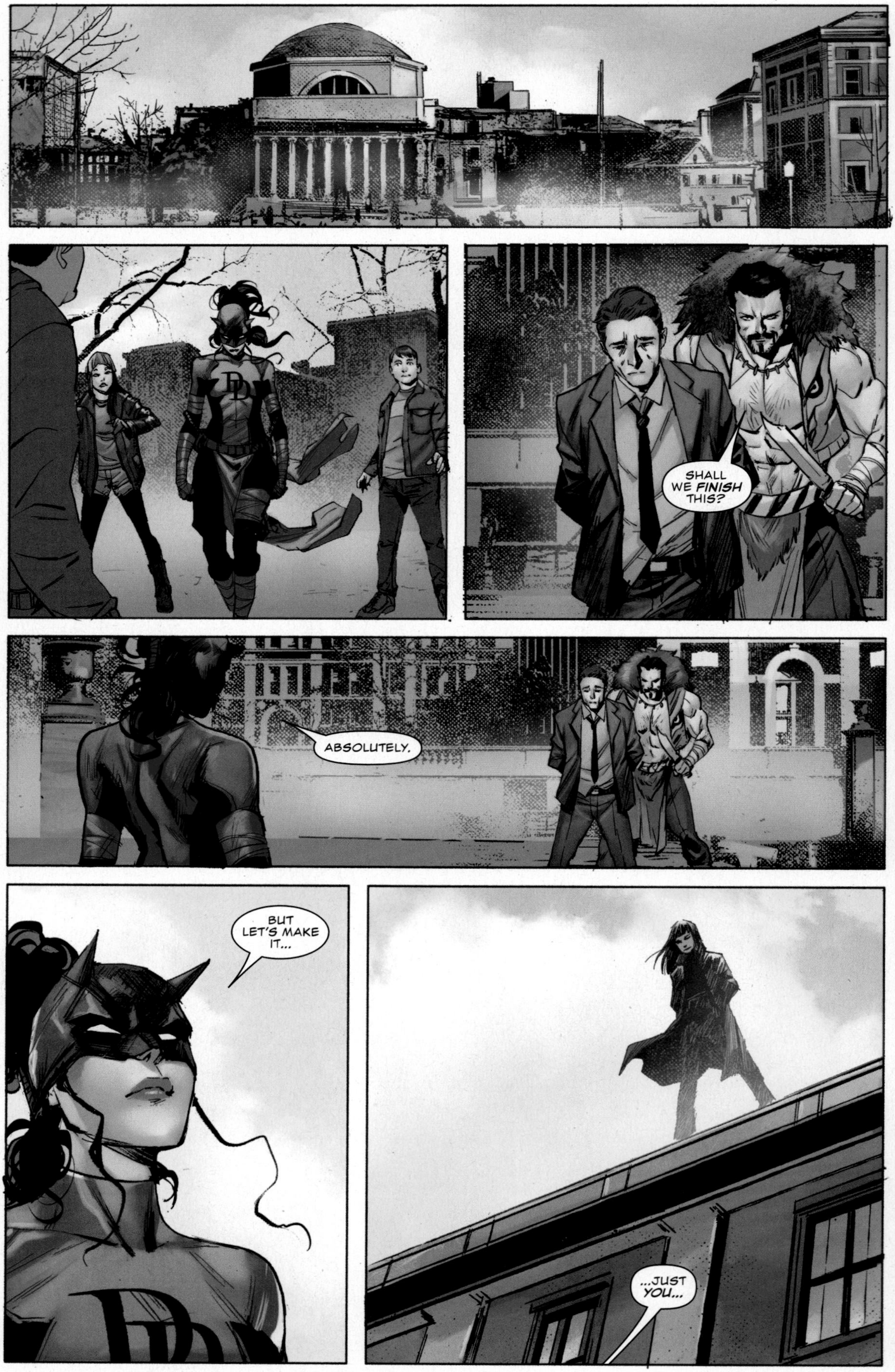
SHALL WE FINISH THIS?
ABSOLUTELY.
BUT LET'S MAKE IT...
...JUST YOU...

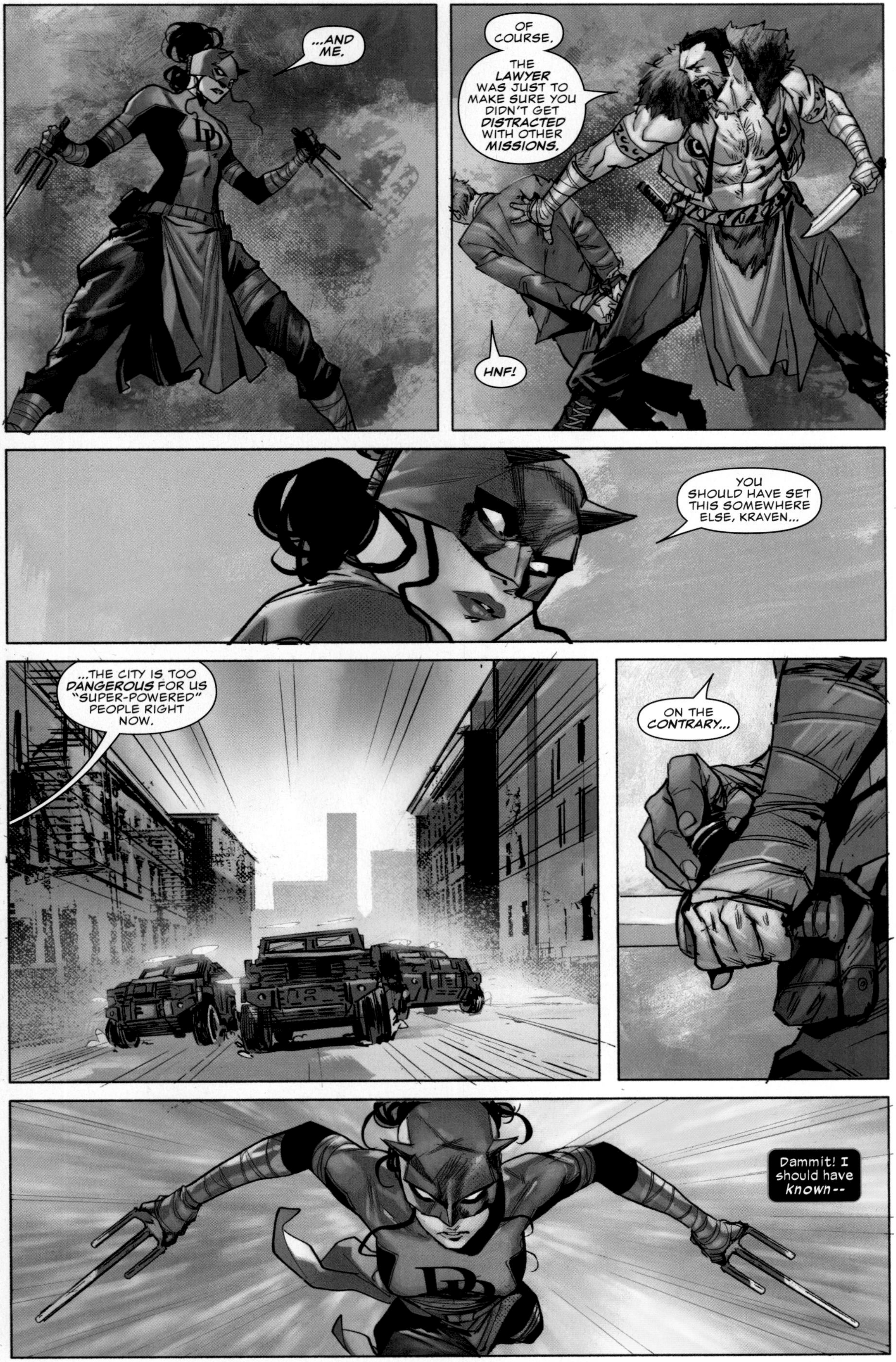
...AND ME.
OF COURSE.
THE LAWYER WAS JUST TO MAKE SURE YOU DIDN'T GET DISTRACTED WITH OTHER MISSIONS.
HNF!
YOU SHOULD HAVE SET THIS SOMEWHERE ELSE, KRAVEN...
...THE CITY IS TOO DANGEROUS FOR US "SUPER-POWERED" PEOPLE RIGHT NOW.
ON THE CONTRARY...
Dammit! I should have known--

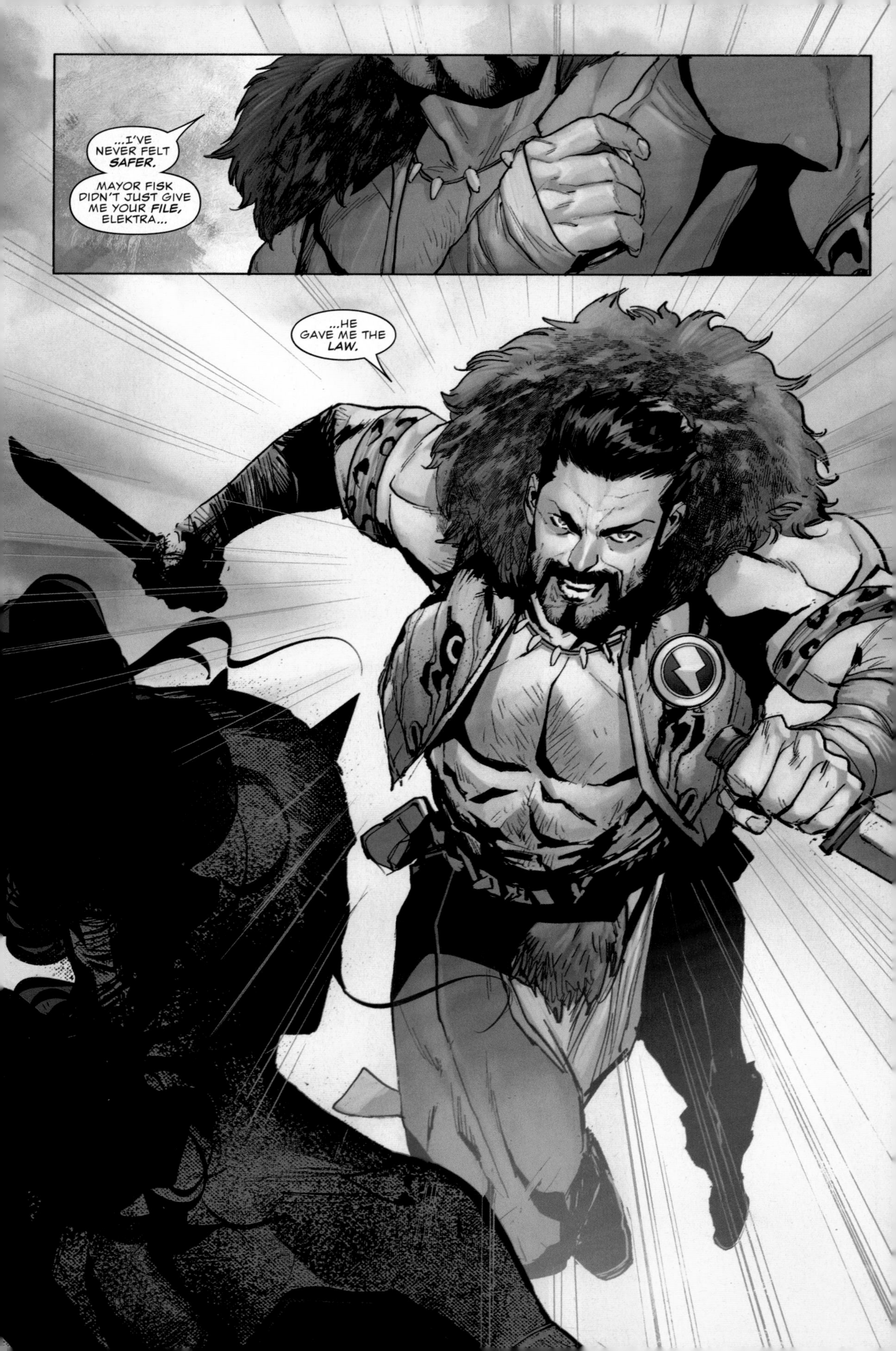
...I'VE NEVER FELT SAFER.
MAYOR FISK DIDN'T JUST GIVE ME YOUR FILE, ELEKTRA...
...HE GAVE ME THE LAW.

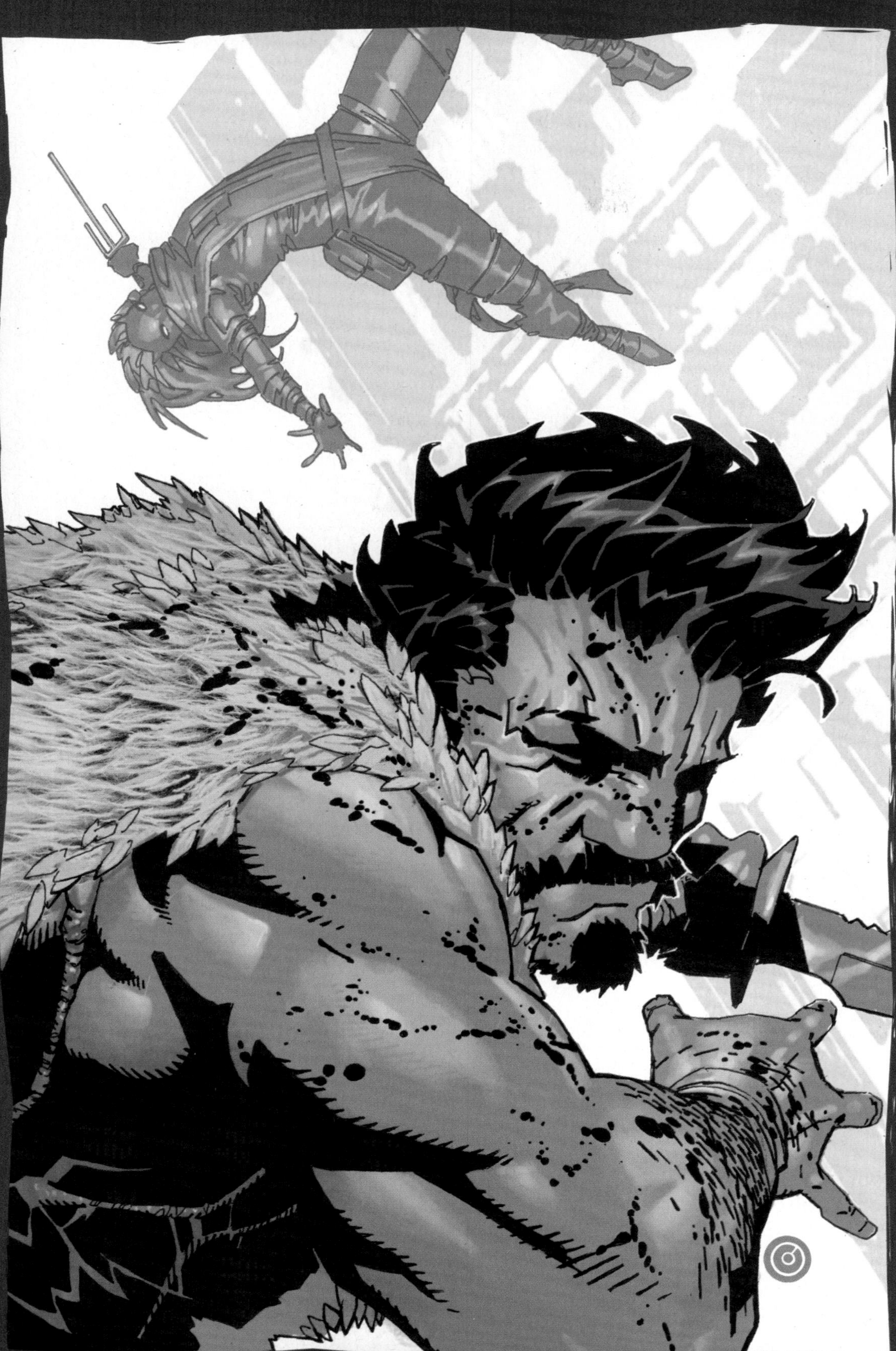

3

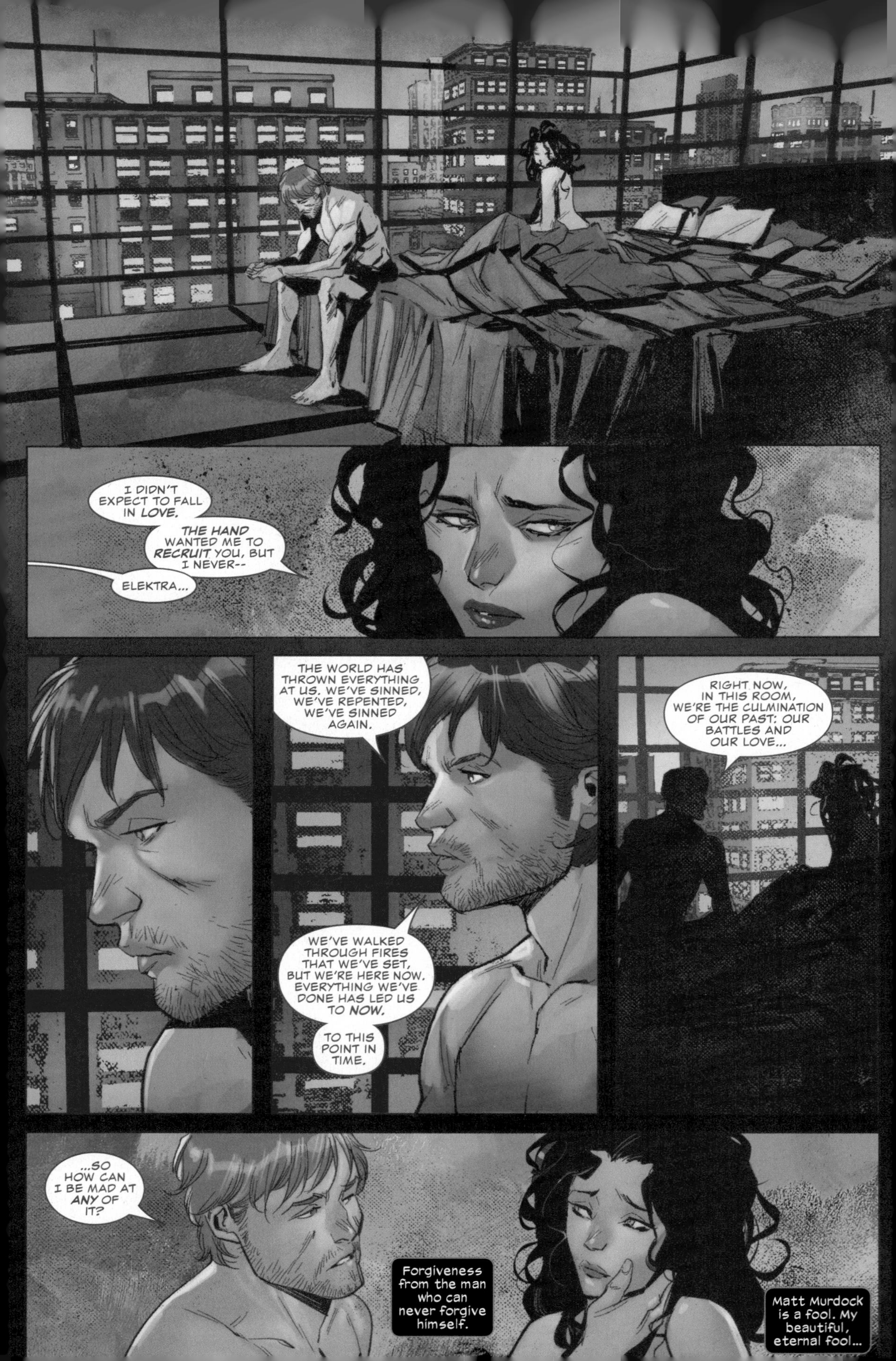
I DIDN'T EXPECT TO FALL IN LOVE.
THE HAND WANTED ME TO RECRUIT YOU, BUT I NEVER--
ELEKTRA...
THE WORLD HAS THROWN EVERYTHING AT US. WE'VE SINNED, WE'VE REPENTED, WE'VE SINNED AGAIN.
WE'VE WALKED THROUGH FIRES THAT WE'VE SET, BUT WE'RE HERE NOW. EVERYTHING WE'VE DONE HAS LED US TO NOW.
TO THIS POINT IN TIME.
RIGHT NOW, IN THIS ROOM, WE'RE THE CULMINATION OF OUR PAST: OUR BATTLES AND OUR LOVE...
...SO HOW CAN I BE MAD AT ANY OF IT?
Forgiveness from the man who can never forgive himself.
Matt Murdock is a fool. My beautiful, eternal fool...

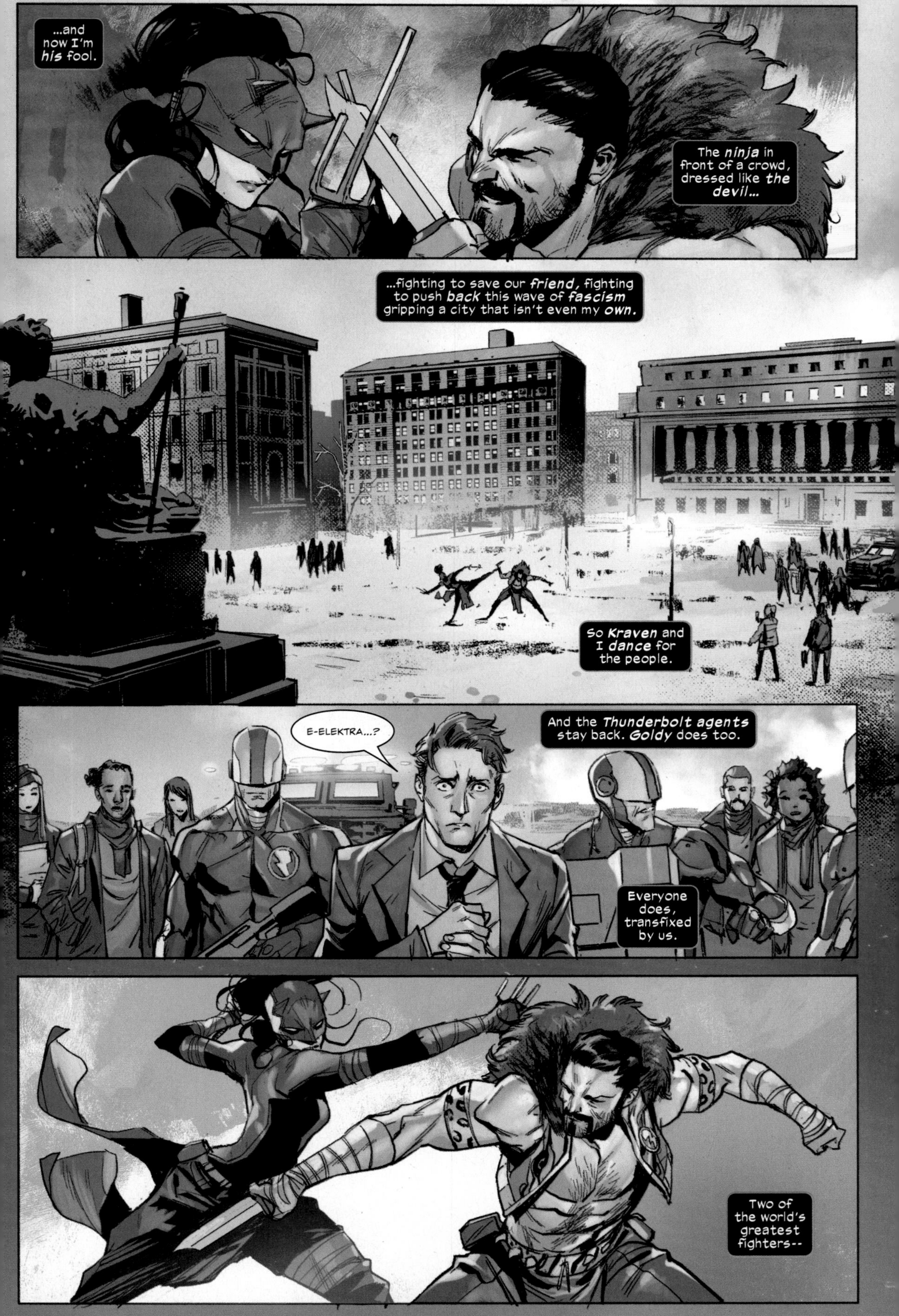

...and now I'm *his* fool.
The *ninja* in front of a crowd, dressed like *the devil...*
...fighting to save our *friend,* fighting to push *back* this wave of *fascism* gripping a city that isn't even my *own.*
So *Kraven* and I *dance* for the people.
E-ELEKTRA...?
And the *Thunderbolt agents* stay back. *Goldy* does too.
Everyone does, transfixed by us.
Two of the world's greatest fighters--

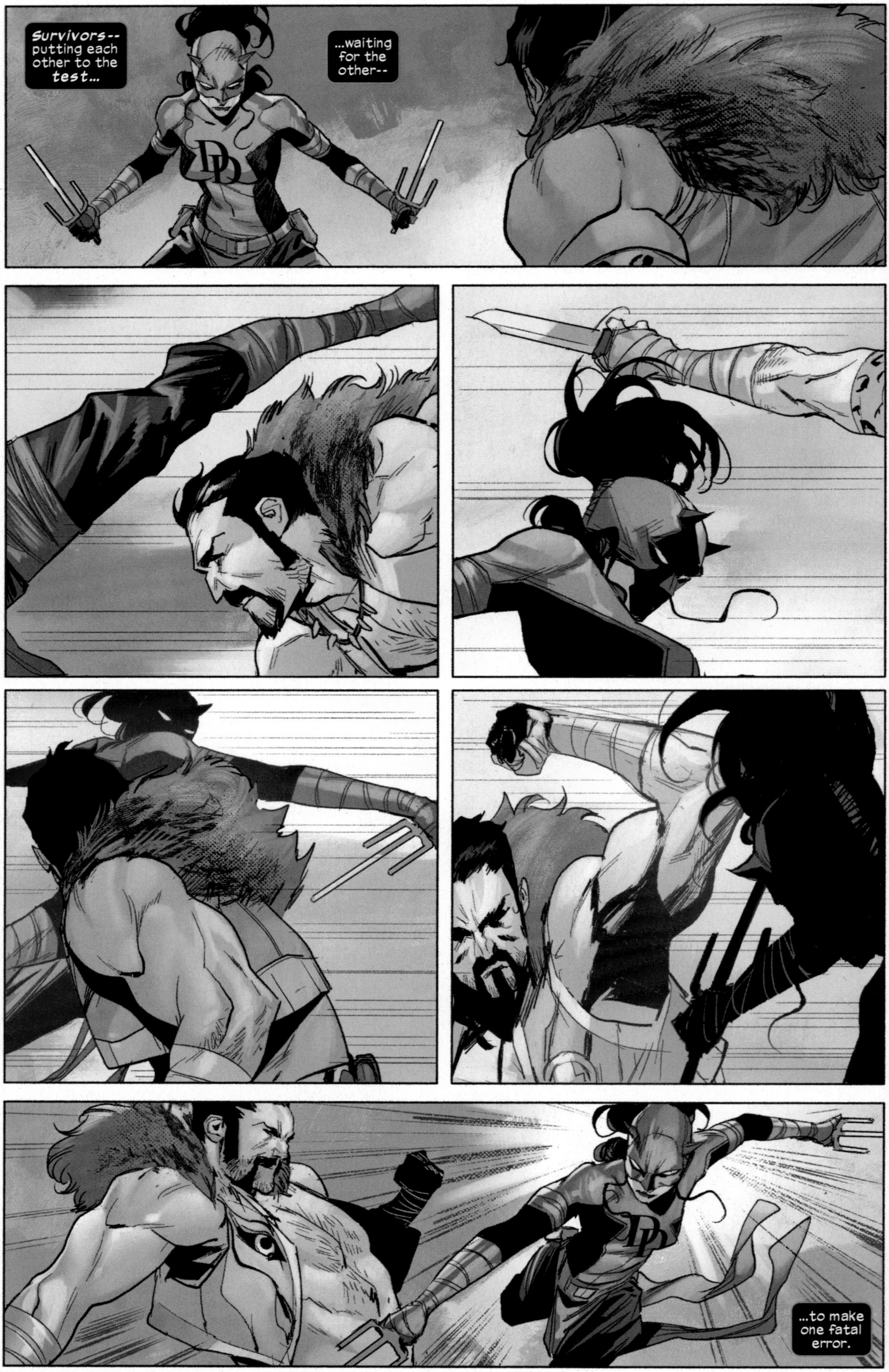
Survivors-- putting each other to the test...
...waiting for the other--
...to make one fatal error.

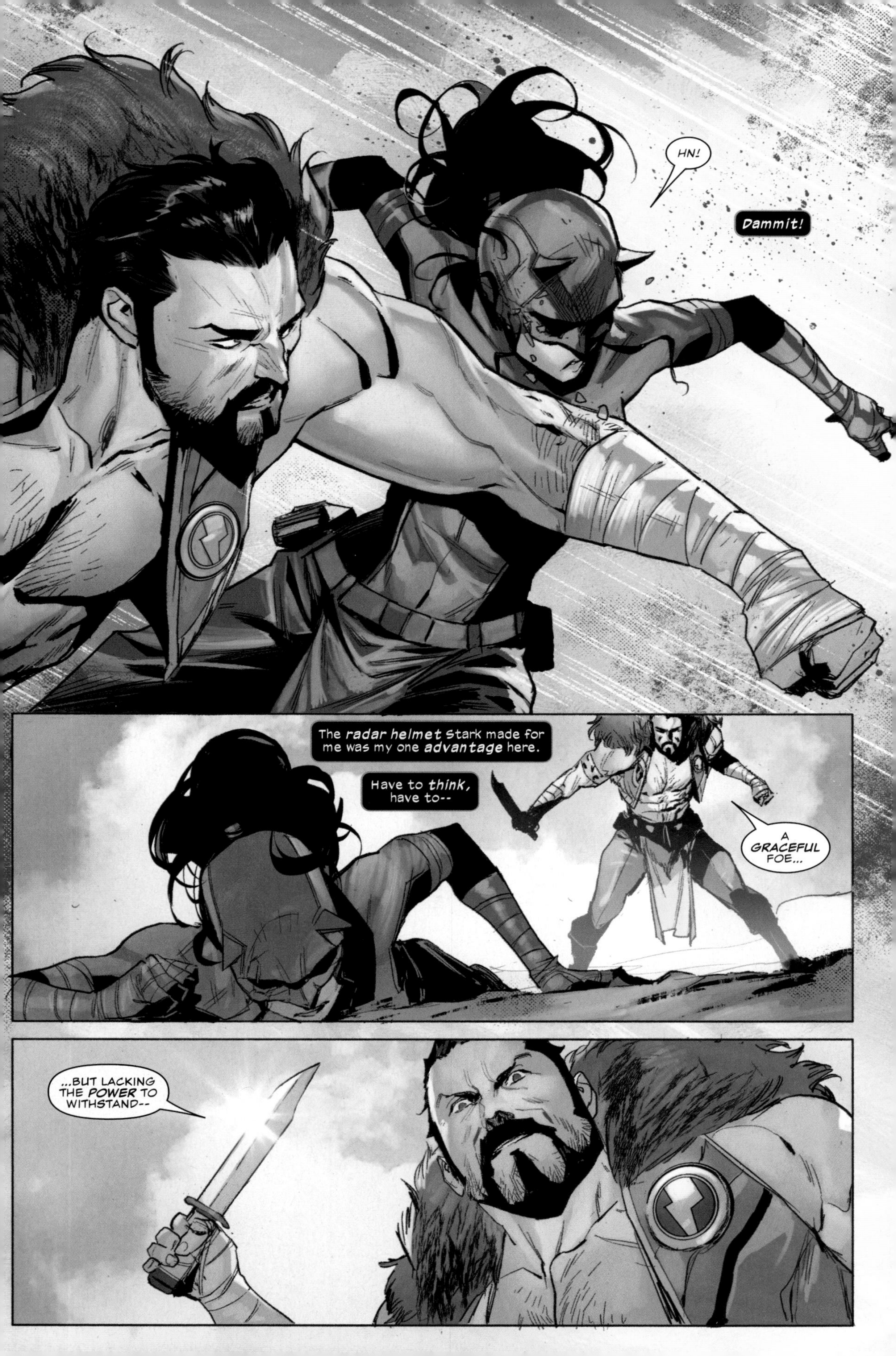
HN!
Dammit!
The radar helmet Stark made for me was my one advantage here.
Have to think, have to--
A GRACEFUL FOE...
...BUT LACKING THE POWER TO WITHSTAND--

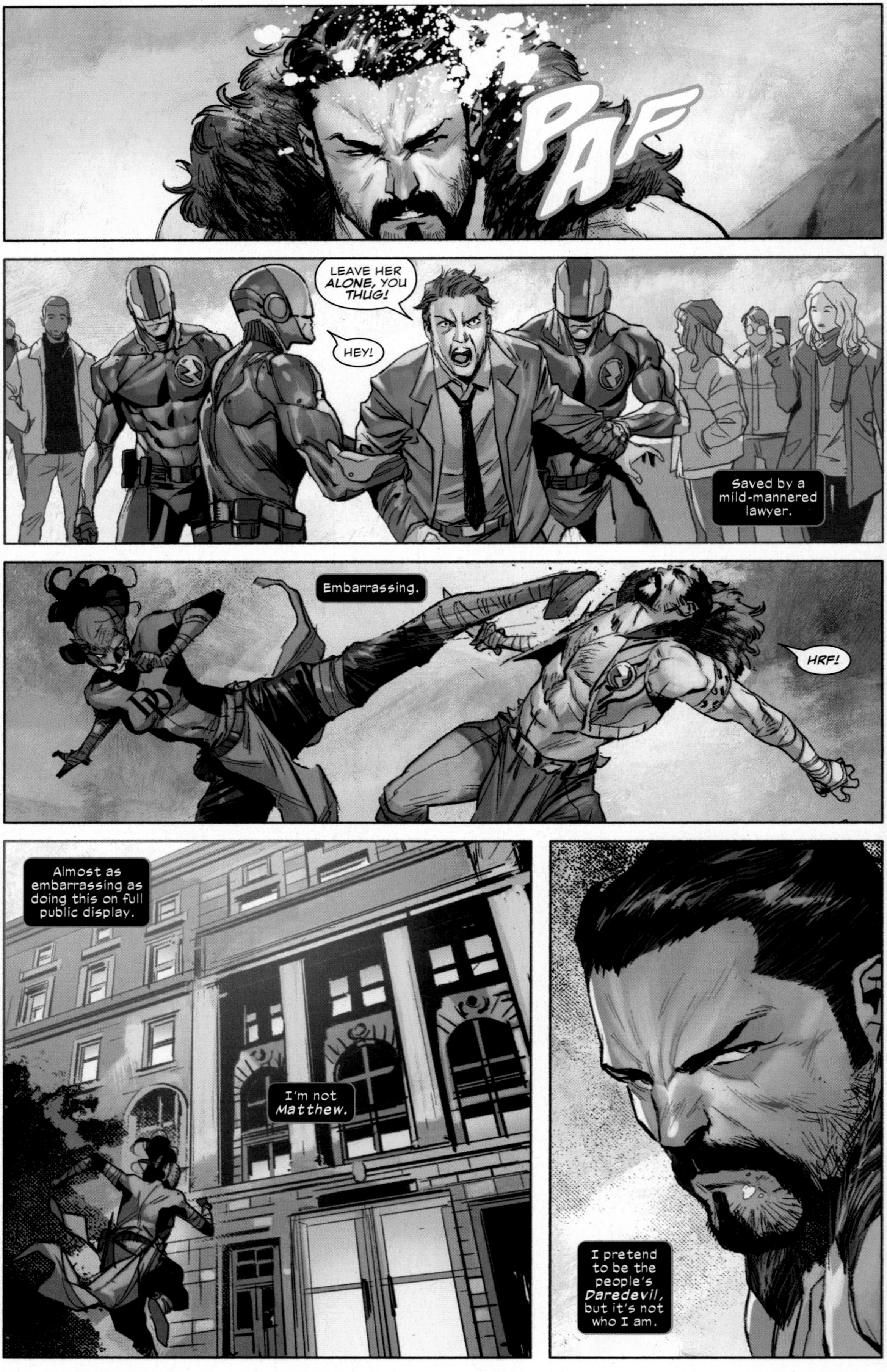
PAF
LEAVE HER ALONE, YOU THUG!
HEY!
Saved by a mild-mannered lawyer.
Embarrassing.
HRF!
Almost as embarrassing as doing this on full public display.
I'm not Matthew.
I pretend to be the people's Daredevil, but it's not who I am.

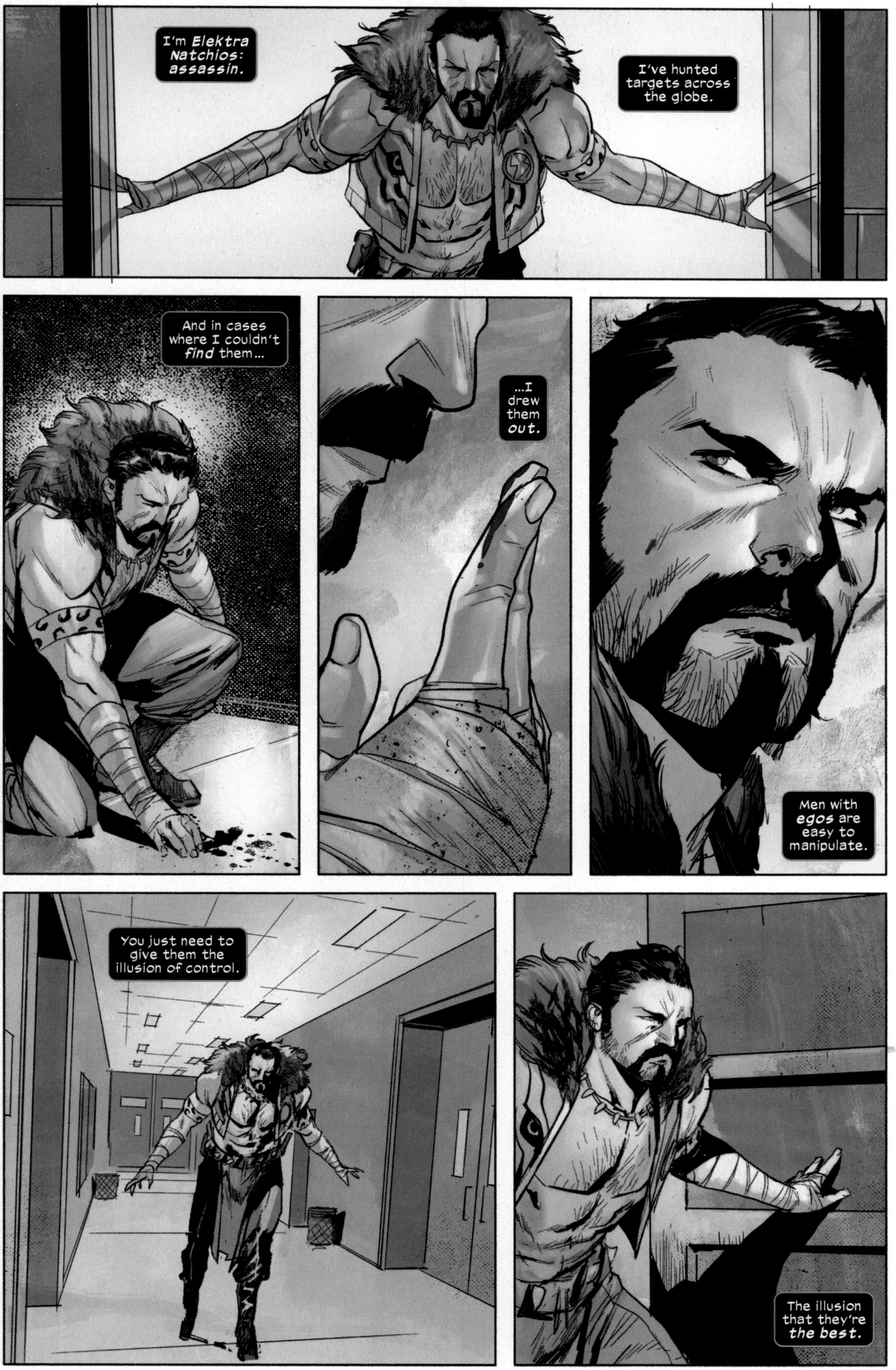

I'm *Elektra Natchios*: *assassin.*
I've hunted targets across the globe.
And in cases where I couldn't *find* them...
...I drew them *out.*
Men with *egos* are easy to manipulate.
You just need to give them the illusion of control.
The illusion that they're *the best.*

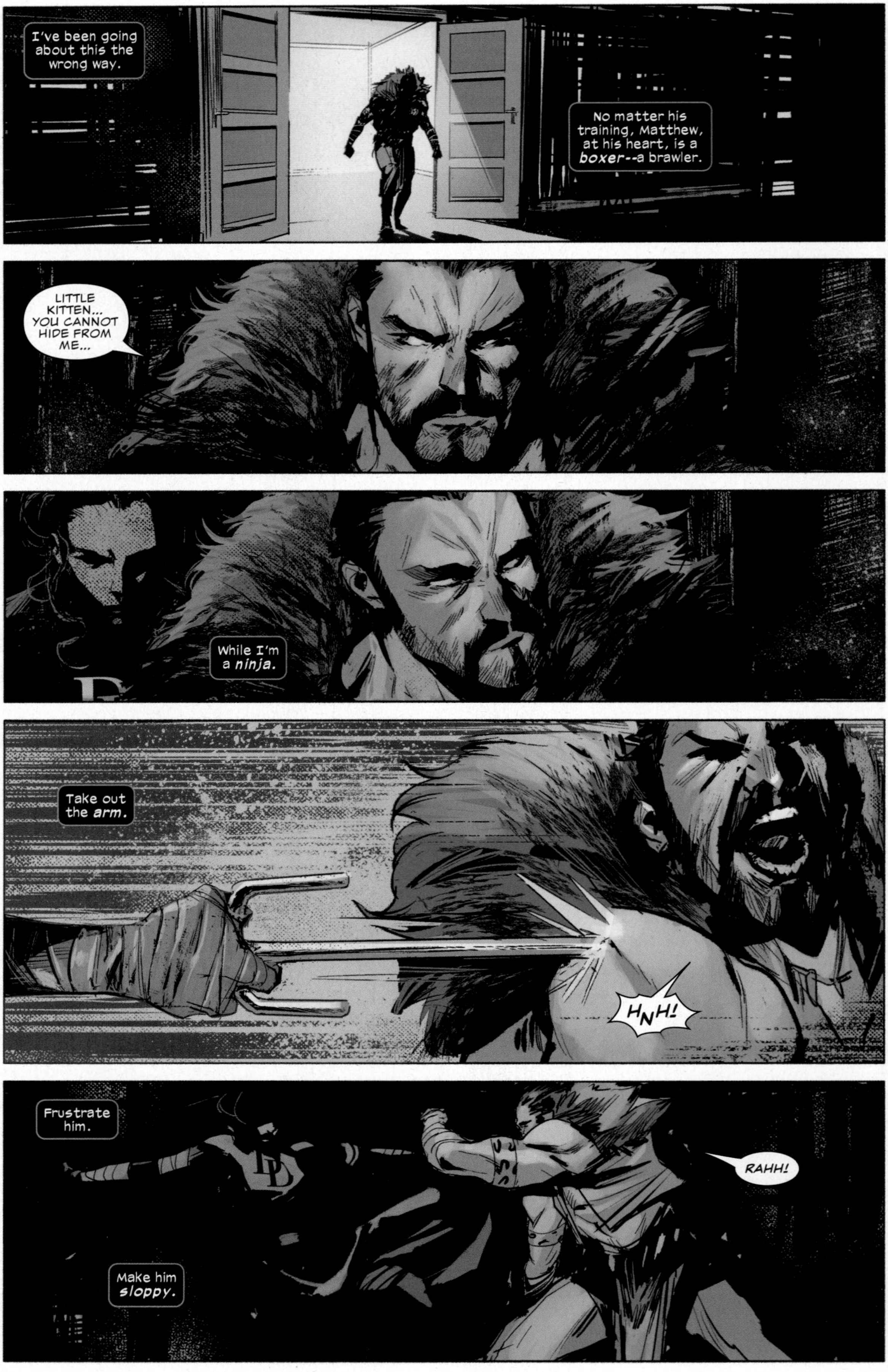

I've been going about this the wrong way.
No matter his training, Matthew, at his heart, is a *boxer*--a brawler.
LITTLE KITTEN... YOU CANNOT HIDE FROM ME...
While I'm a *ninja*.
Take out the *arm*.
HNH!
Frustrate him.
RAHH!
Make him *sloppy*.

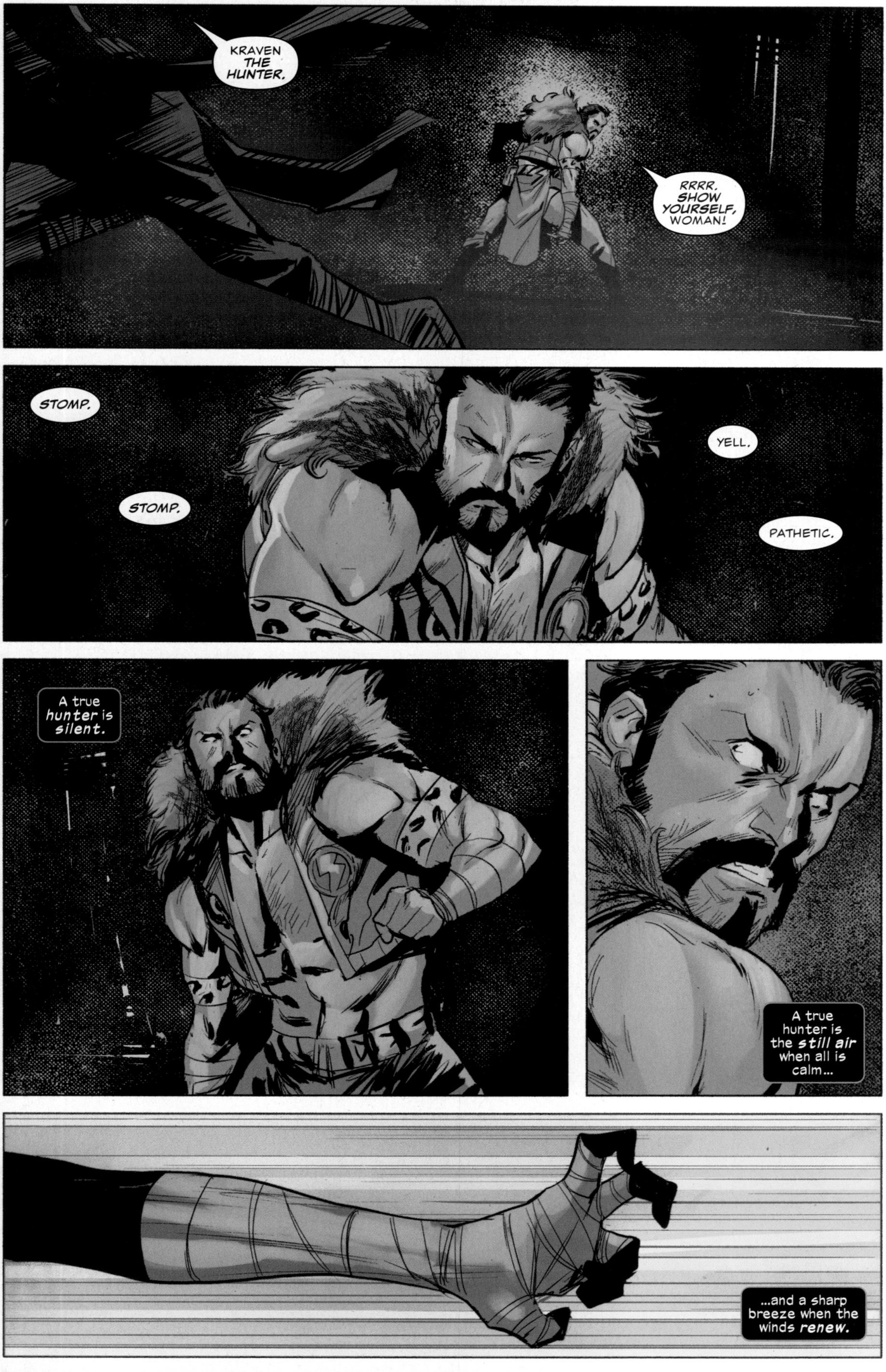
KRAVEN THE HUNTER.
RRRR. SHOW YOURSELF, WOMAN!
STOMP.
STOMP.
YELL.
PATHETIC.
A true hunter is silent.
A true hunter is the still air when all is calm...
...and a sharp breeze when the winds renew.

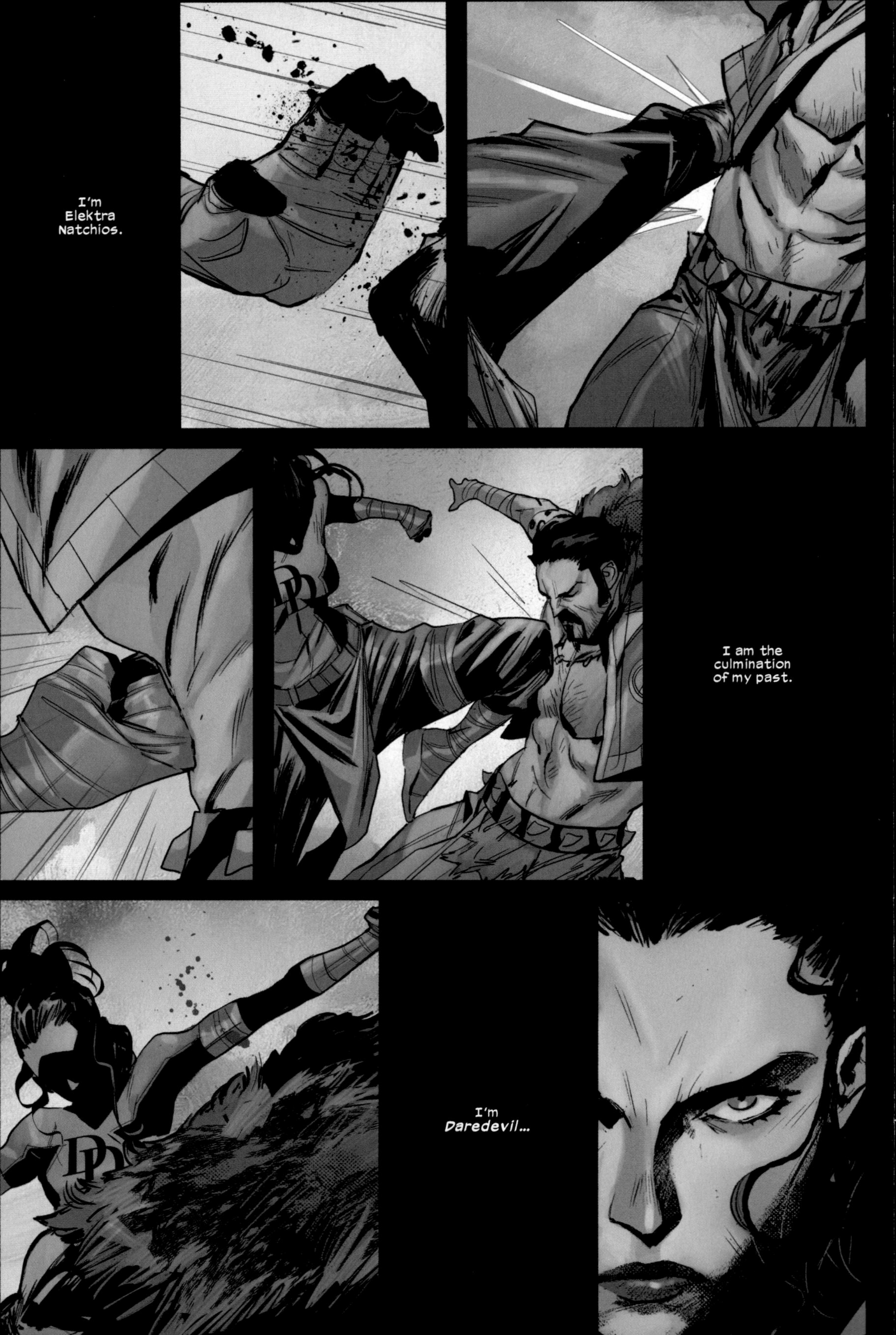
I'm Elektra Natchios.
I am the culmination of my past.
I'm *Daredevil*...

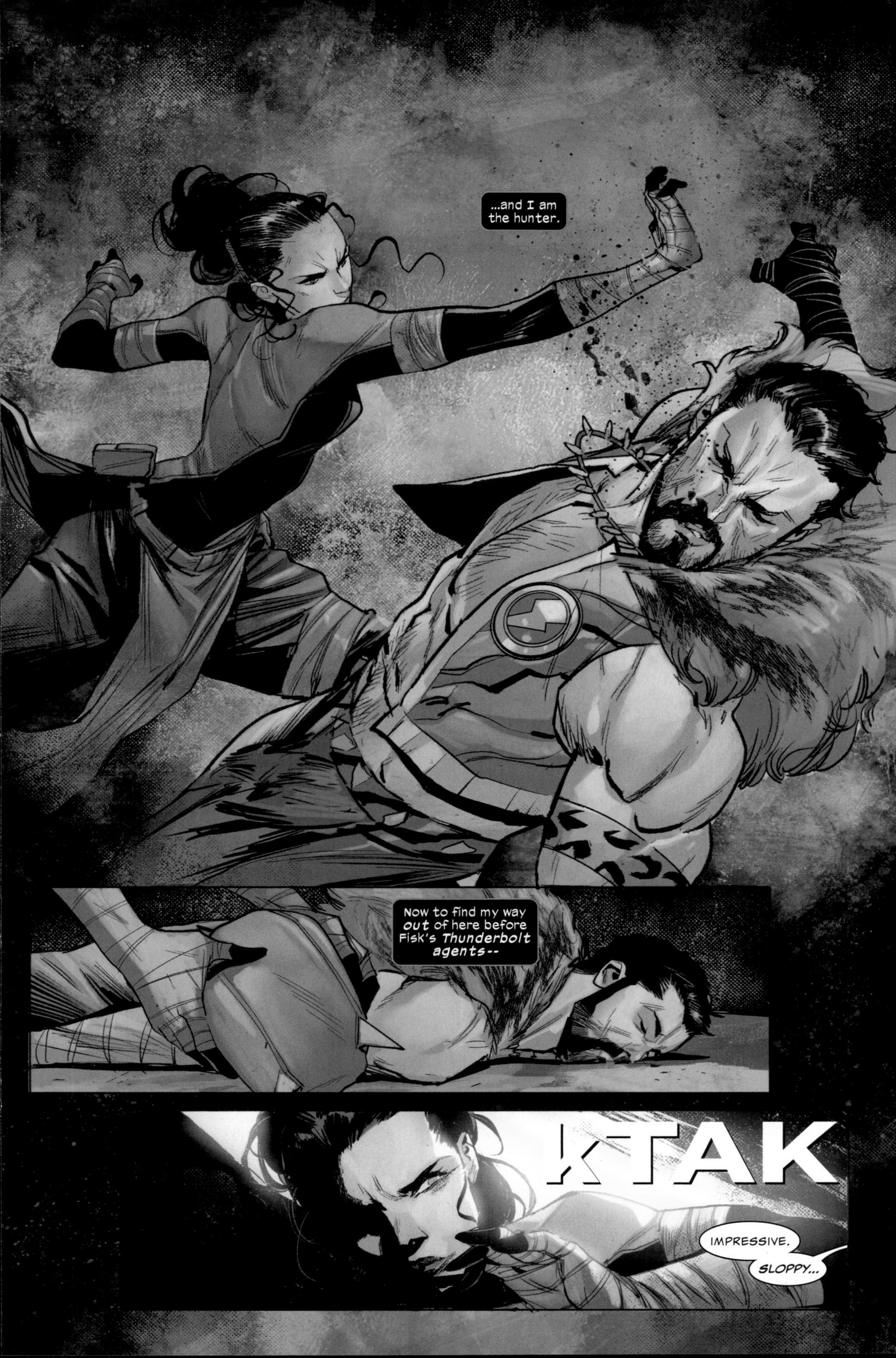
...and I am the hunter.
Now to find my way out of here before Fisk's Thunderbolt agents--
KTAK
IMPRESSIVE.
SLOPPY...

...BUT IMPRESSIVE. THE ELEKTRA NATCHIOS STORY.

AKA, SO I HAVEN'T BEEN SEEING *GHOSTS.*

JUST *MONSTERS.*

YOU SENT *KRAVEN* AFTER ME THROUGH *FISK?* WHY?

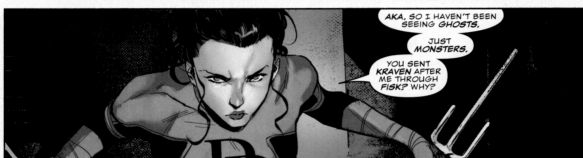

I HAVE MY REASONS. ONE OF WHICH IS *DELIGHT.*

AFTER ALL THIS TIME, YOU'RE STILL *RECRUITING MATTHEW MURDOCK.*

NOW FOR *THE FIST,* SOME *EONS-DEAD* CULT.

HOW MARVELOUS.

WE'VE BEEN UNDER THE THUMBS OF DELUSIONAL *SENSEIS* AND *MASTERS* FOR TOO LONG.

I DON'T NEED TO "RECRUIT" MATTHEW. HE SEES WHAT NEEDS TO BE DONE, AS DO I.

THE END OF *THE HAND?*

AFTER ALL THIS TIME, YOU KNOW SO LITTLE ABOUT US, DEAR.

WE MAKE THE WORLD RUN. IT SITS WITHIN US, OUR FINGERS GENTLY CRADLING IT.

THE *HAND* IS *DEATH.*

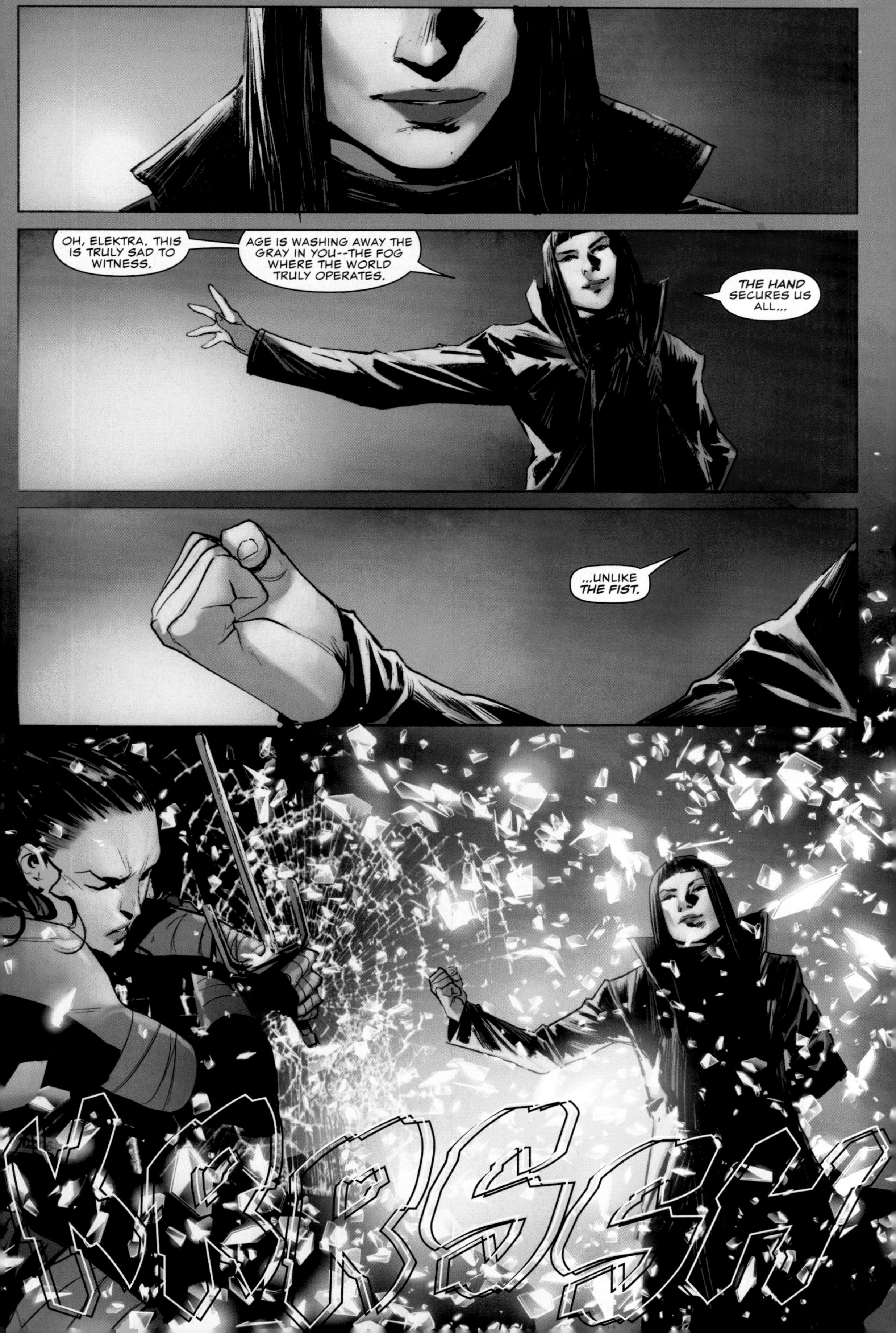
OH, ELEKTRA, THIS IS TRULY SAD TO WITNESS.
AGE IS WASHING AWAY THE GRAY IN YOU--THE FOG WHERE THE WORLD TRULY OPERATES.
THE HAND SECURES US ALL...
...UNLIKE THE FIST.

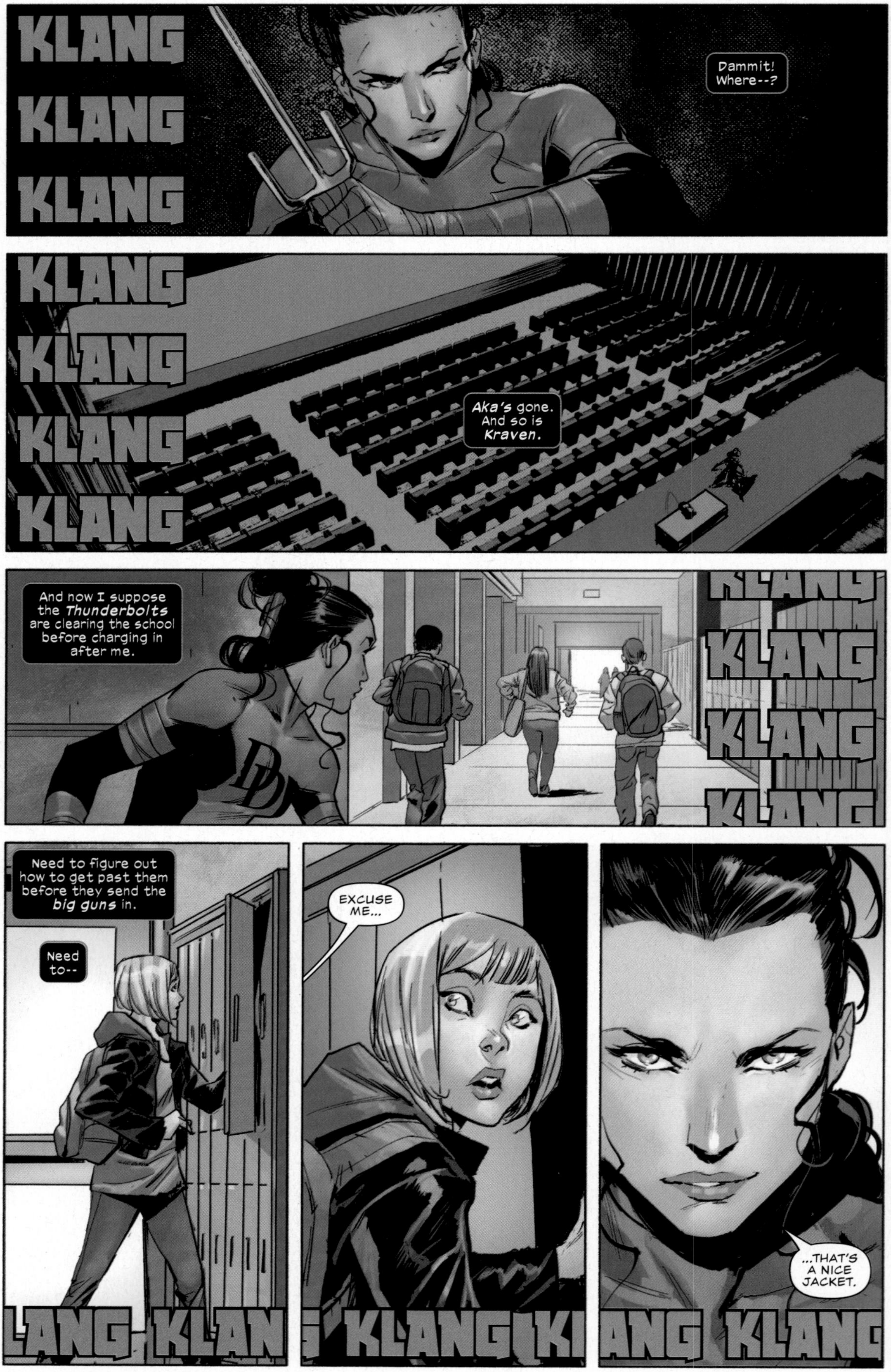
KLANG
KLANG
KLANG
Dammit! Where--?
KLANG
KLANG
KLANG
KLANG
Aka's gone. And so is Kraven.
And now I suppose the Thunderbolts are clearing the school before charging in after me.
KLANG
KLANG
KLANG
Need to figure out how to get past them before they send the big guns in.
Need to--
EXCUSE ME...
...THAT'S A NICE JACKET.
KLANG KLANG KLANG KLANG KLANG

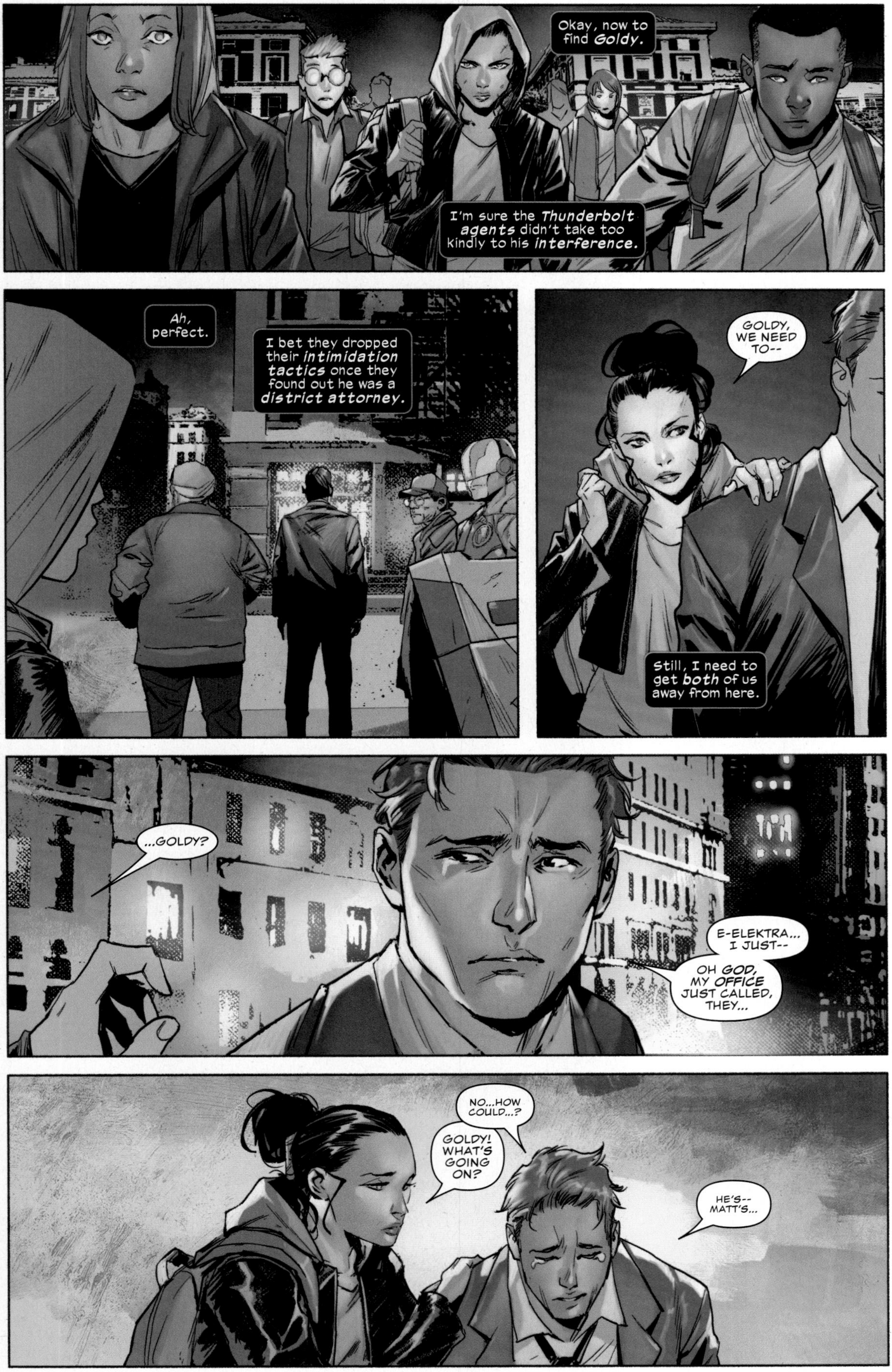
Okay, now to find Goldy.
I'm sure the Thunderbolt agents didn't take too kindly to his interference.
Ah, perfect.
I bet they dropped their intimidation tactics once they found out he was a district attorney.
GOLDY, WE NEED TO--
Still, I need to get both of us away from here.
...GOLDY?
E-ELEKTRA... I JUST--
OH GOD, MY OFFICE JUST CALLED, THEY...
NO...HOW COULD...?
GOLDY! WHAT'S GOING ON?
HE'S-- MATT'S...

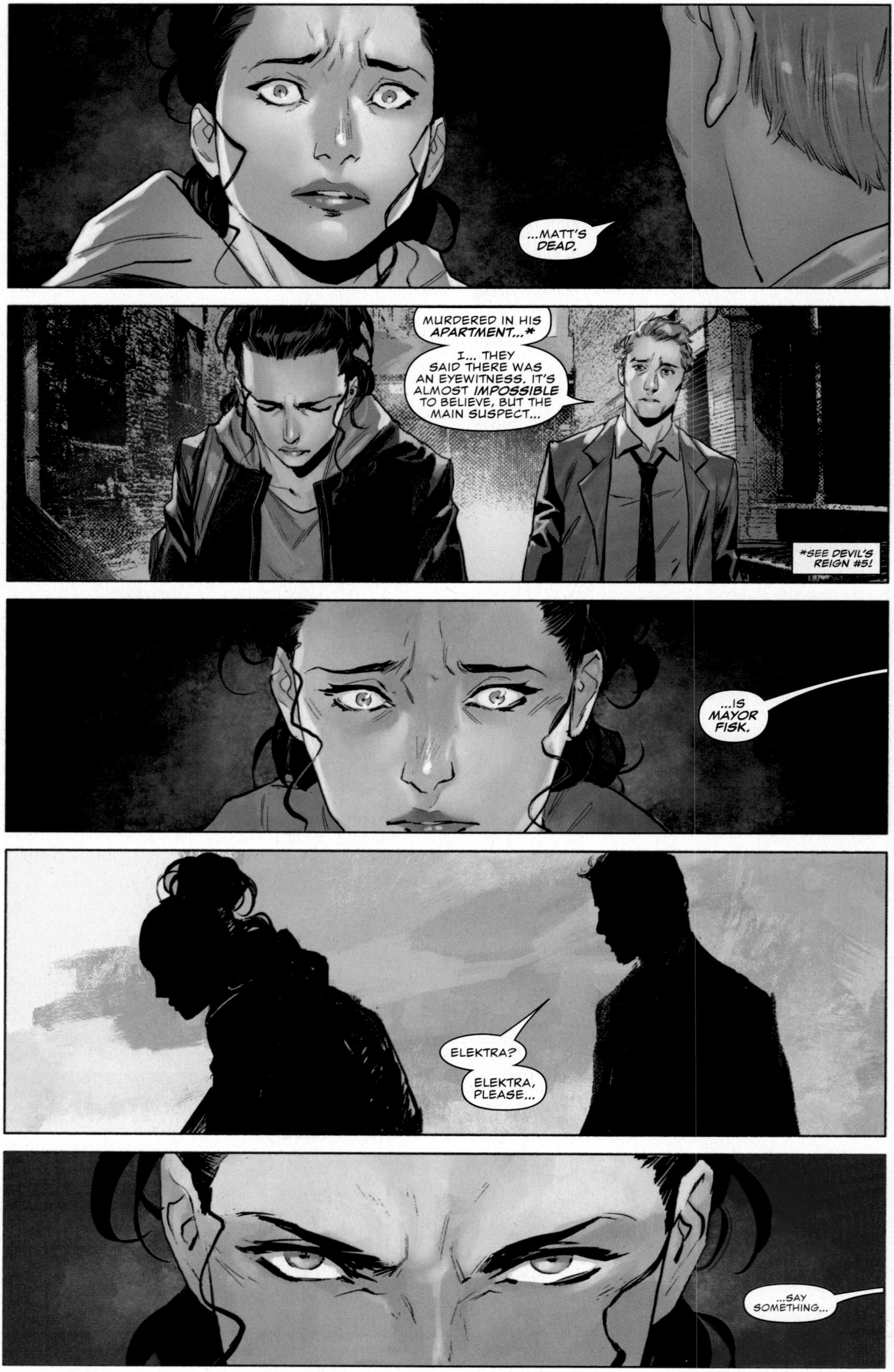
...MATT'S DEAD.
MURDERED IN HIS APARTMENT...*
I... THEY SAID THERE WAS AN EYEWITNESS. IT'S ALMOST IMPOSSIBLE TO BELIEVE, BUT THE MAIN SUSPECT...
*SEE DEVIL'S REIGN #5!
...IS MAYOR FISK.
ELEKTRA?
ELEKTRA, PLEASE...
...SAY SOMETHING...

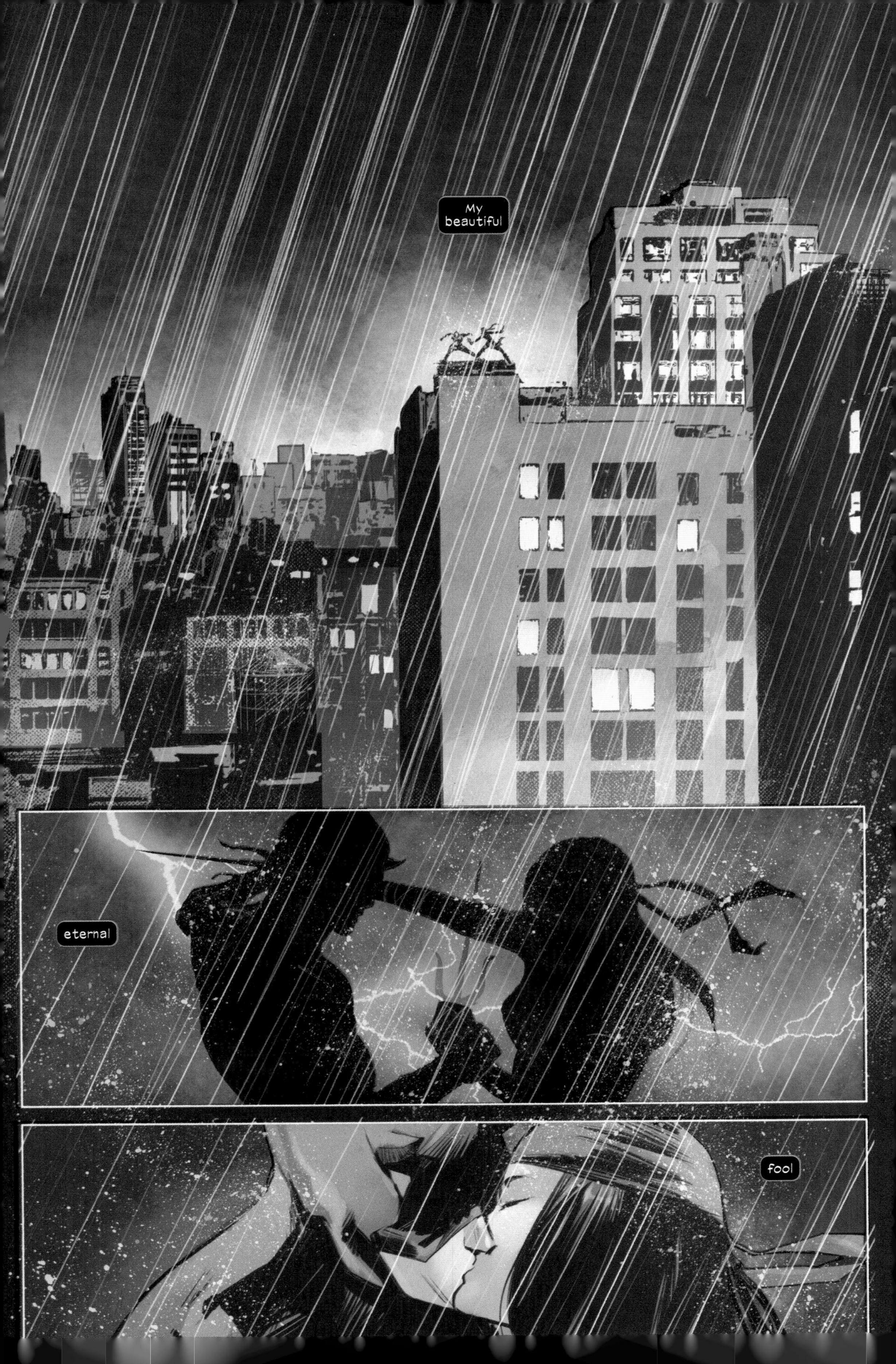
My
beautiful
eternal
fool

ELEKTRA...?

KRSH

It could be a lie.

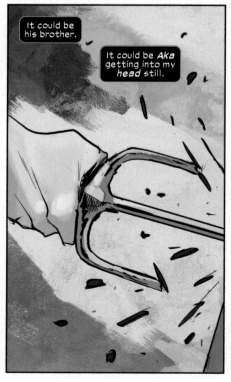

It could be his brother.

It could be *Aka* getting into my *head* still.

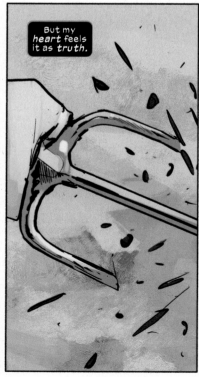

But my *heart* feels it as *truth*.

And my heart also feels something I haven't felt in a *long time*. A *pure* feeling:

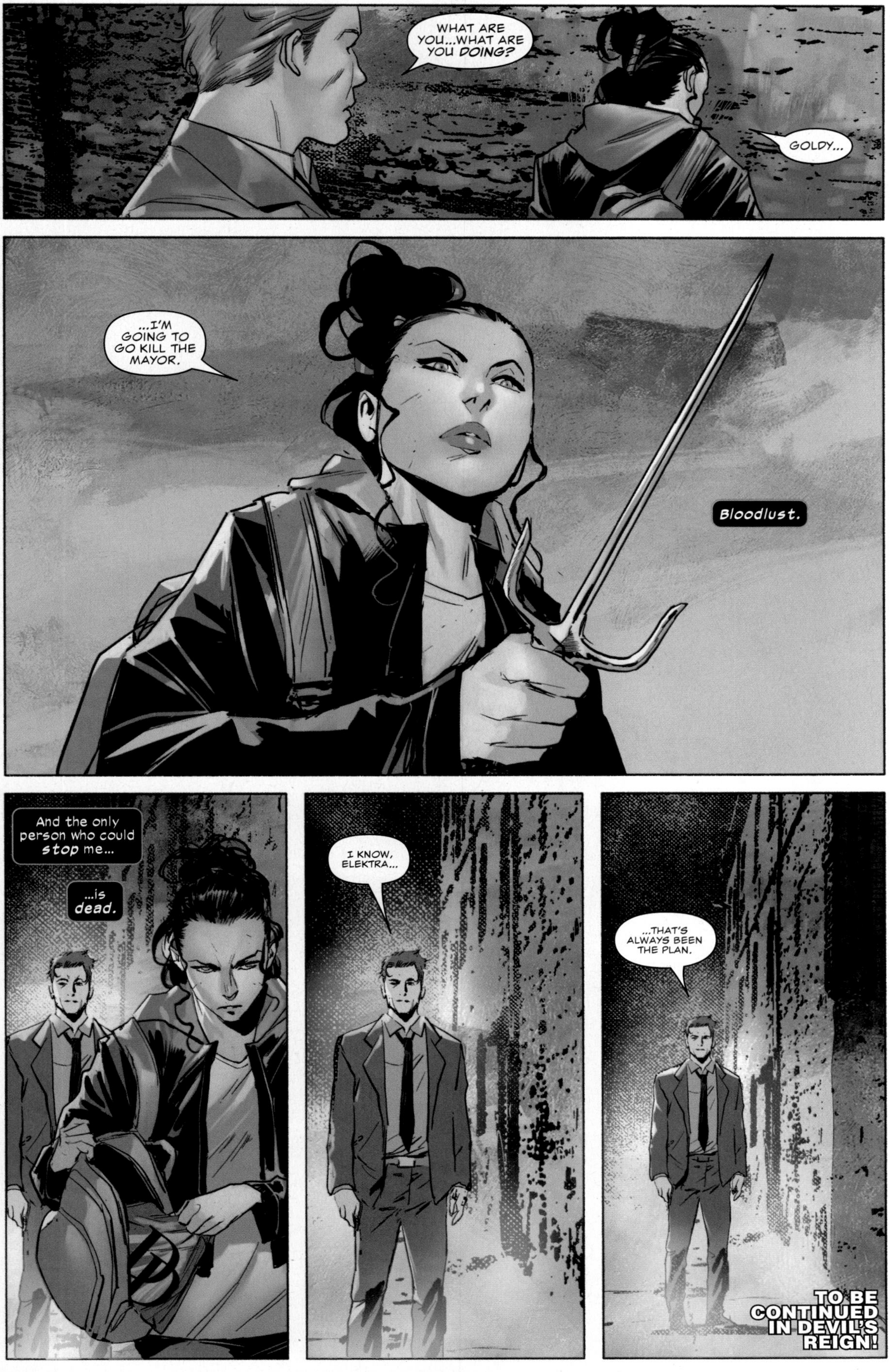
WHAT ARE YOU...WHAT ARE YOU DOING?
GOLDY...
...I'M GOING TO GO KILL THE MAYOR.
Bloodlust.
And the only person who could stop me...
...is dead.
I KNOW, ELEKTRA...
...THAT'S ALWAYS BEEN THE PLAN.
TO BE CONTINUED IN DEVIL'S REIGN!

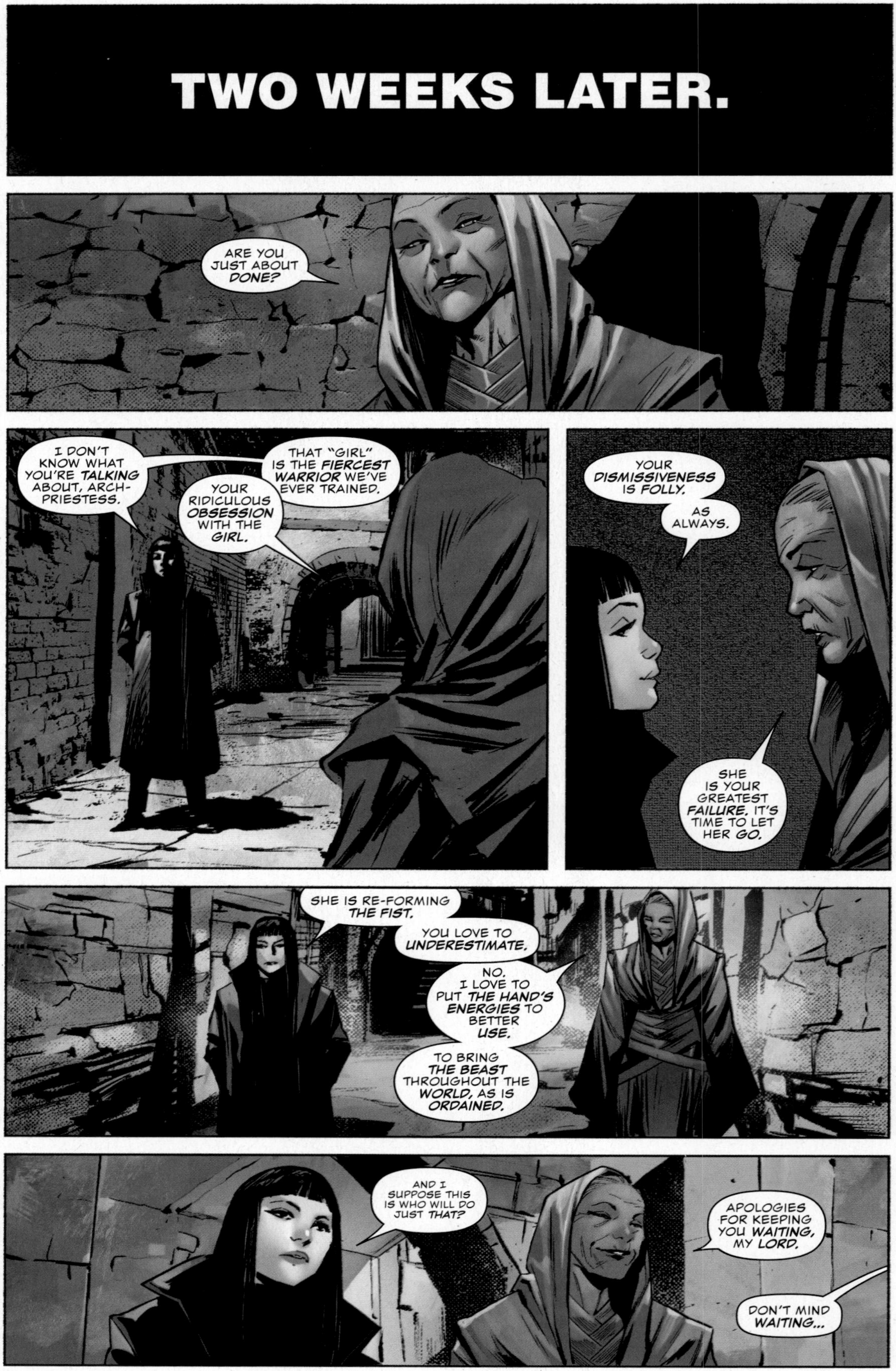

TWO WEEKS LATER.
ARE YOU JUST ABOUT DONE?
I DON'T KNOW WHAT YOU'RE TALKING ABOUT, ARCH-PRIESTESS.
YOUR RIDICULOUS OBSESSION WITH THE GIRL.
THAT "GIRL" IS THE FIERCEST WARRIOR WE'VE EVER TRAINED.
YOUR DISMISSIVENESS IS FOLLY.
AS ALWAYS.
SHE IS YOUR GREATEST FAILURE. IT'S TIME TO LET HER GO.
SHE IS RE-FORMING THE FIST.
YOU LOVE TO UNDERESTIMATE.
NO. I LOVE TO PUT THE HAND'S ENERGIES TO BETTER USE.
TO BRING THE BEAST THROUGHOUT THE WORLD, AS IS ORDAINED.
AND I SUPPOSE THIS IS WHO WILL DO JUST THAT?
APOLOGIES FOR KEEPING YOU WAITING, MY LORD.
DON'T MIND WAITING...

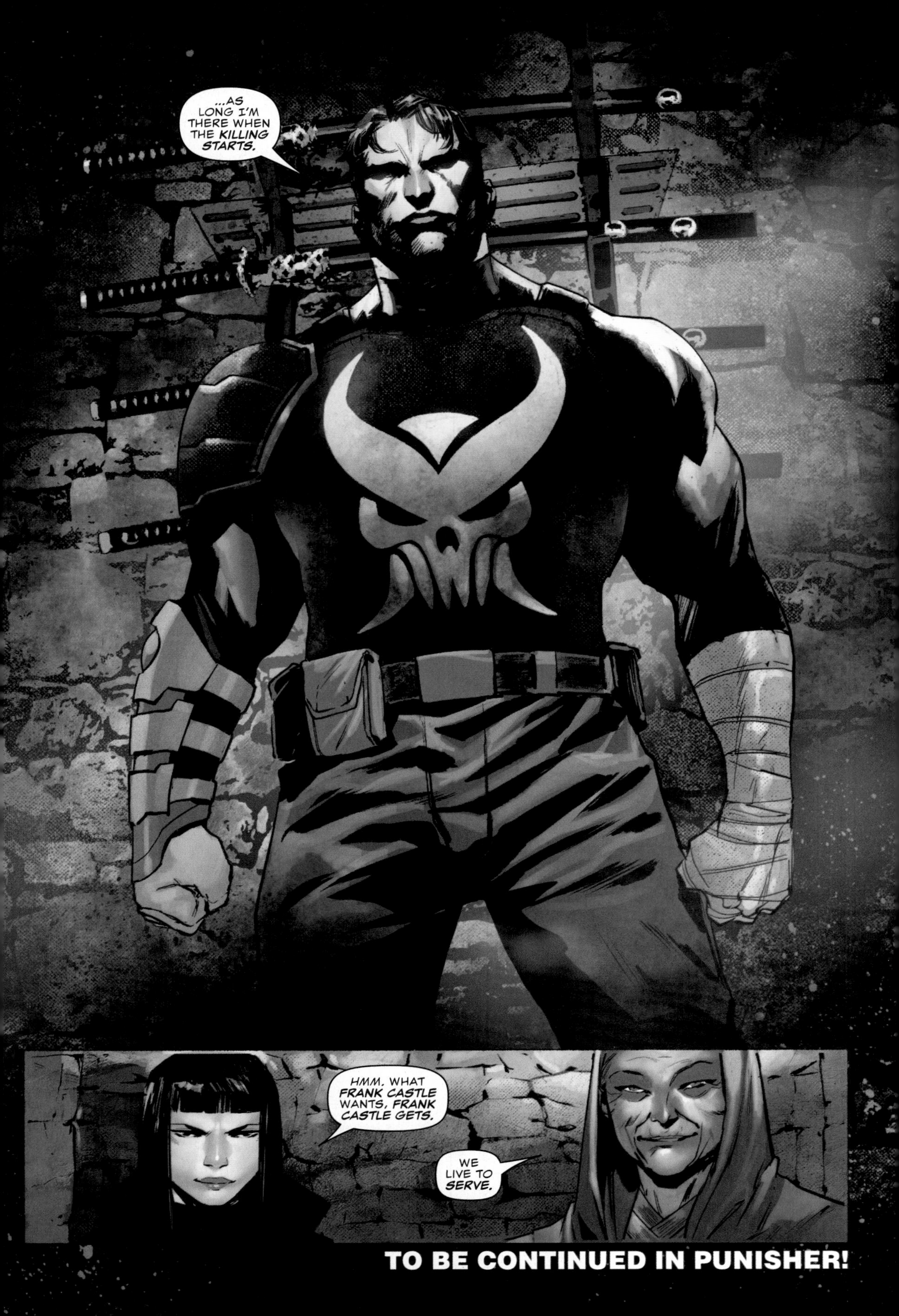
...AS LONG I'M THERE WHEN THE KILLING STARTS.
HMM. WHAT FRANK CASTLE WANTS, FRANK CASTLE GETS.
WE LIVE TO SERVE.

TO BE CONTINUED IN PUNISHER!

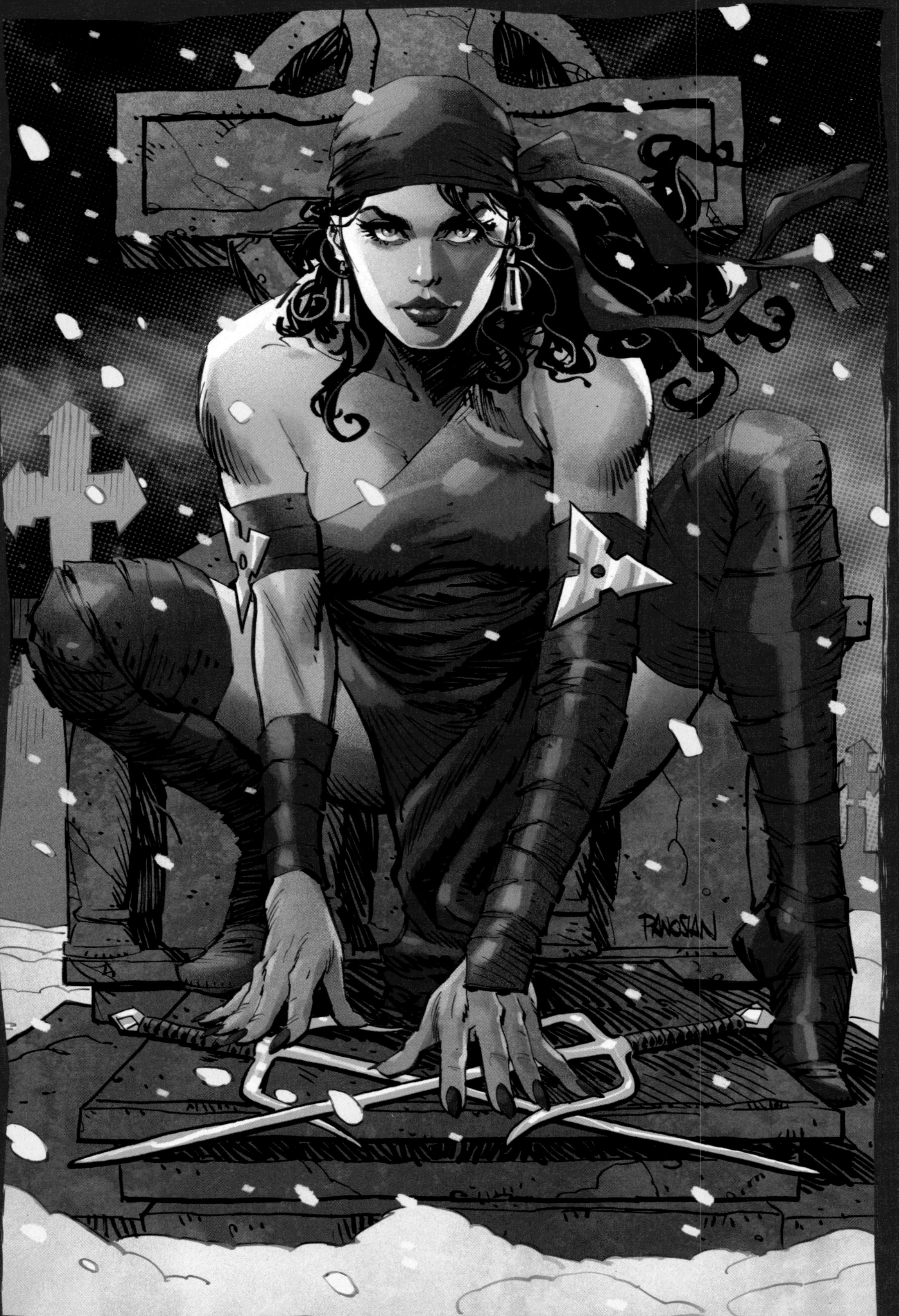
PANOSIAN

ELEKTRA #100

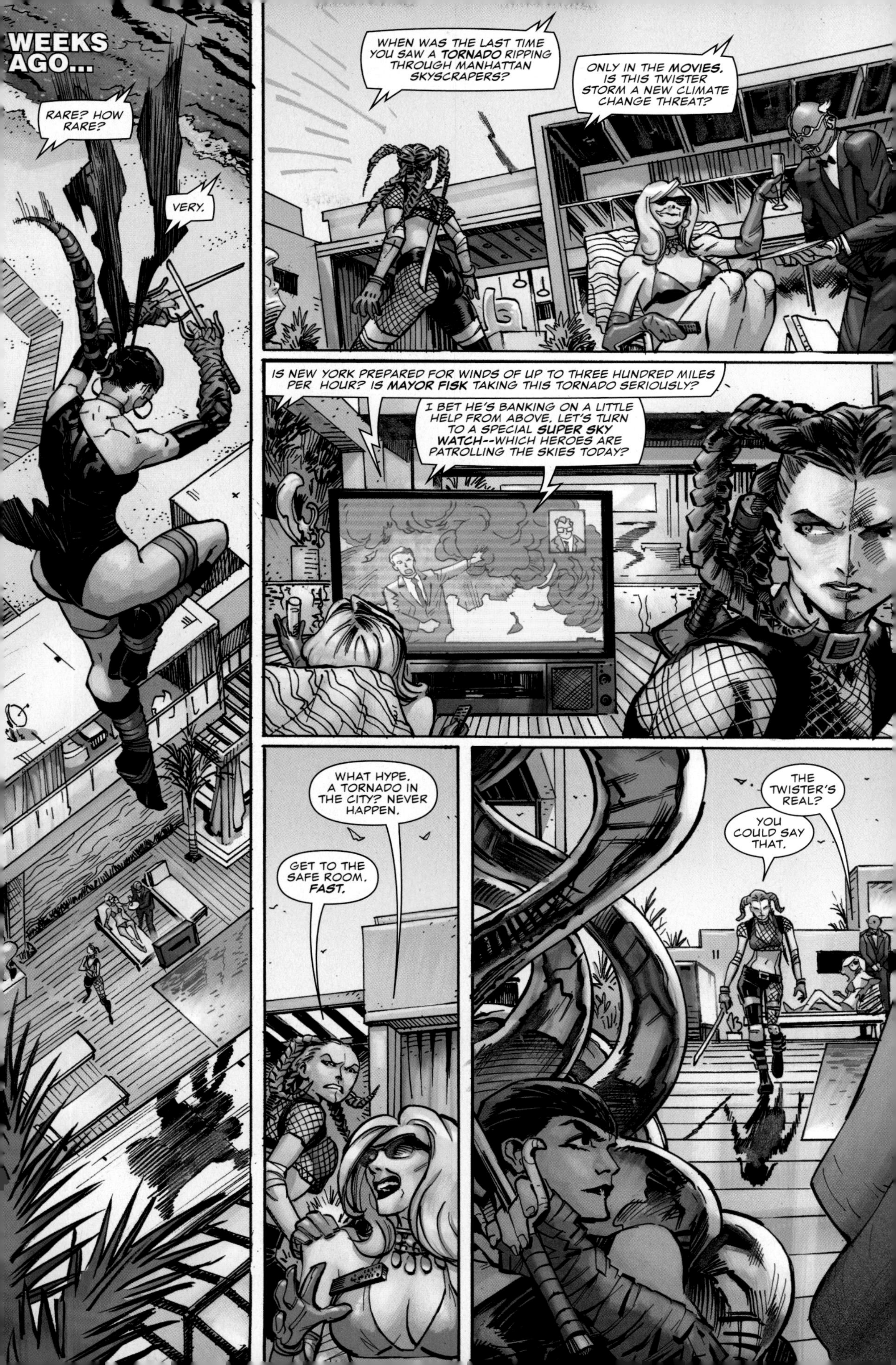
WEEKS AGO...
RARE? HOW RARE?
VERY.
WHEN WAS THE LAST TIME YOU SAW A TORNADO RIPPING THROUGH MANHATTAN SKYSCRAPERS?
ONLY IN THE MOVIES. IS THIS TWISTER STORM A NEW CLIMATE CHANGE THREAT?
IS NEW YORK PREPARED FOR WINDS OF UP TO THREE HUNDRED MILES PER HOUR? IS MAYOR FISK TAKING THIS TORNADO SERIOUSLY?
I BET HE'S BANKING ON A LITTLE HELP FROM ABOVE. LET'S TURN TO A SPECIAL SUPER SKY WATCH--WHICH HEROES ARE PATROLLING THE SKIES TODAY?
WHAT HYPE. A TORNADO IN THE CITY? NEVER HAPPEN.
GET TO THE SAFE ROOM. FAST.
THE TWISTER'S REAL?
YOU COULD SAY THAT.

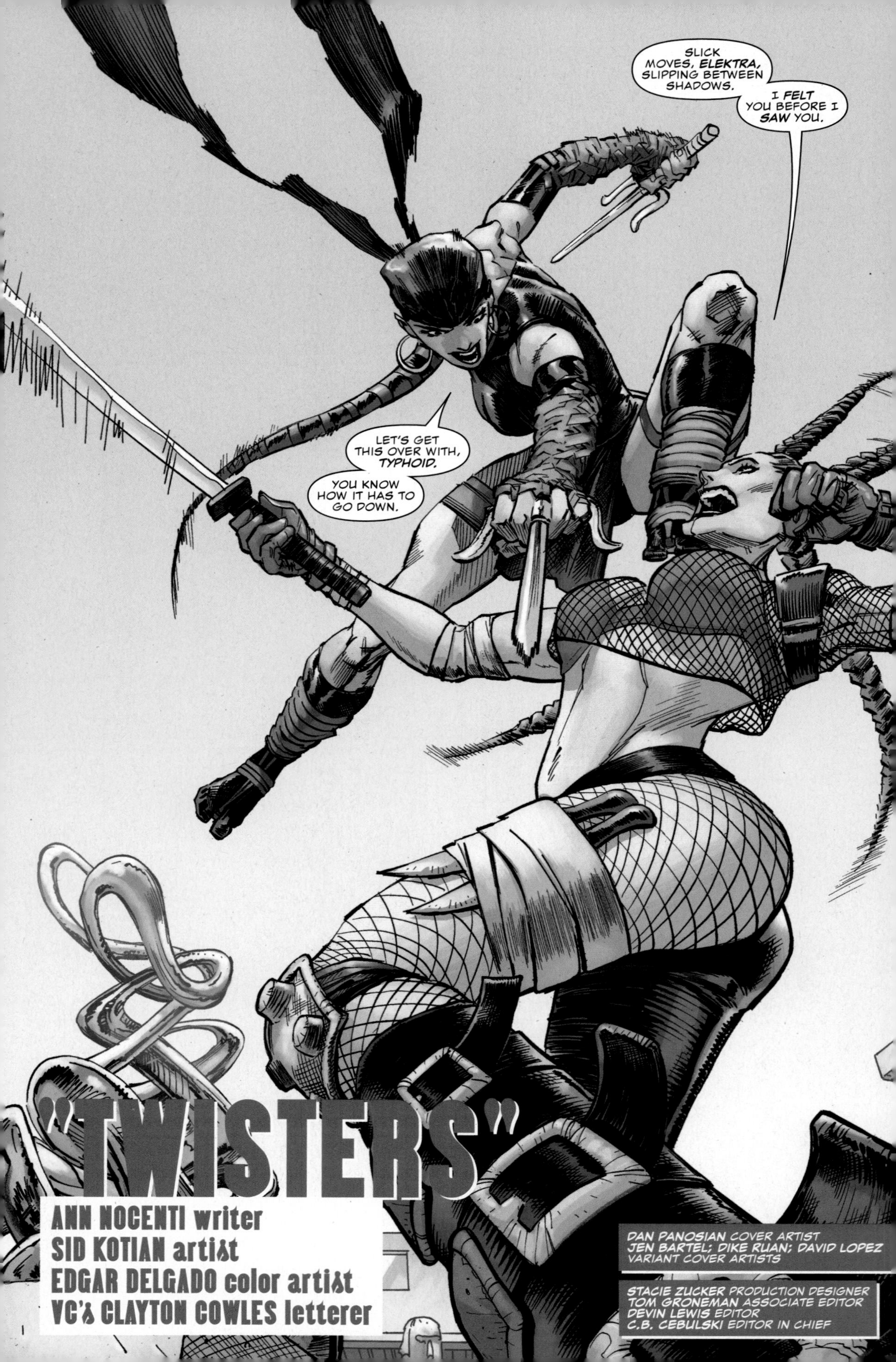
SLICK MOVES, ELEKTRA, SLIPPING BETWEEN SHADOWS.
I FELT YOU BEFORE I SAW YOU.
LET'S GET THIS OVER WITH, TYPHOID.
YOU KNOW HOW IT HAS TO GO DOWN.
"TWISTERS"
ANN NOCENTI writer
SID KOTIAN artist
EDGAR DELGADO color artist
VC's CLAYTON COWLES letterer
DAN PANOSIAN COVER ARTIST
JEN BARTEL; DIKE RUAN; DAVID LOPEZ
VARIANT COVER ARTISTS
STACIE ZUCKER PRODUCTION DESIGNER
TOM GRONEMAN ASSOCIATE EDITOR
DEVIN LEWIS EDITOR
C.B. CEBULSKI EDITOR IN CHIEF

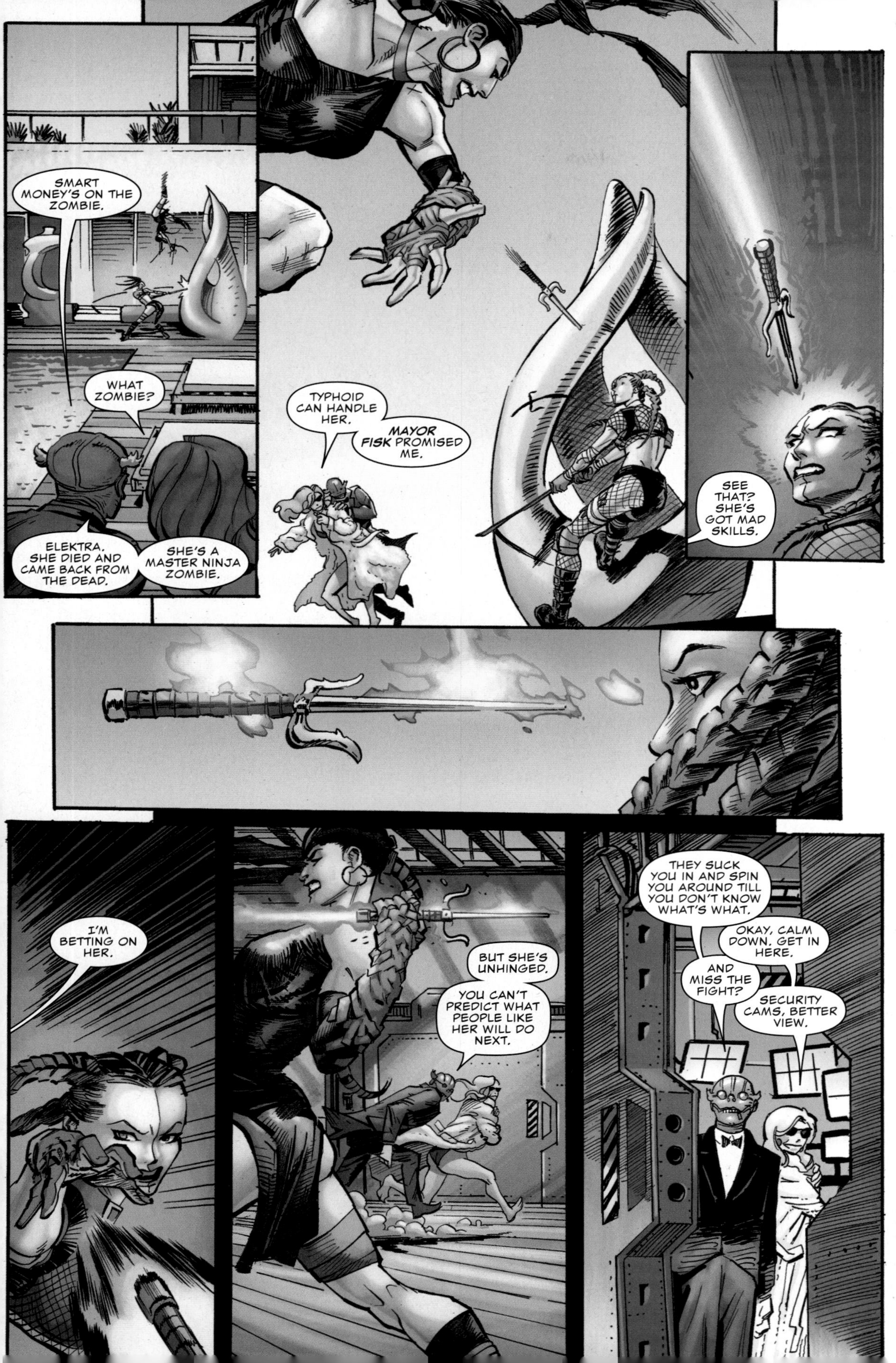

SMART MONEY'S ON THE ZOMBIE.
WHAT ZOMBIE?
ELEKTRA. SHE DIED AND CAME BACK FROM THE DEAD.
SHE'S A MASTER NINJA ZOMBIE.
TYPHOID CAN HANDLE HER.
MAYOR FISK PROMISED ME.
SEE THAT? SHE'S GOT MAD SKILLS.
I'M BETTING ON HER.
BUT SHE'S UNHINGED.
YOU CAN'T PREDICT WHAT PEOPLE LIKE HER WILL DO NEXT.
THEY SUCK YOU IN AND SPIN YOU AROUND TILL YOU DON'T KNOW WHAT'S WHAT.
OKAY, CALM DOWN. GET IN HERE.
AND MISS THE FIGHT?
SECURITY CAMS, BETTER VIEW.

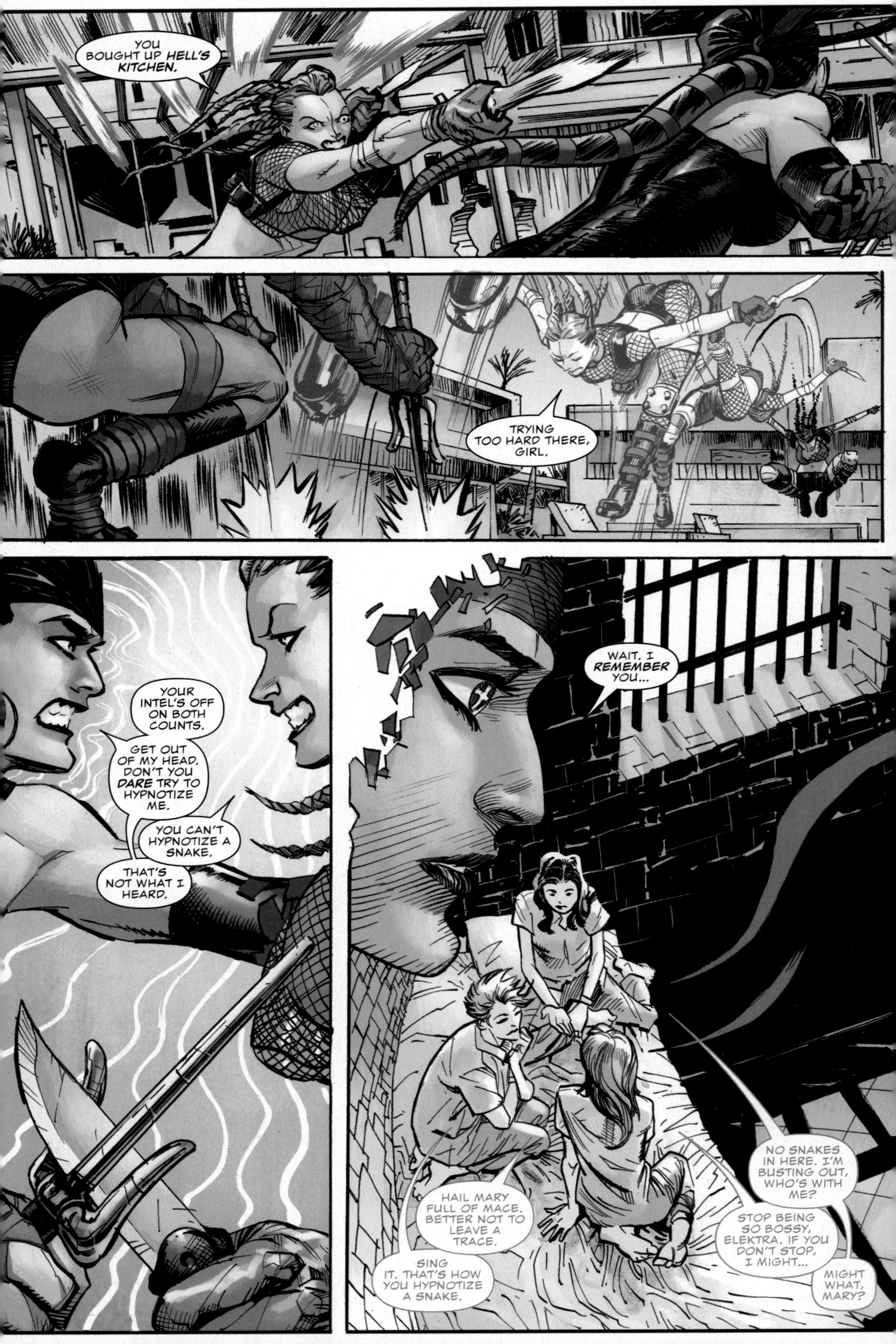
YOU BOUGHT UP HELL'S KITCHEN.
TRYING TOO HARD THERE, GIRL.
YOUR INTEL'S OFF ON BOTH COUNTS.
GET OUT OF MY HEAD. DON'T YOU DARE TRY TO HYPNOTIZE ME.
YOU CAN'T HYPNOTIZE A SNAKE.
THAT'S NOT WHAT I HEARD.
WAIT. I REMEMBER YOU...
NO SNAKES IN HERE. I'M BUSTING OUT, WHO'S WITH ME?
HAIL MARY FULL OF MACE. BETTER NOT TO LEAVE A TRACE.
SING IT. THAT'S HOW YOU HYPNOTIZE A SNAKE.
STOP BEING SO BOSSY, ELEKTRA. IF YOU DON'T STOP, I MIGHT...
MIGHT WHAT, MARY?

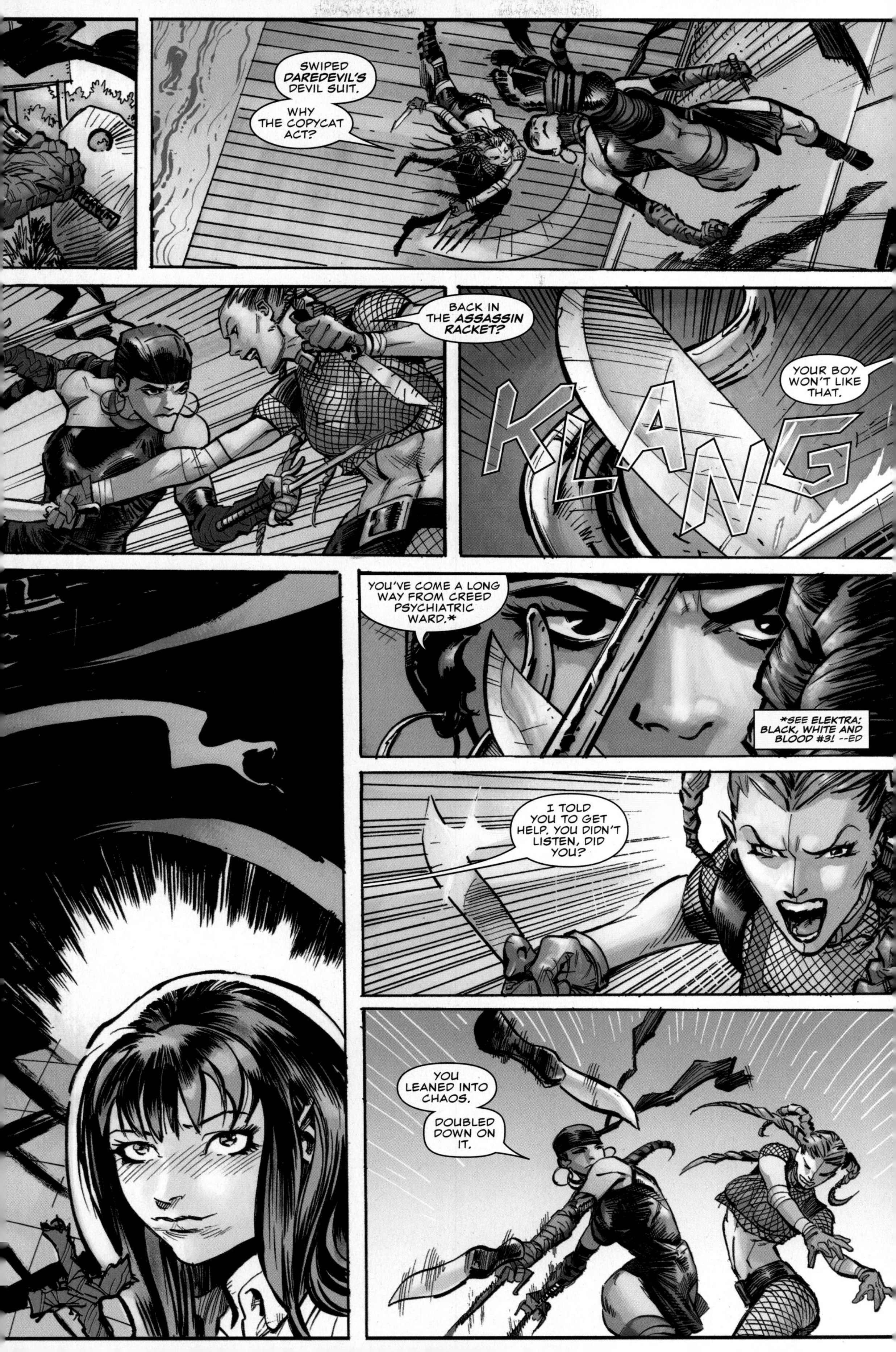
SWIPED DAREDEVIL'S DEVIL SUIT.
WHY THE COPYCAT ACT?
BACK IN THE ASSASSIN RACKET?
KLANG
YOUR BOY WON'T LIKE THAT.
YOU'VE COME A LONG WAY FROM CREED PSYCHIATRIC WARD.*
*SEE ELEKTRA: BLACK, WHITE AND BLOOD #3! --ED
I TOLD YOU TO GET HELP. YOU DIDN'T LISTEN, DID YOU?
YOU LEANED INTO CHAOS.
DOUBLED DOWN ON IT.

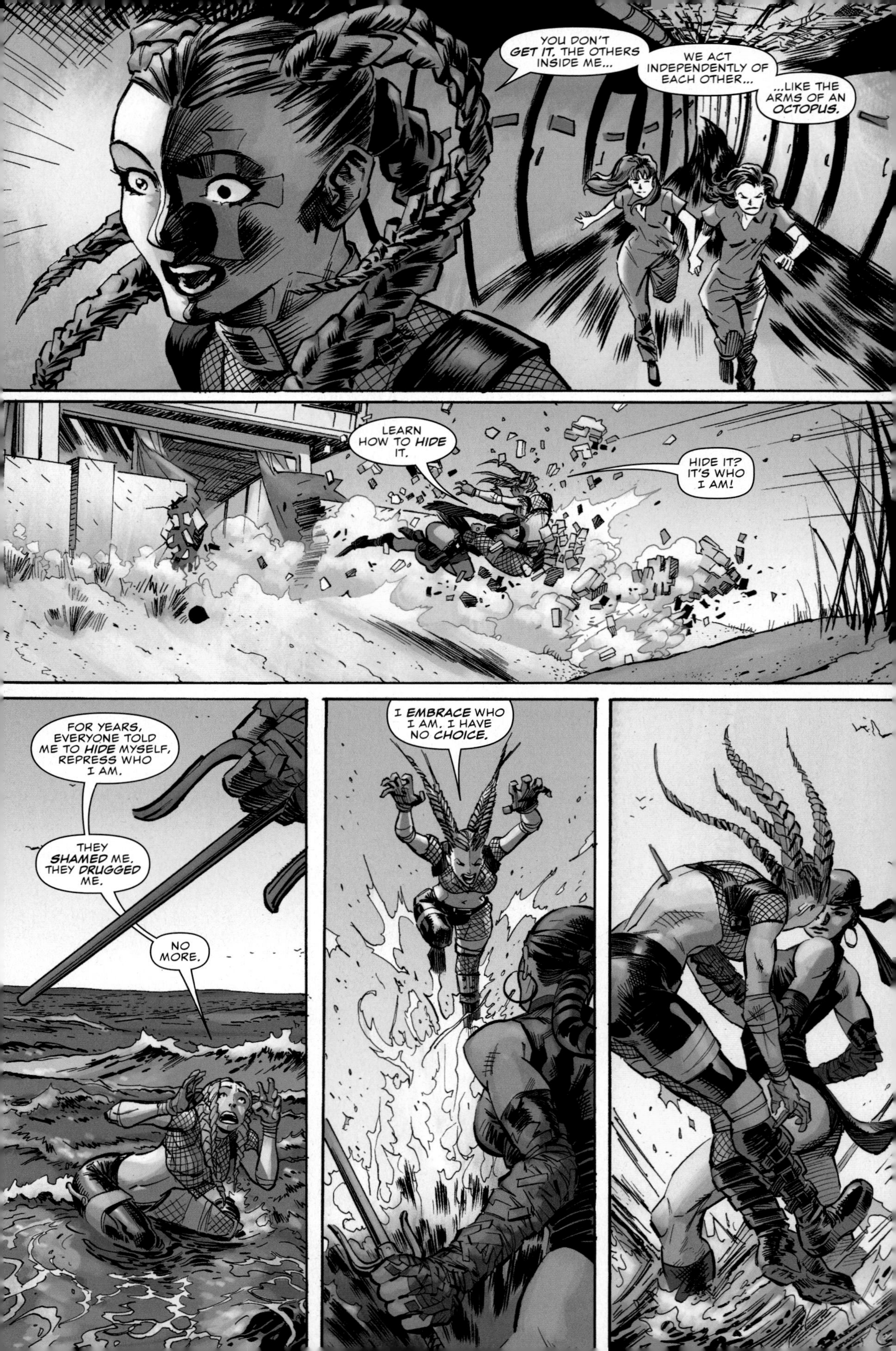
YOU DON'T GET IT. THE OTHERS INSIDE ME...
WE ACT INDEPENDENTLY OF EACH OTHER...
...LIKE THE ARMS OF AN OCTOPUS.
LEARN HOW TO HIDE IT.
HIDE IT? IT'S WHO I AM!
FOR YEARS, EVERYONE TOLD ME TO HIDE MYSELF, REPRESS WHO I AM.
THEY SHAMED ME. THEY DRUGGED ME.
NO MORE.
I EMBRACE WHO I AM. I HAVE NO CHOICE.

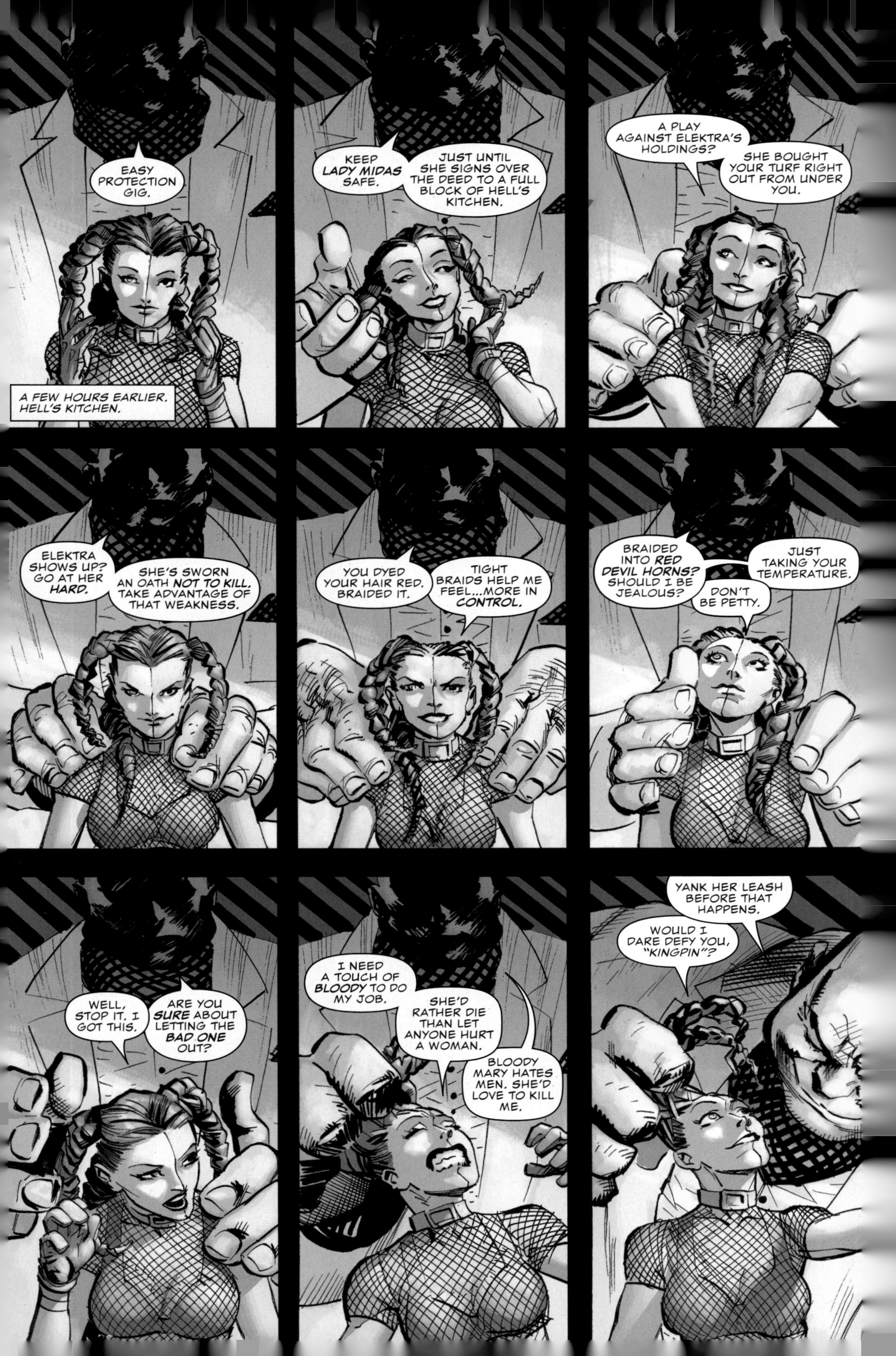
EASY PROTECTION GIG.
A FEW HOURS EARLIER. HELL'S KITCHEN.
KEEP LADY MIDAS SAFE.
JUST UNTIL SHE SIGNS OVER THE DEED TO A FULL BLOCK OF HELL'S KITCHEN.
A PLAY AGAINST ELEKTRA'S HOLDINGS?
SHE BOUGHT YOUR TURF RIGHT OUT FROM UNDER YOU.
ELEKTRA SHOWS UP? GO AT HER HARD.
SHE'S SWORN AN OATH NOT TO KILL. TAKE ADVANTAGE OF THAT WEAKNESS.
YOU DYED YOUR HAIR RED. BRAIDED IT.
TIGHT BRAIDS HELP ME FEEL...MORE IN CONTROL.
BRAIDED INTO RED DEVIL HORNS? SHOULD I BE JEALOUS?
JUST TAKING YOUR TEMPERATURE.
DON'T BE PETTY.
WELL, STOP IT. I GOT THIS.
ARE YOU SURE ABOUT LETTING THE BAD ONE OUT?
I NEED A TOUCH OF BLOODY TO DO MY JOB.
SHE'D RATHER DIE THAN LET ANYONE HURT A WOMAN.
BLOODY MARY HATES MEN. SHE'D LOVE TO KILL ME.
YANK HER LEASH BEFORE THAT HAPPENS.
WOULD I DARE DEFY YOU, "KINGPIN"?

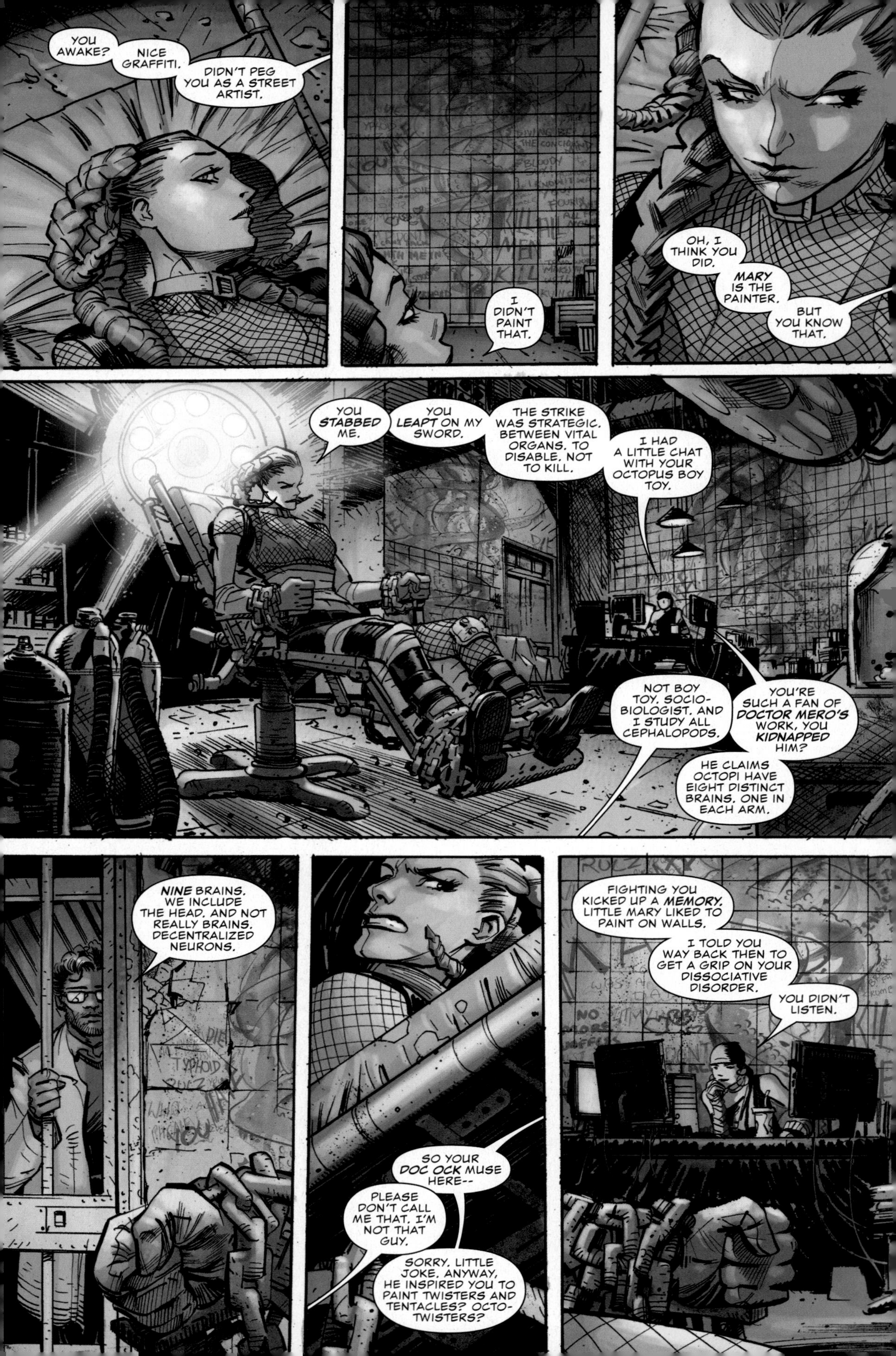

YOU AWAKE?
NICE GRAFFITI.
DIDN'T PEG YOU AS A STREET ARTIST.
I DIDN'T PAINT THAT.
OH, I THINK YOU DID.
MARY IS THE PAINTER.
BUT YOU KNOW THAT.
YOU STABBED ME.
YOU LEAPT ON MY SWORD.
THE STRIKE WAS STRATEGIC. BETWEEN VITAL ORGANS. TO DISABLE. NOT TO KILL.
I HAD A LITTLE CHAT WITH YOUR OCTOPUS BOY TOY.
NOT BOY TOY. SOCIO-BIOLOGIST. AND I STUDY ALL CEPHALOPODS.
YOU'RE SUCH A FAN OF DOCTOR MERO'S WORK, YOU KIDNAPPED HIM?
HE CLAIMS OCTOPI HAVE EIGHT DISTINCT BRAINS. ONE IN EACH ARM.
NINE BRAINS. WE INCLUDE THE HEAD. AND NOT REALLY BRAINS. DECENTRALIZED NEURONS.
SO YOUR DOC OCK MUSE HERE--
PLEASE DON'T CALL ME THAT. I'M NOT THAT GUY.
SORRY, LITTLE JOKE. ANYWAY, HE INSPIRED YOU TO PAINT TWISTERS AND TENTACLES? OCTO-TWISTERS?
FIGHTING YOU KICKED UP A MEMORY. LITTLE MARY LIKED TO PAINT ON WALLS.
I TOLD YOU WAY BACK THEN TO GET A GRIP ON YOUR DISSOCIATIVE DISORDER.
YOU DIDN'T LISTEN.

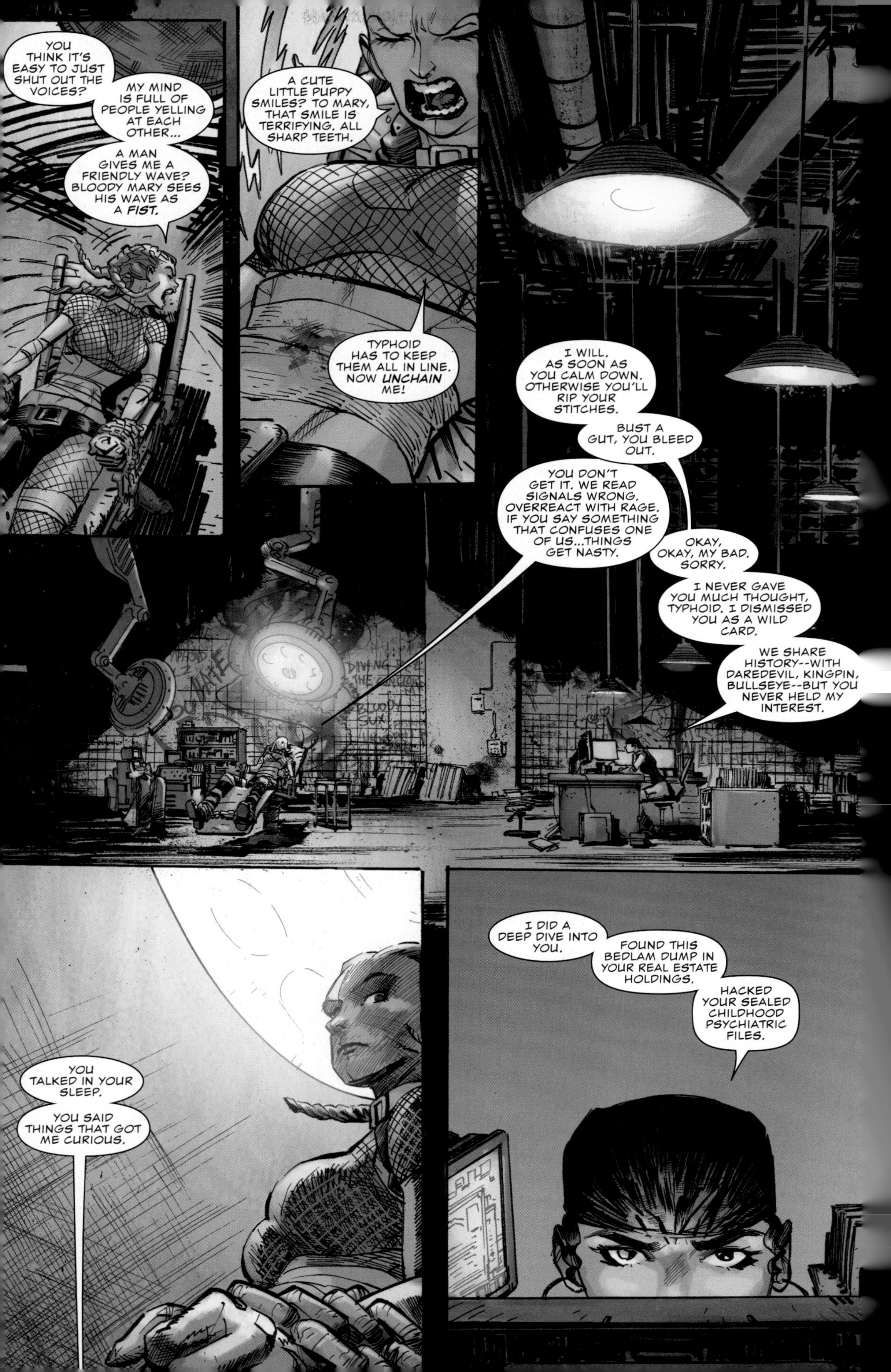
YOU THINK IT'S EASY TO JUST SHUT OUT THE VOICES?
MY MIND IS FULL OF PEOPLE YELLING AT EACH OTHER...
A MAN GIVES ME A FRIENDLY WAVE? BLOODY MARY SEES HIS WAVE AS A FIST.
A CUTE LITTLE PUPPY SMILES? TO MARY, THAT SMILE IS TERRIFYING, ALL SHARP TEETH.
TYPHOID HAS TO KEEP THEM ALL IN LINE. NOW UNCHAIN ME!
I WILL, AS SOON AS YOU CALM DOWN. OTHERWISE YOU'LL RIP YOUR STITCHES.
BUST A GUT, YOU BLEED OUT.
YOU DON'T GET IT. WE READ SIGNALS WRONG. OVERREACT WITH RAGE. IF YOU SAY SOMETHING THAT CONFUSES ONE OF US...THINGS GET NASTY.
OKAY, OKAY, MY BAD. SORRY.
I NEVER GAVE YOU MUCH THOUGHT, TYPHOID. I DISMISSED YOU AS A WILD CARD.
WE SHARE HISTORY--WITH DAREDEVIL, KINGPIN, BULLSEYE--BUT YOU NEVER HELD MY INTEREST.
YOU TALKED IN YOUR SLEEP.
YOU SAID THINGS THAT GOT ME CURIOUS.
I DID A DEEP DIVE INTO YOU.
FOUND THIS BEDLAM DUMP IN YOUR REAL ESTATE HOLDINGS.
HACKED YOUR SEALED CHILDHOOD PSYCHIATRIC FILES.

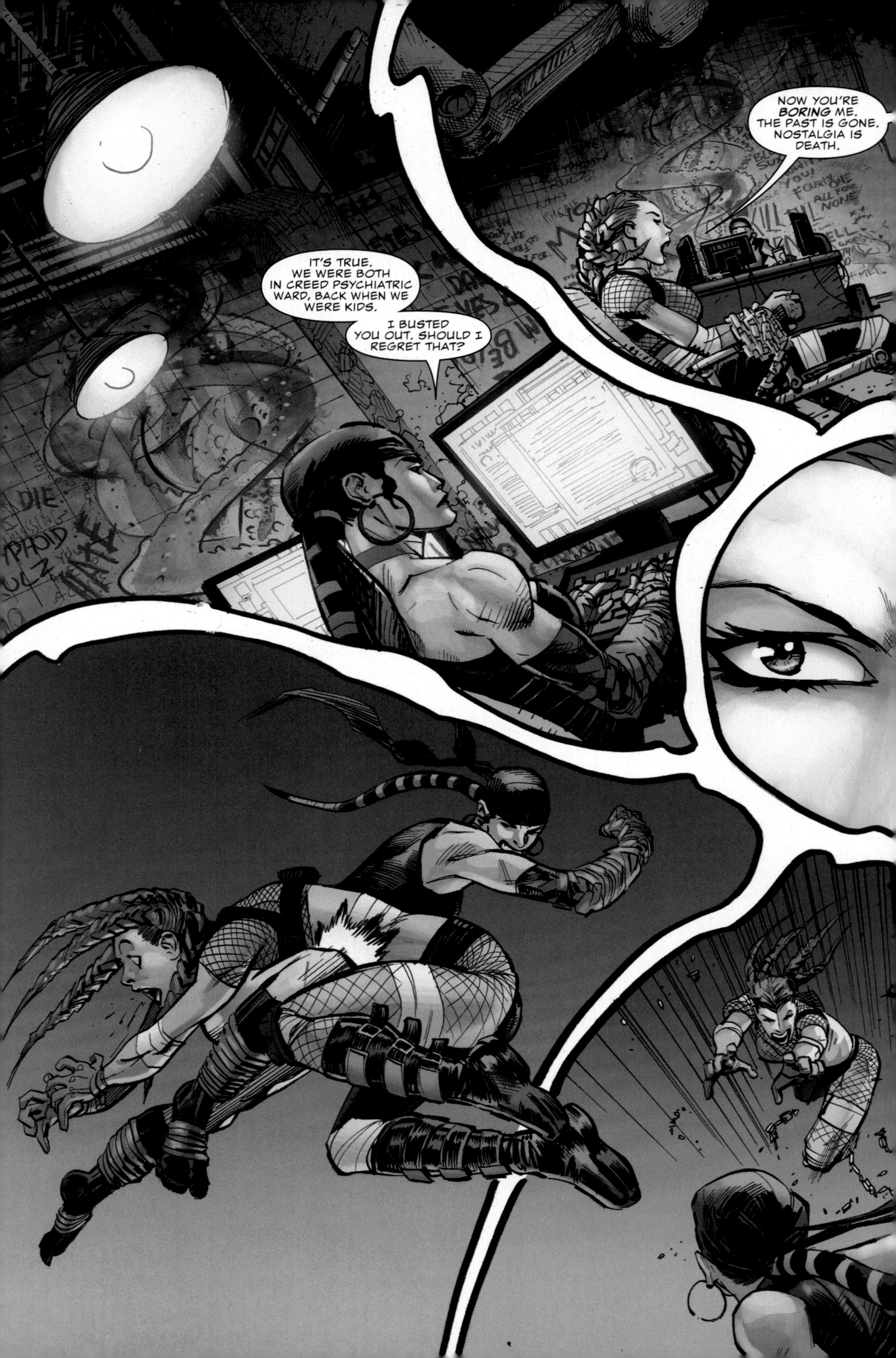
NOW YOU'RE *BORING* ME. THE PAST IS GONE. NOSTALGIA IS DEATH.
IT'S TRUE. WE WERE BOTH IN CREED PSYCHIATRIC WARD, BACK WHEN WE WERE KIDS.
I BUSTED YOU OUT. SHOULD I REGRET THAT?

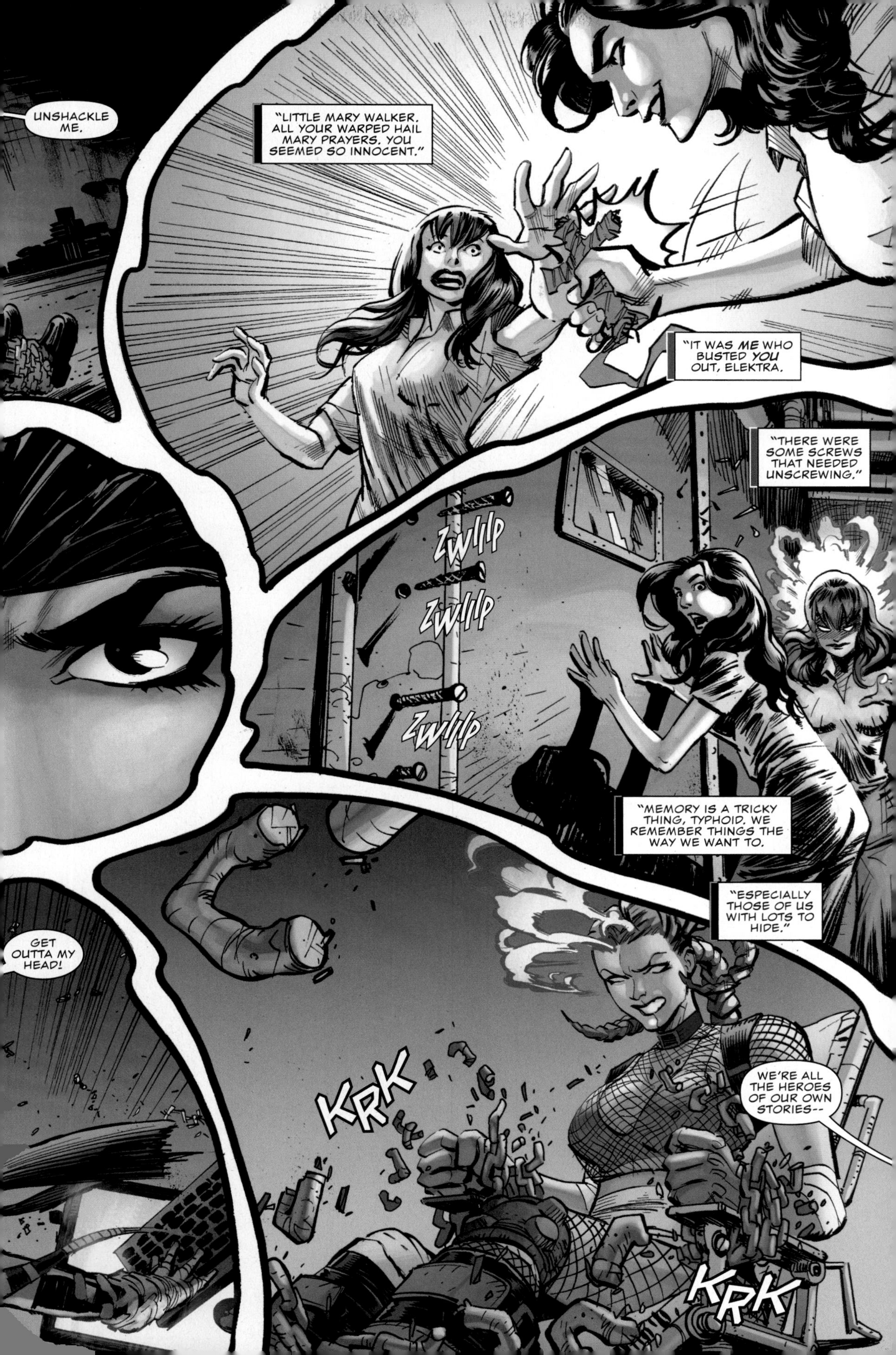
UNSHACKLE ME.
"LITTLE MARY WALKER. ALL YOUR WARPED HAIL MARY PRAYERS. YOU SEEMED SO INNOCENT."
"IT WAS ME WHO BUSTED YOU OUT, ELEKTRA.
"THERE WERE SOME SCREWS THAT NEEDED UNSCREWING."
ZWIIP
ZWIIP
ZWIIP
"MEMORY IS A TRICKY THING, TYPHOID. WE REMEMBER THINGS THE WAY WE WANT TO.
"ESPECIALLY THOSE OF US WITH LOTS TO HIDE."
GET OUTTA MY HEAD!
KRK
WE'RE ALL THE HEROES OF OUR OWN STORIES--
KRK

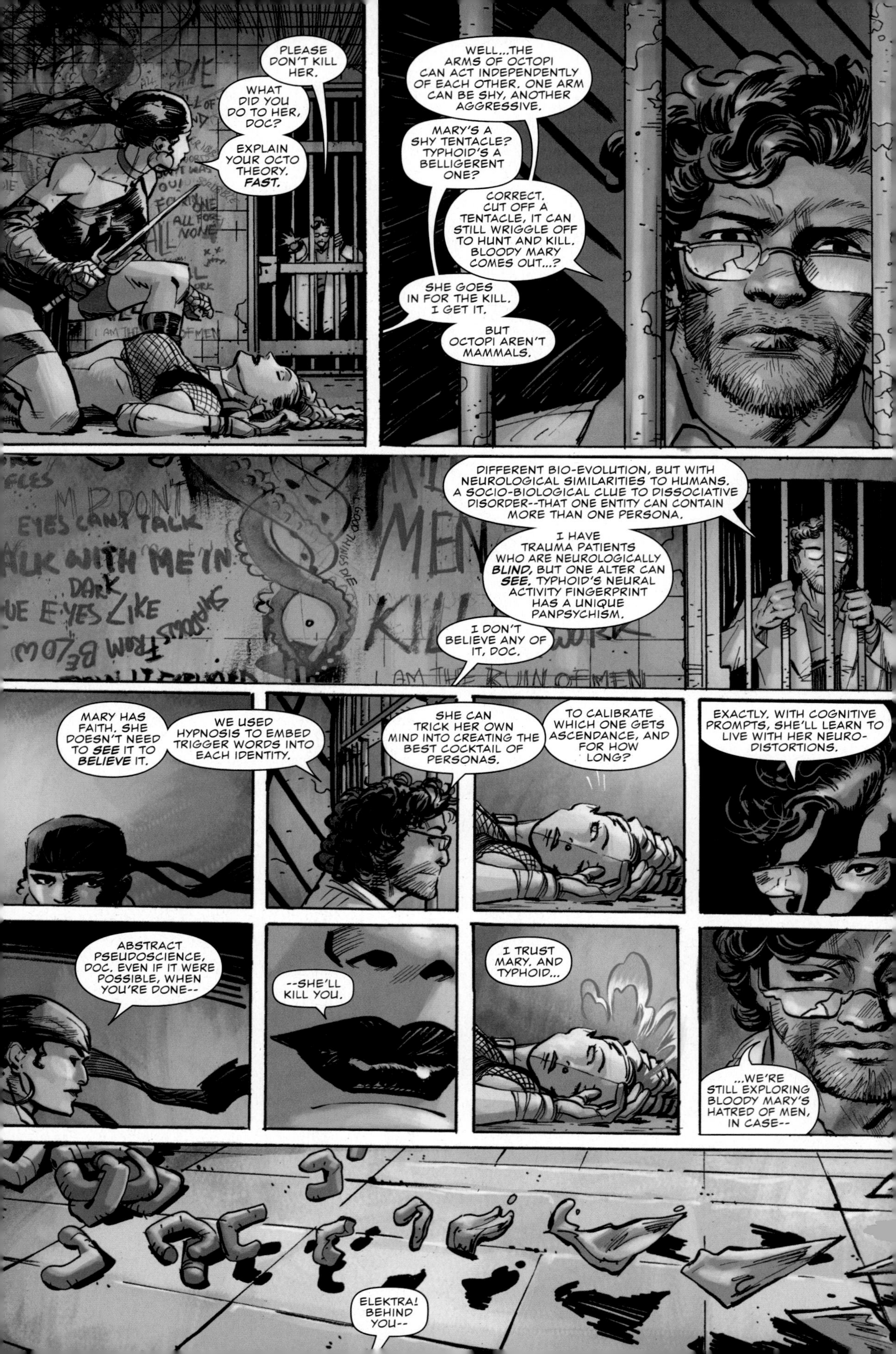

PLEASE DON'T KILL HER.
WHAT DID YOU DO TO HER, DOC?
EXPLAIN YOUR OCTO THEORY. *FAST.*
WELL...THE ARMS OF OCTOPI CAN ACT INDEPENDENTLY OF EACH OTHER. ONE ARM CAN BE SHY, ANOTHER AGGRESSIVE.
MARY'S A SHY TENTACLE? TYPHOID'S A BELLIGERENT ONE?
CORRECT. CUT OFF A TENTACLE, IT CAN STILL WRIGGLE OFF TO HUNT AND KILL. BLOODY MARY COMES OUT...?
SHE GOES IN FOR THE KILL. I GET IT.
BUT OCTOPI AREN'T MAMMALS.
DIFFERENT BIO-EVOLUTION, BUT WITH NEUROLOGICAL SIMILARITIES TO HUMANS. A SOCIO-BIOLOGICAL CLUE TO DISSOCIATIVE DISORDER--THAT ONE ENTITY CAN CONTAIN MORE THAN ONE PERSONA.
I HAVE TRAUMA PATIENTS WHO ARE NEUROLOGICALLY *BLIND*, BUT ONE ALTER CAN *SEE*. TYPHOID'S NEURAL ACTIVITY FINGERPRINT HAS A UNIQUE PANPSYCHISM.
I DON'T BELIEVE ANY OF IT, DOC.
MARY HAS FAITH. SHE DOESN'T NEED TO *SEE* IT TO *BELIEVE* IT.
WE USED HYPNOSIS TO EMBED TRIGGER WORDS INTO EACH IDENTITY.
SHE CAN TRICK HER OWN MIND INTO CREATING THE BEST COCKTAIL OF PERSONAS.
TO CALIBRATE WHICH ONE GETS ASCENDANCE, AND FOR HOW LONG?
EXACTLY. WITH COGNITIVE PROMPTS, SHE'LL LEARN TO LIVE WITH HER NEURO-DISTORTIONS.
ABSTRACT PSEUDOSCIENCE, DOC. EVEN IF IT WERE POSSIBLE, WHEN YOU'RE DONE--
--SHE'LL KILL YOU.
I TRUST MARY. AND TYPHOID...
...WE'RE STILL EXPLORING BLOODY MARY'S HATRED OF MEN, IN CASE--
ELEKTRA! BEHIND YOU--

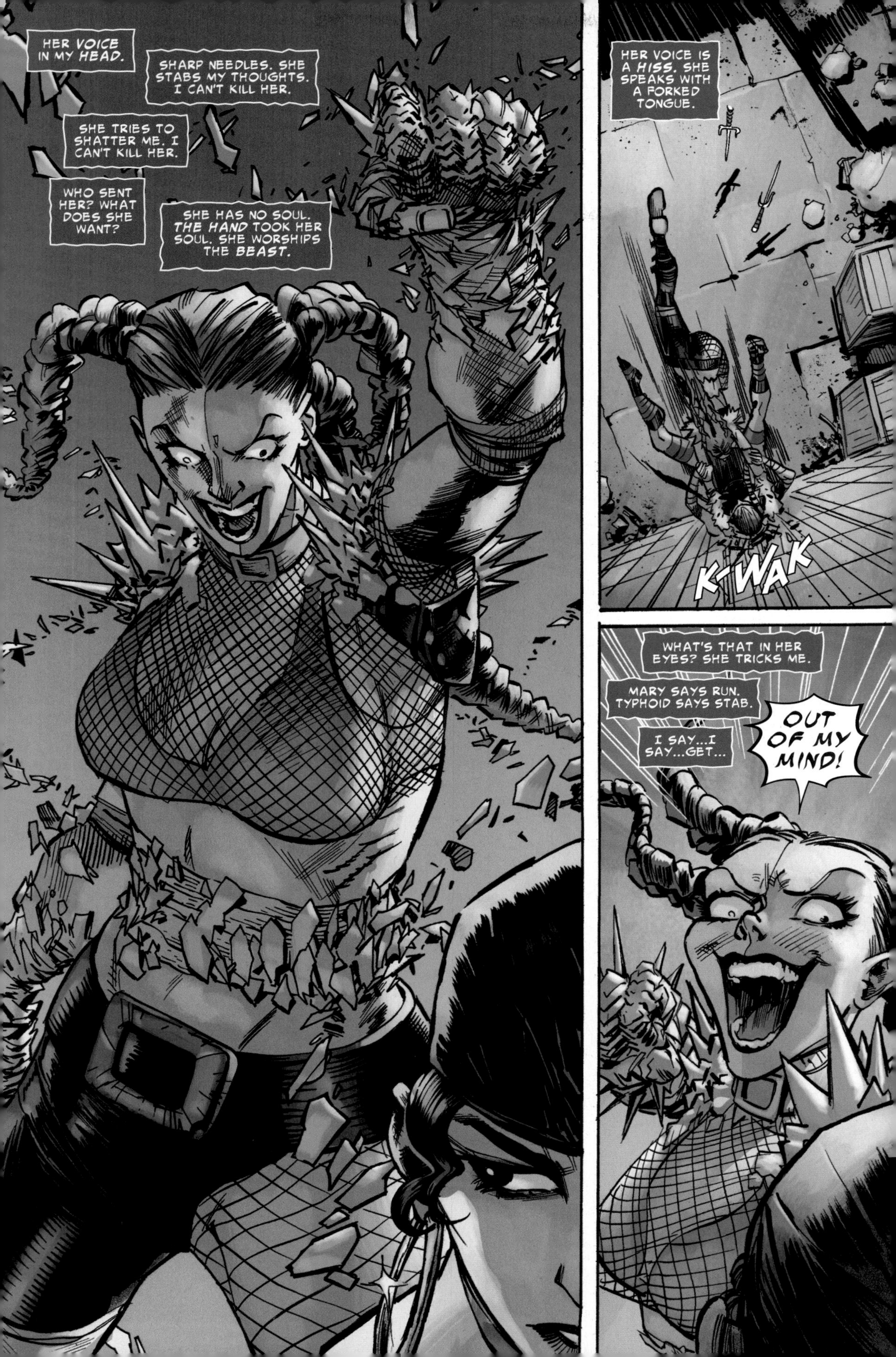

HER VOICE IN MY HEAD.
SHARP NEEDLES. SHE STABS MY THOUGHTS. I CAN'T KILL HER.
SHE TRIES TO SHATTER ME. I CAN'T KILL HER.
WHO SENT HER? WHAT DOES SHE WANT?
SHE HAS NO SOUL. THE HAND TOOK HER SOUL. SHE WORSHIPS THE BEAST.
HER VOICE IS A HISS. SHE SPEAKS WITH A FORKED TONGUE.
K-WAK
WHAT'S THAT IN HER EYES? SHE TRICKS ME.
MARY SAYS RUN. TYPHOID SAYS STAB.
I SAY...I SAY...GET...
OUT OF MY MIND!

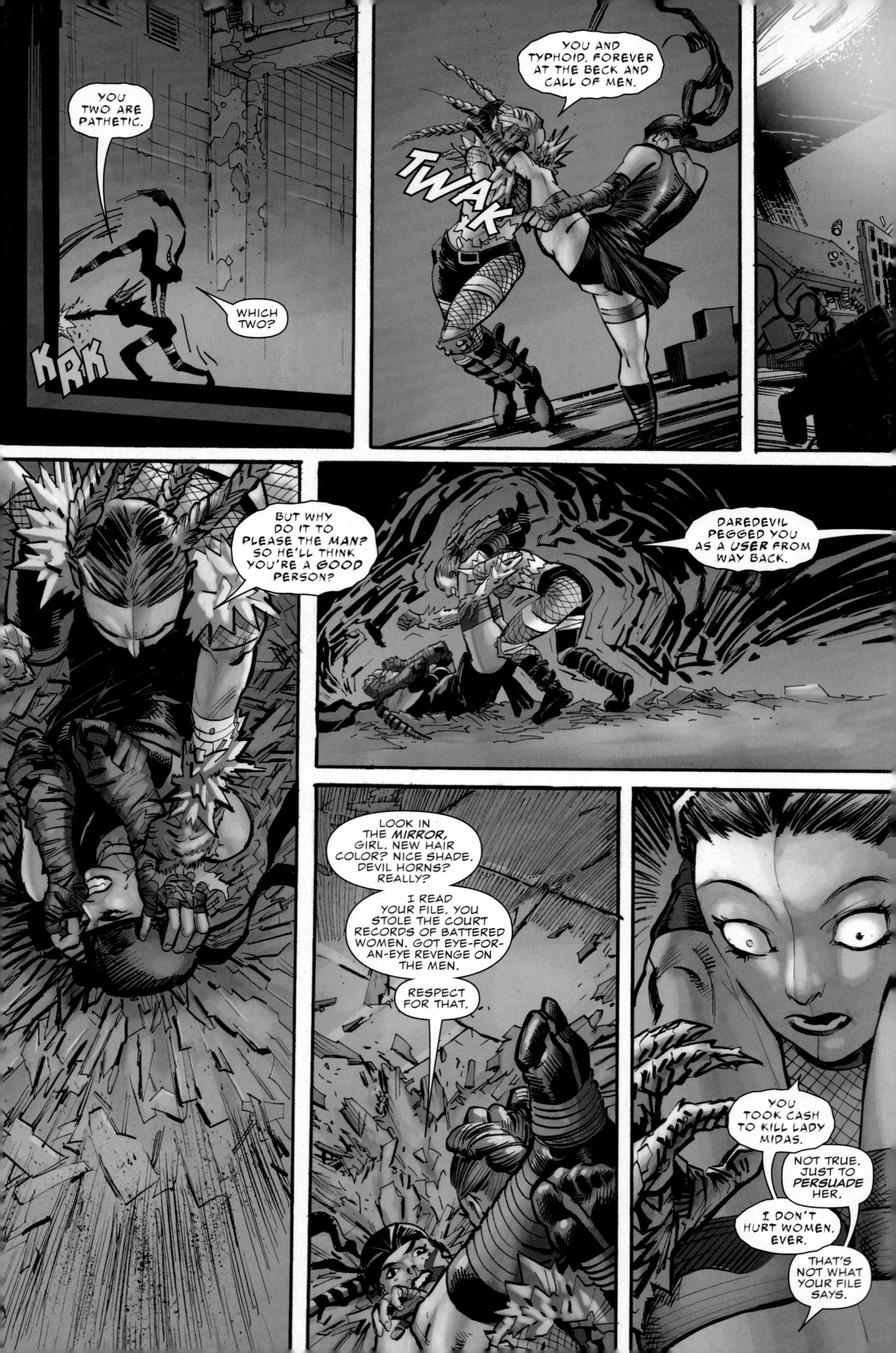

YOU TWO ARE PATHETIC.
WHICH TWO?
KRK
YOU AND TYPHOID. FOREVER AT THE BECK AND CALL OF MEN.
TWAK
BUT WHY DO IT TO PLEASE THE MAN? SO HE'LL THINK YOU'RE A GOOD PERSON?
DAREDEVIL PEGGED YOU AS A USER FROM WAY BACK.
LOOK IN THE MIRROR, GIRL. NEW HAIR COLOR? NICE SHADE. DEVIL HORNS? REALLY?
I READ YOUR FILE. YOU STOLE THE COURT RECORDS OF BATTERED WOMEN. GOT EYE-FOR-AN-EYE REVENGE ON THE MEN.
RESPECT FOR THAT.
YOU TOOK CASH TO KILL LADY MIDAS.
NOT TRUE. JUST TO PERSUADE HER.
I DON'T HURT WOMEN. EVER.
THAT'S NOT WHAT YOUR FILE SAYS.

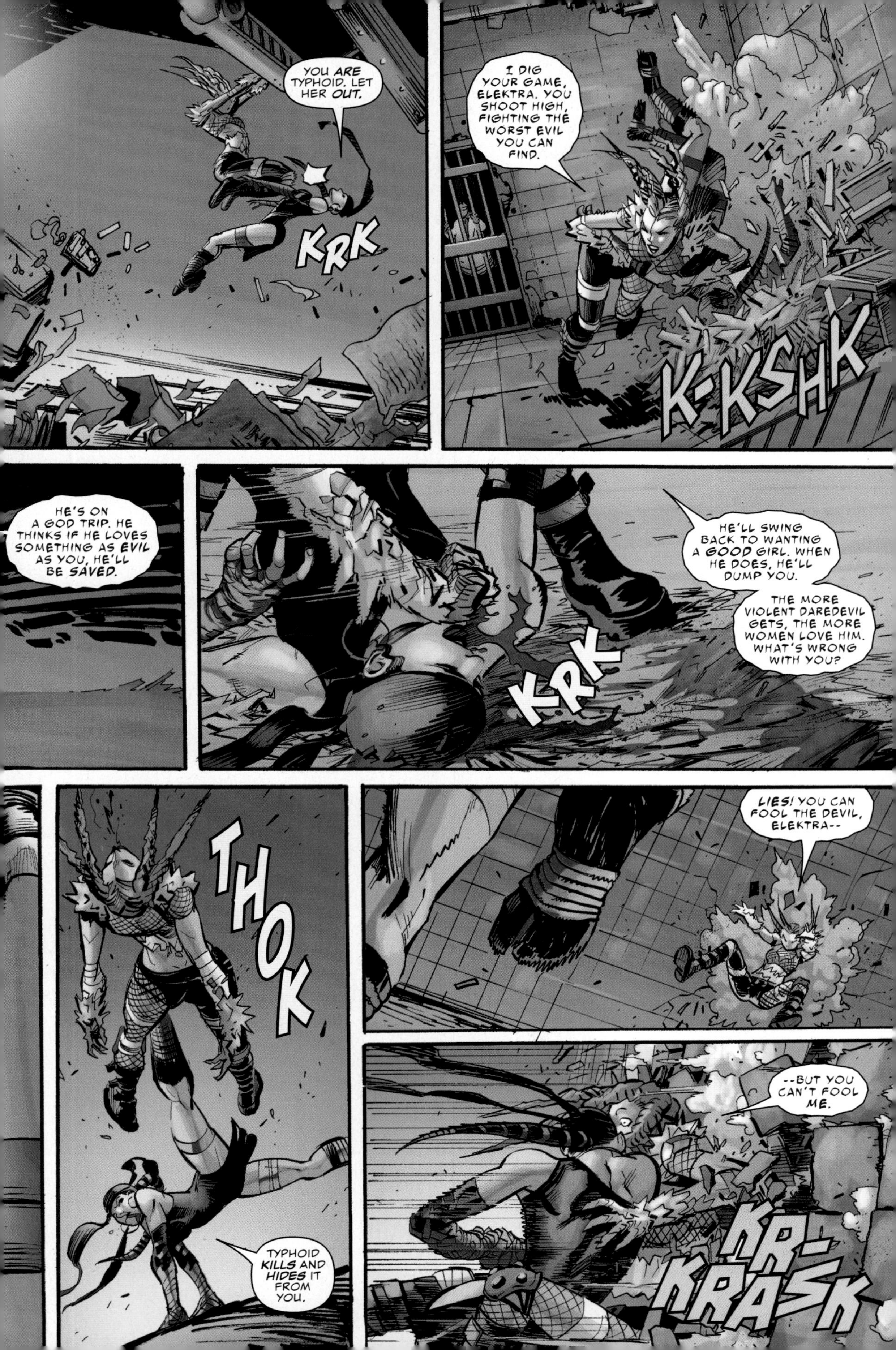
YOU ARE TYPHOID. LET HER OUT.
KRK
I DIG YOUR GAME, ELEKTRA. YOU SHOOT HIGH, FIGHTING THE WORST EVIL YOU CAN FIND.
K-KSHK
HE'S ON A GOD TRIP. HE THINKS IF HE LOVES SOMETHING AS EVIL AS YOU, HE'LL BE SAVED.
HE'LL SWING BACK TO WANTING A GOOD GIRL. WHEN HE DOES, HE'LL DUMP YOU.
THE MORE VIOLENT DAREDEVIL GETS, THE MORE WOMEN LOVE HIM. WHAT'S WRONG WITH YOU?
KRK
THOK
TYPHOID KILLS AND HIDES IT FROM YOU.
LIES! YOU CAN FOOL THE DEVIL, ELEKTRA--
--BUT YOU CAN'T FOOL ME.
KR-KRASK

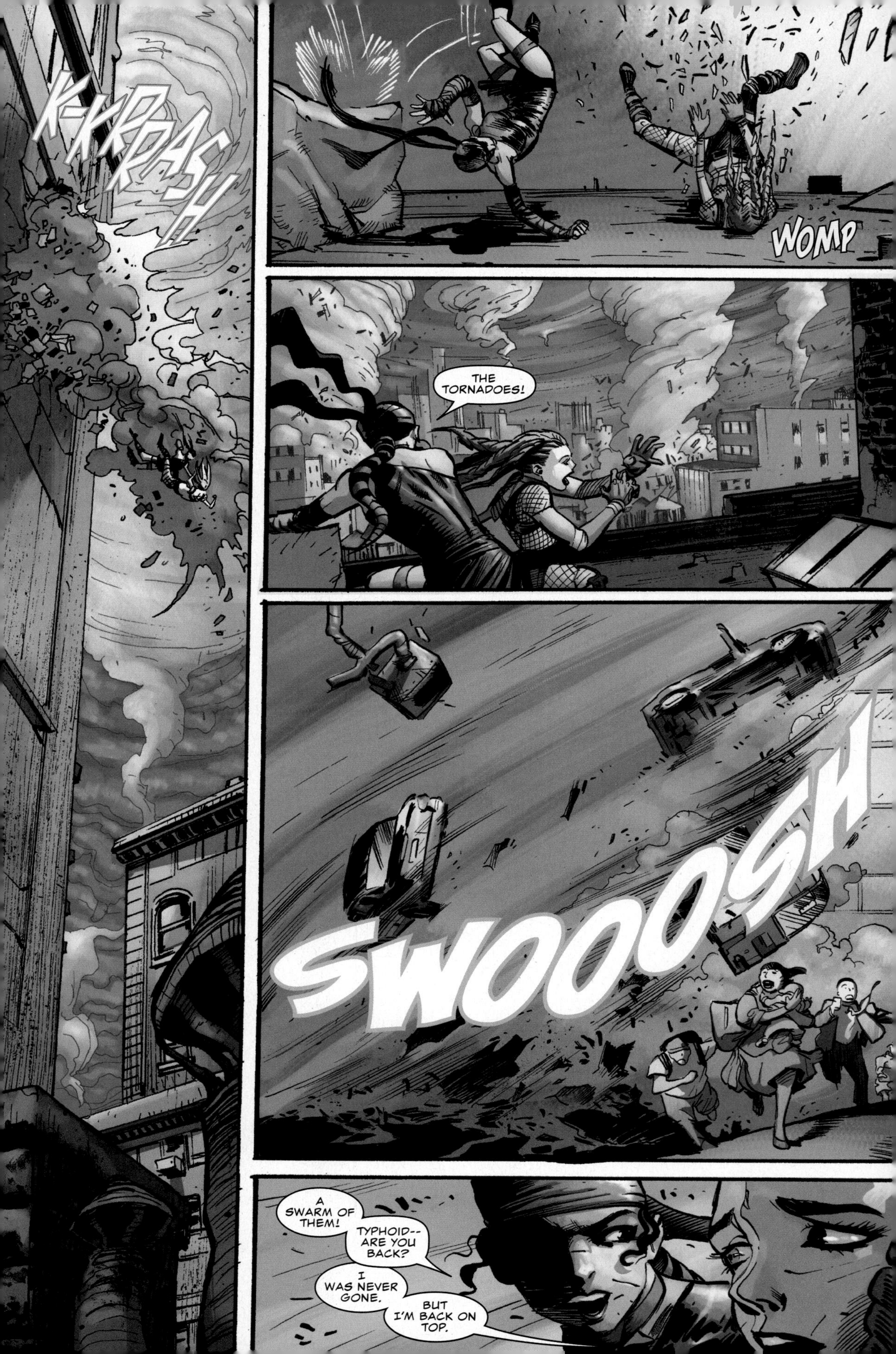
K-KRRASH
WOMP
THE TORNADOES!
SWOOOSH
A SWARM OF THEM!
TYPHOID-- ARE YOU BACK?
I WAS NEVER GONE.
BUT I'M BACK ON TOP.

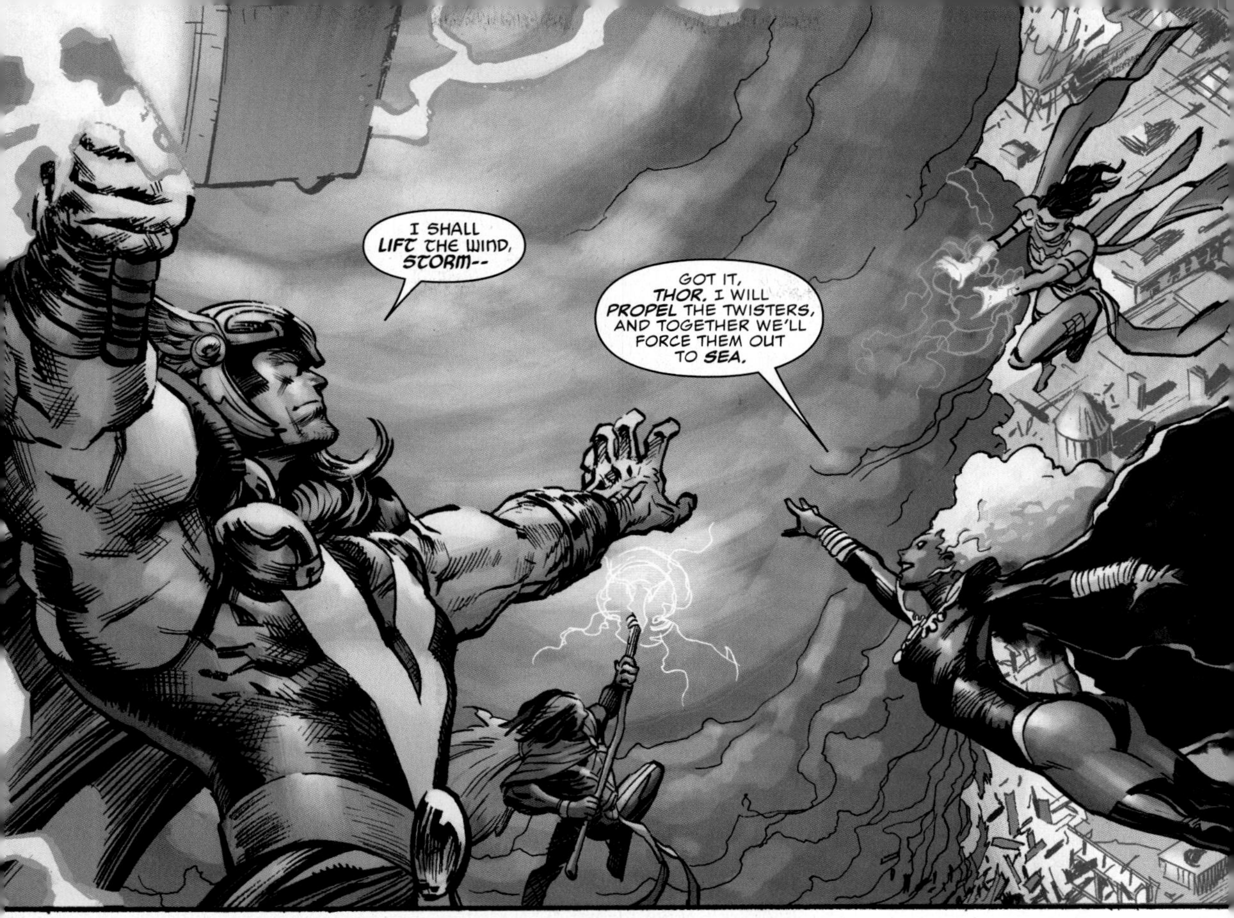
I SHALL LIFT THE WIND, STORM--
GOT IT, THOR. I WILL PROPEL THE TWISTERS, AND TOGETHER WE'LL FORCE THEM OUT TO SEA.

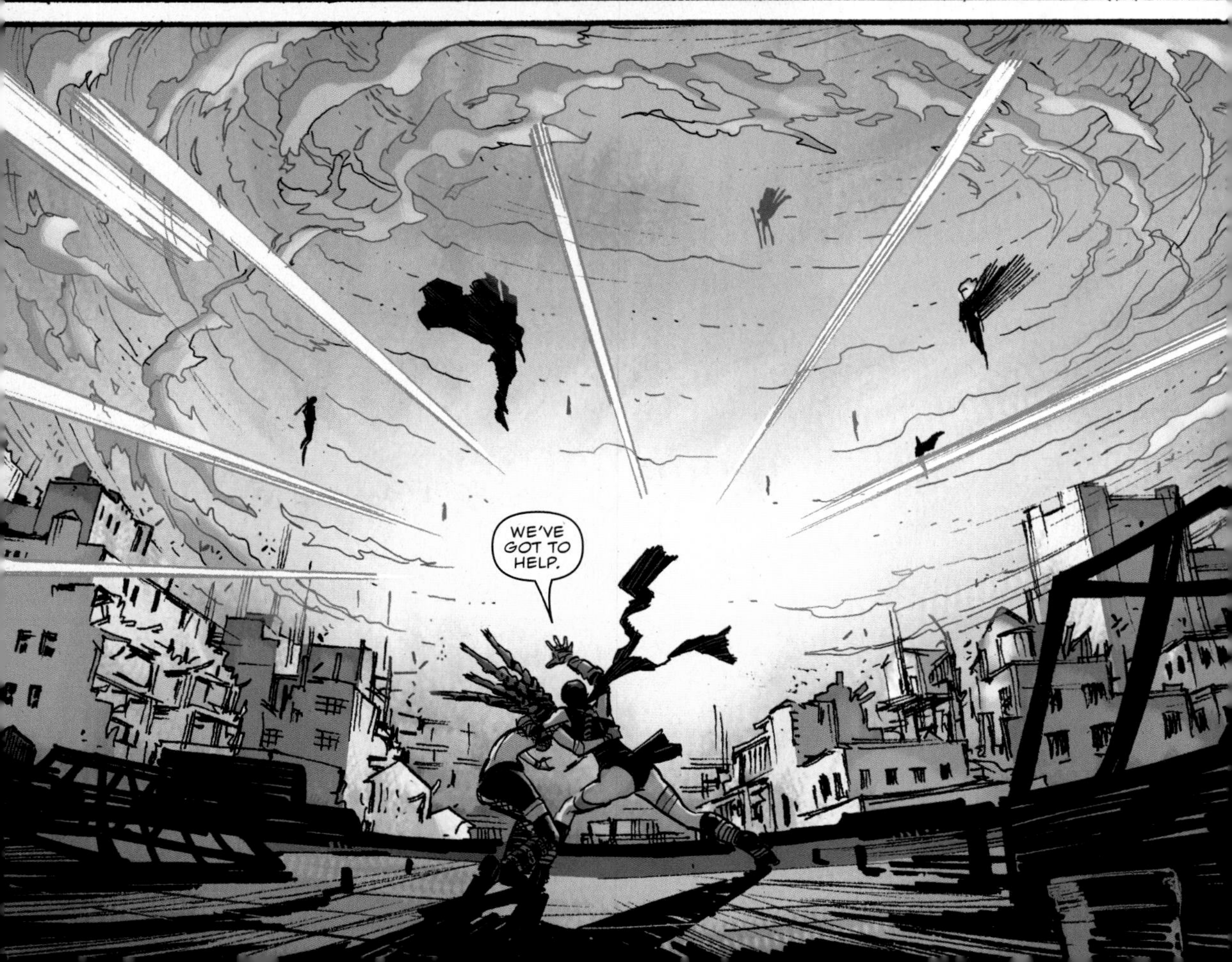
WE'VE GOT TO HELP.

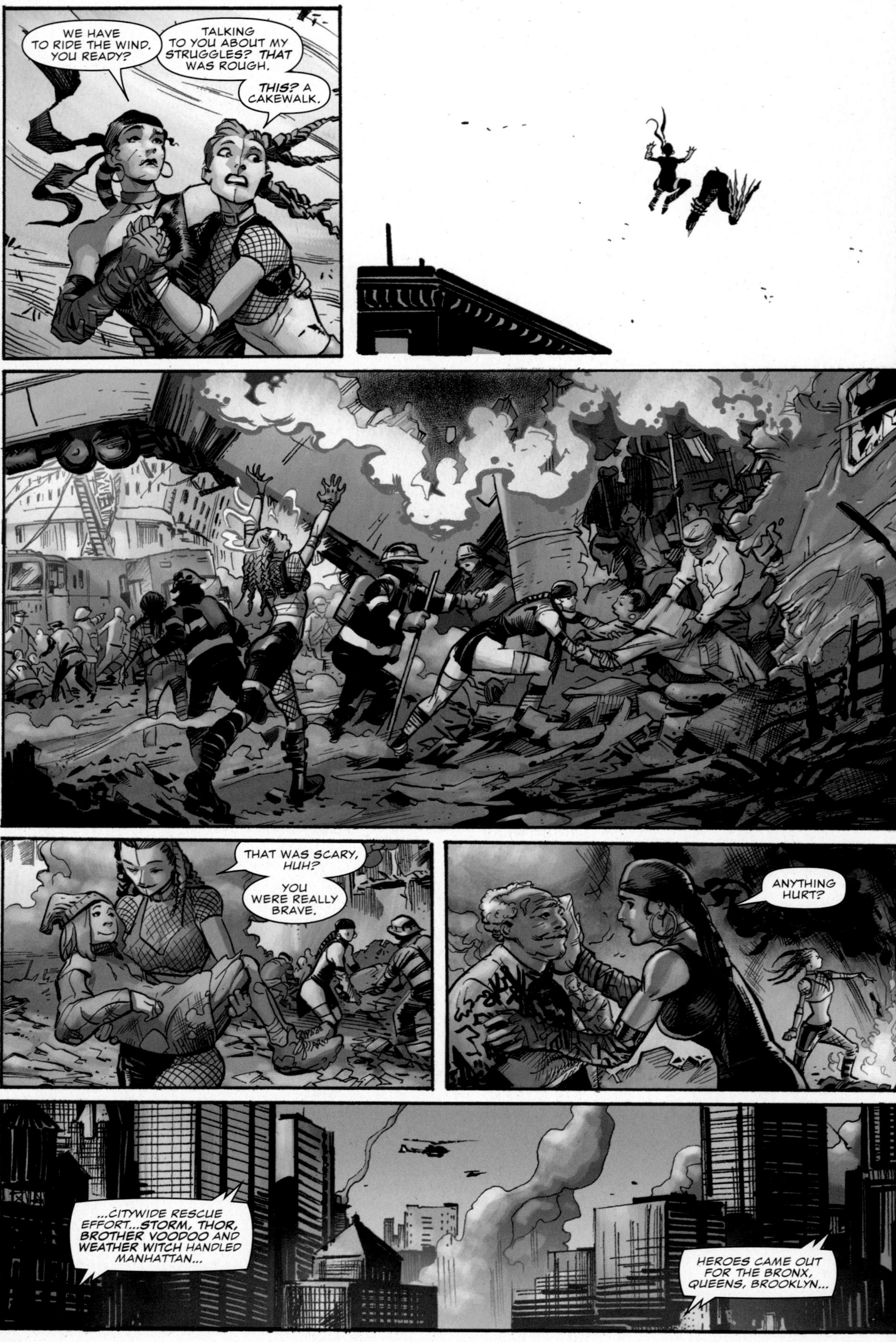
WE HAVE TO RIDE THE WIND. YOU READY?
TALKING TO YOU ABOUT MY STRUGGLES? THAT WAS ROUGH.
THIS? A CAKEWALK.
THAT WAS SCARY, HUH?
YOU WERE REALLY BRAVE.
ANYTHING HURT?
...CITYWIDE RESCUE EFFORT...STORM, THOR, BROTHER VOODOO AND WEATHER WITCH HANDLED MANHATTAN...
HEROES CAME OUT FOR THE BRONX, QUEENS, BROOKLYN...

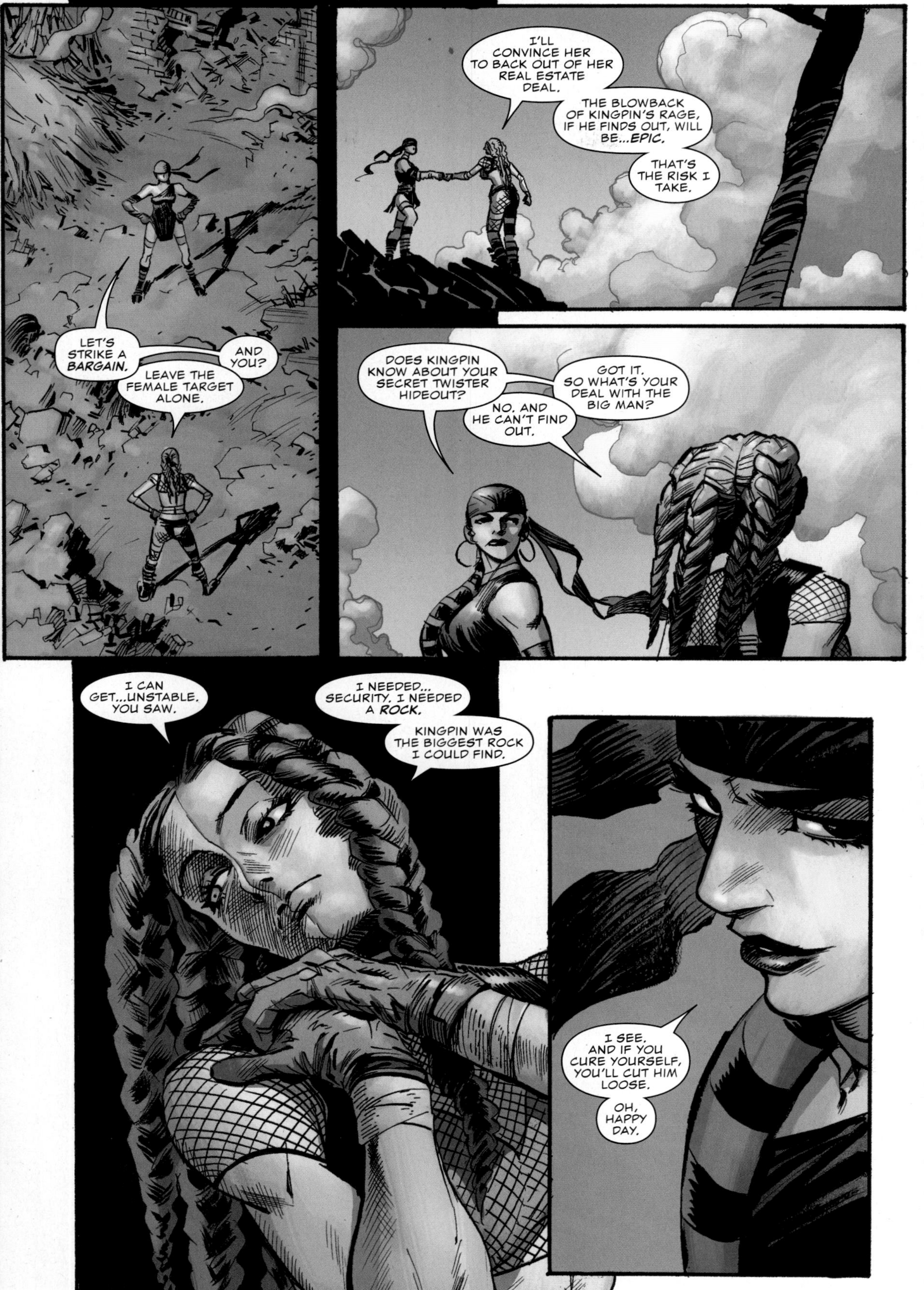
LET'S STRIKE A BARGAIN.
LEAVE THE FEMALE TARGET ALONE.
AND YOU?
I'LL CONVINCE HER TO BACK OUT OF HER REAL ESTATE DEAL.
THE BLOWBACK OF KINGPIN'S RAGE, IF HE FINDS OUT, WILL BE...EPIC.
THAT'S THE RISK I TAKE.
DOES KINGPIN KNOW ABOUT YOUR SECRET TWISTER HIDEOUT?
NO. AND HE CAN'T FIND OUT.
GOT IT. SO WHAT'S YOUR DEAL WITH THE BIG MAN?
I CAN GET...UNSTABLE. YOU SAW.
I NEEDED... SECURITY. I NEEDED A ROCK.
KINGPIN WAS THE BIGGEST ROCK I COULD FIND.
I SEE. AND IF YOU CURE YOURSELF, YOU'LL CUT HIM LOOSE.
OH, HAPPY DAY.

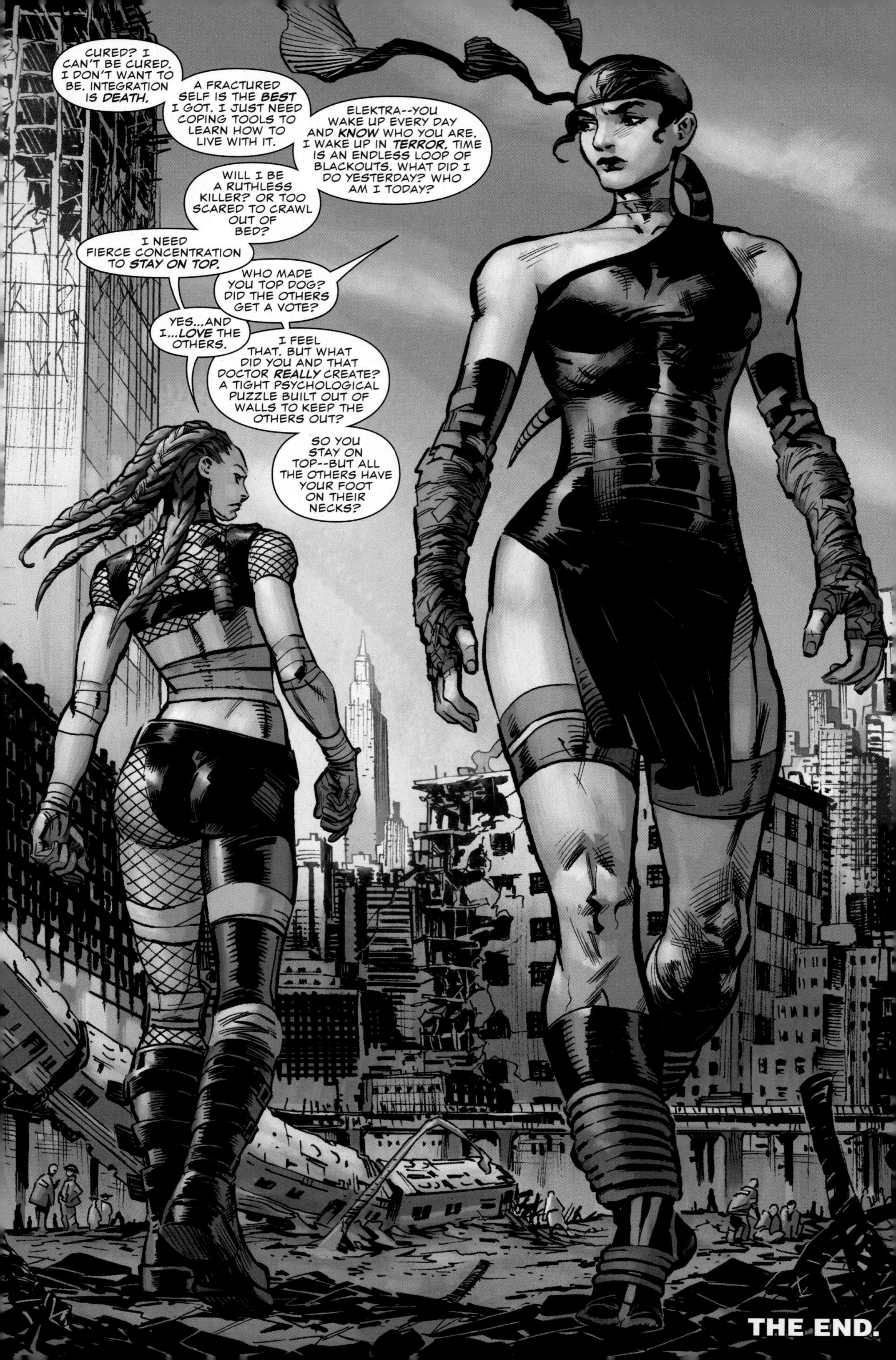
CURED? I CAN'T BE CURED. I DON'T WANT TO BE. INTEGRATION IS DEATH.
A FRACTURED SELF IS THE BEST I GOT. I JUST NEED COPING TOOLS TO LEARN HOW TO LIVE WITH IT.
ELEKTRA--YOU WAKE UP EVERY DAY AND KNOW WHO YOU ARE. I WAKE UP IN TERROR. TIME IS AN ENDLESS LOOP OF BLACKOUTS. WHAT DID I DO YESTERDAY? WHO AM I TODAY?
WILL I BE A RUTHLESS KILLER? OR TOO SCARED TO CRAWL OUT OF BED?
I NEED FIERCE CONCENTRATION TO STAY ON TOP.
WHO MADE YOU TOP DOG? DID THE OTHERS GET A VOTE?
YES...AND I...LOVE THE OTHERS.
I FEEL THAT. BUT WHAT DID YOU AND THAT DOCTOR REALLY CREATE? A TIGHT PSYCHOLOGICAL PUZZLE BUILT OUT OF WALLS TO KEEP THE OTHERS OUT?
SO YOU STAY ON TOP--BUT ALL THE OTHERS HAVE YOUR FOOT ON THEIR NECKS?
THE END.

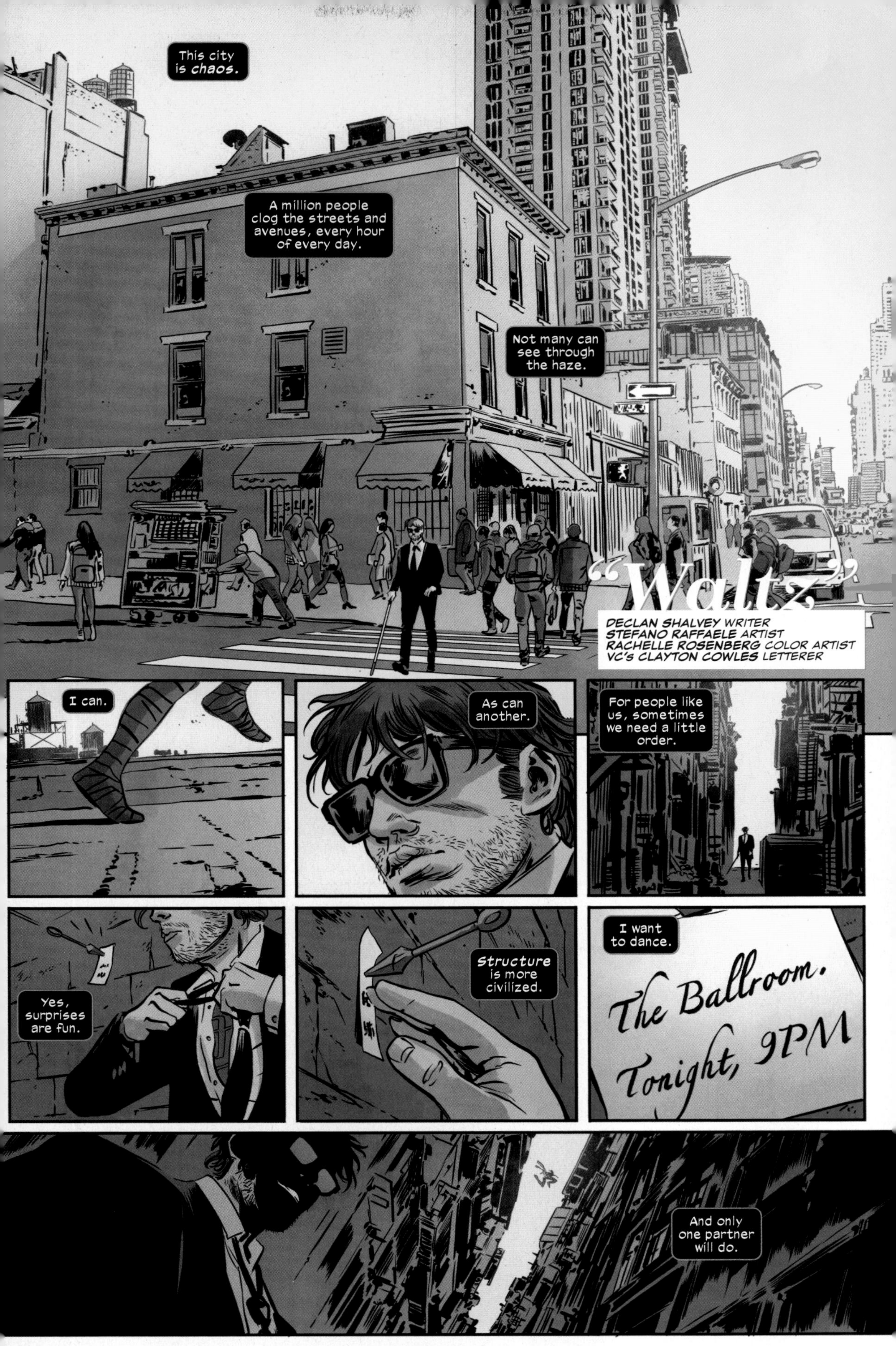

This city is *chaos.*
A million people clog the streets and avenues, every hour of every day.
Not many can see through the haze.
"Waltz"
DECLAN SHALVEY WRITER
STEFANO RAFFAELE ARTIST
RACHELLE ROSENBERG COLOR ARTIST
VC'S CLAYTON COWLES LETTERER
I can.
As can another.
For people like us, sometimes we need a little order.
Yes, surprises are fun.
Structure is more civilized.
I want to dance.
The Ballroom. Tonight, 9PM
And only one partner will do.

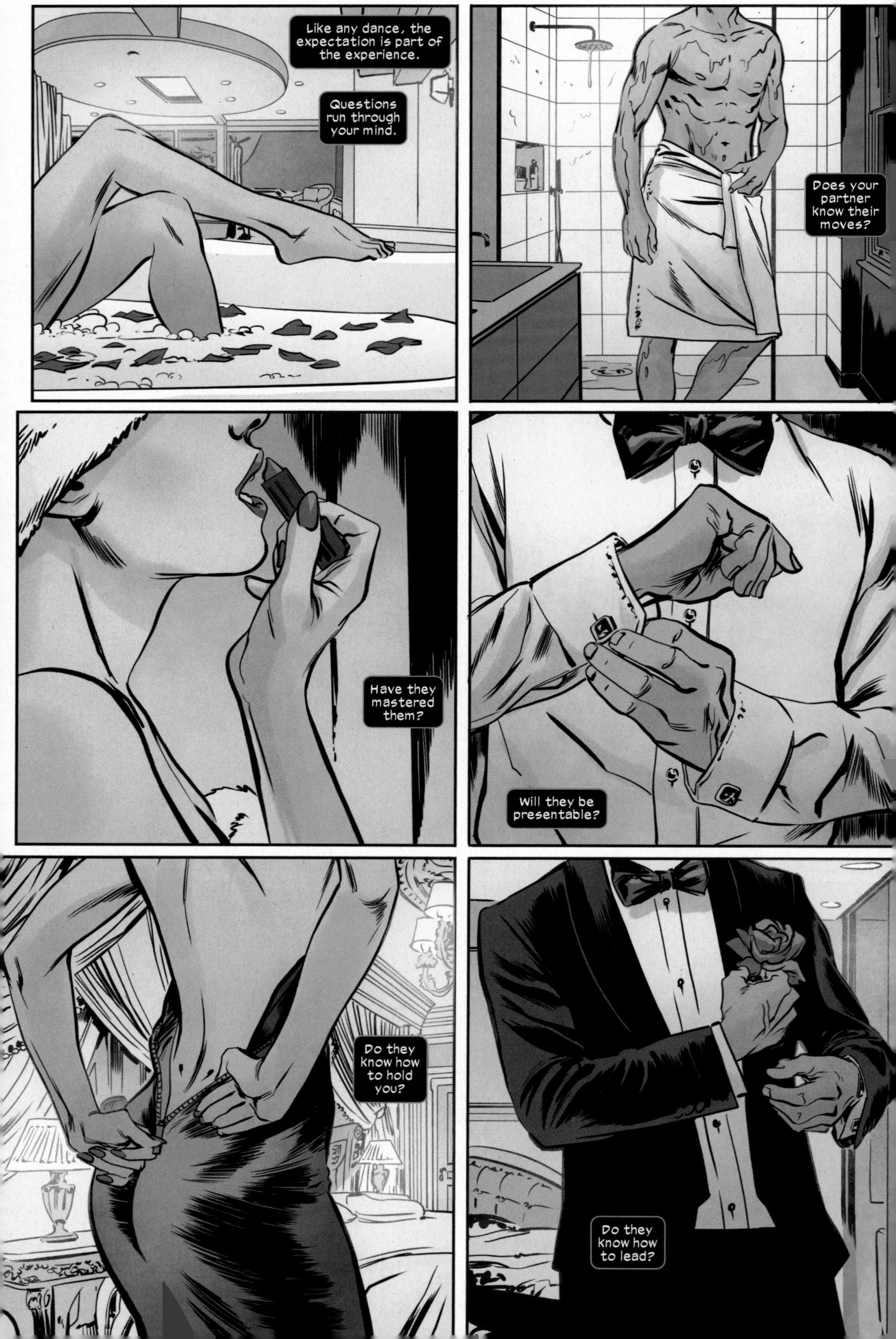
Like any dance, the expectation is part of the experience.
Questions run through your mind.
Does your partner know their moves?
Have they mastered them?
Will they be presentable?
Do they know how to hold you?
Do they know how to lead?

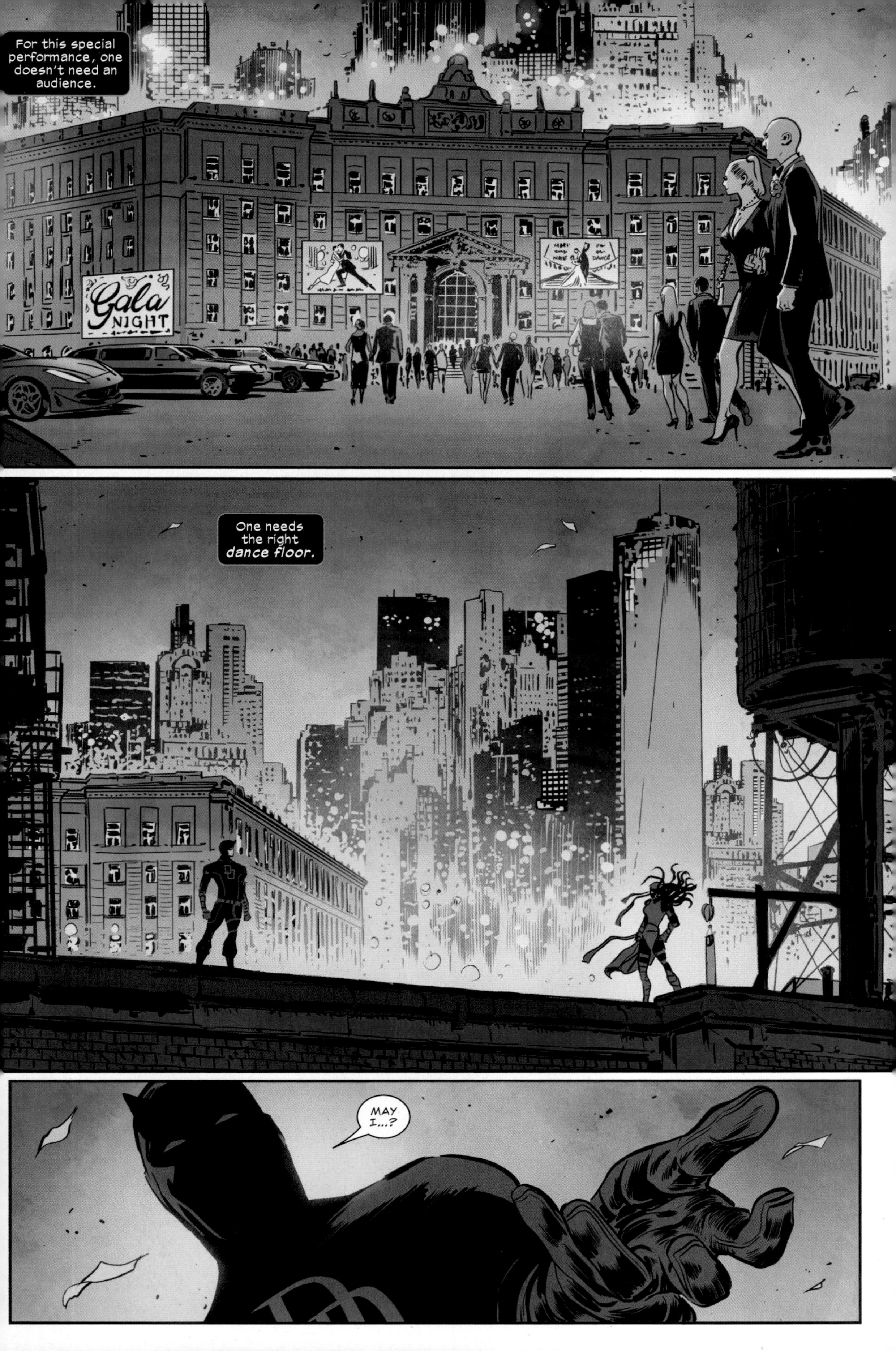
For this special performance, one doesn't need an audience.
Gala NIGHT
One needs the right *dance floor*.
MAY I...?

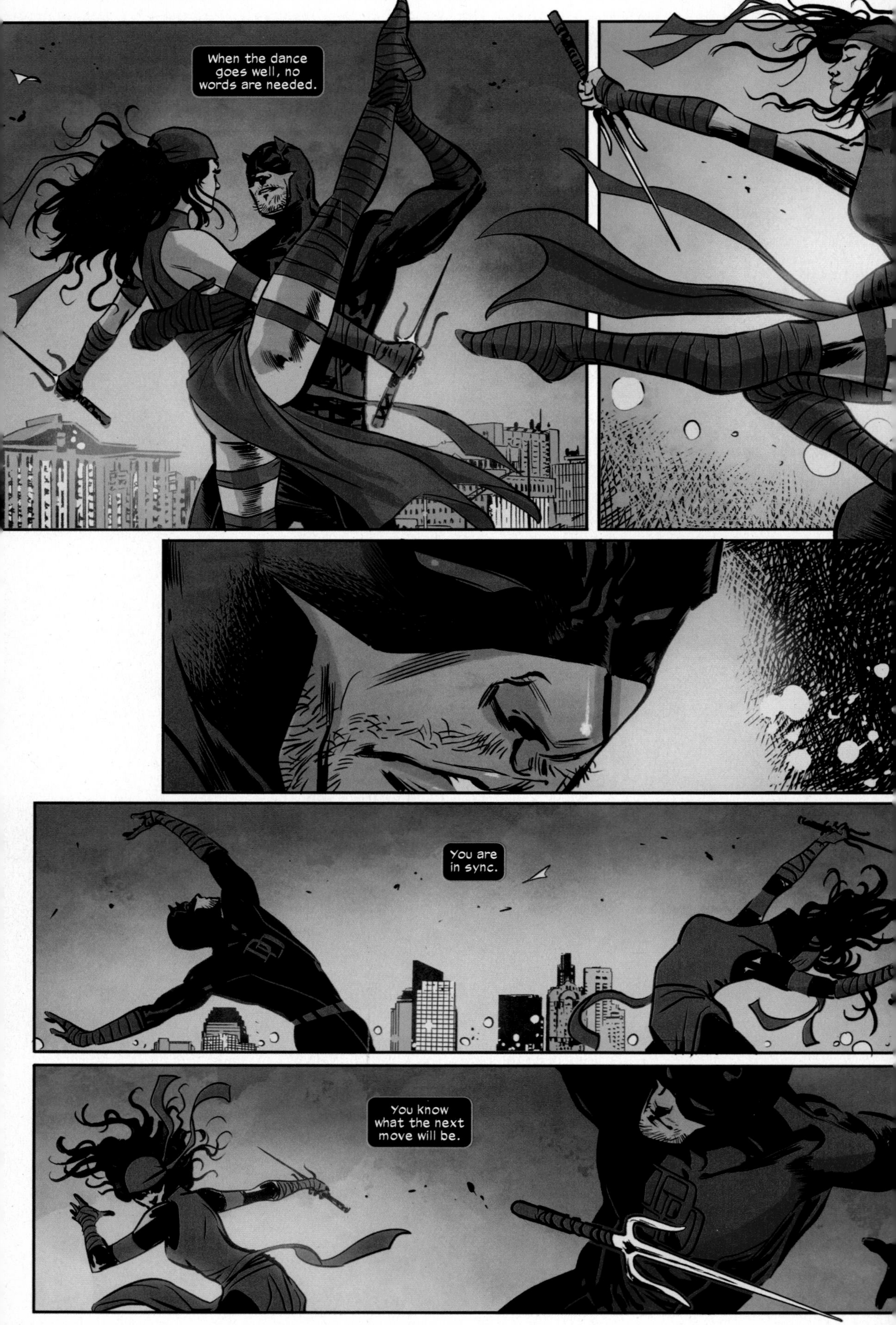
When the dance goes well, no words are needed.
You are in sync.
You know what the next move will be.

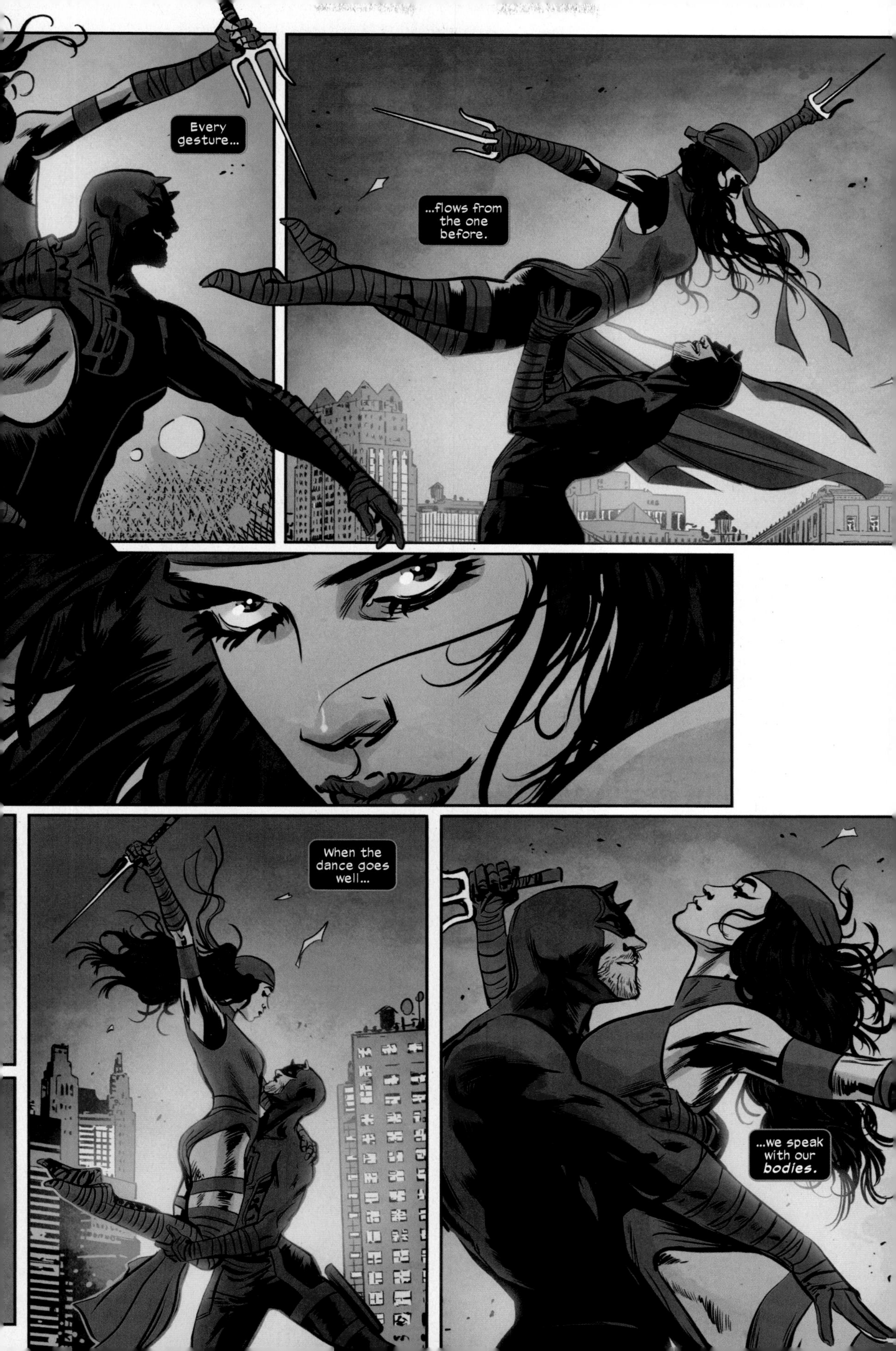
Every gesture...
...flows from the one before.
When the dance goes well...
...we speak with our *bodies*.

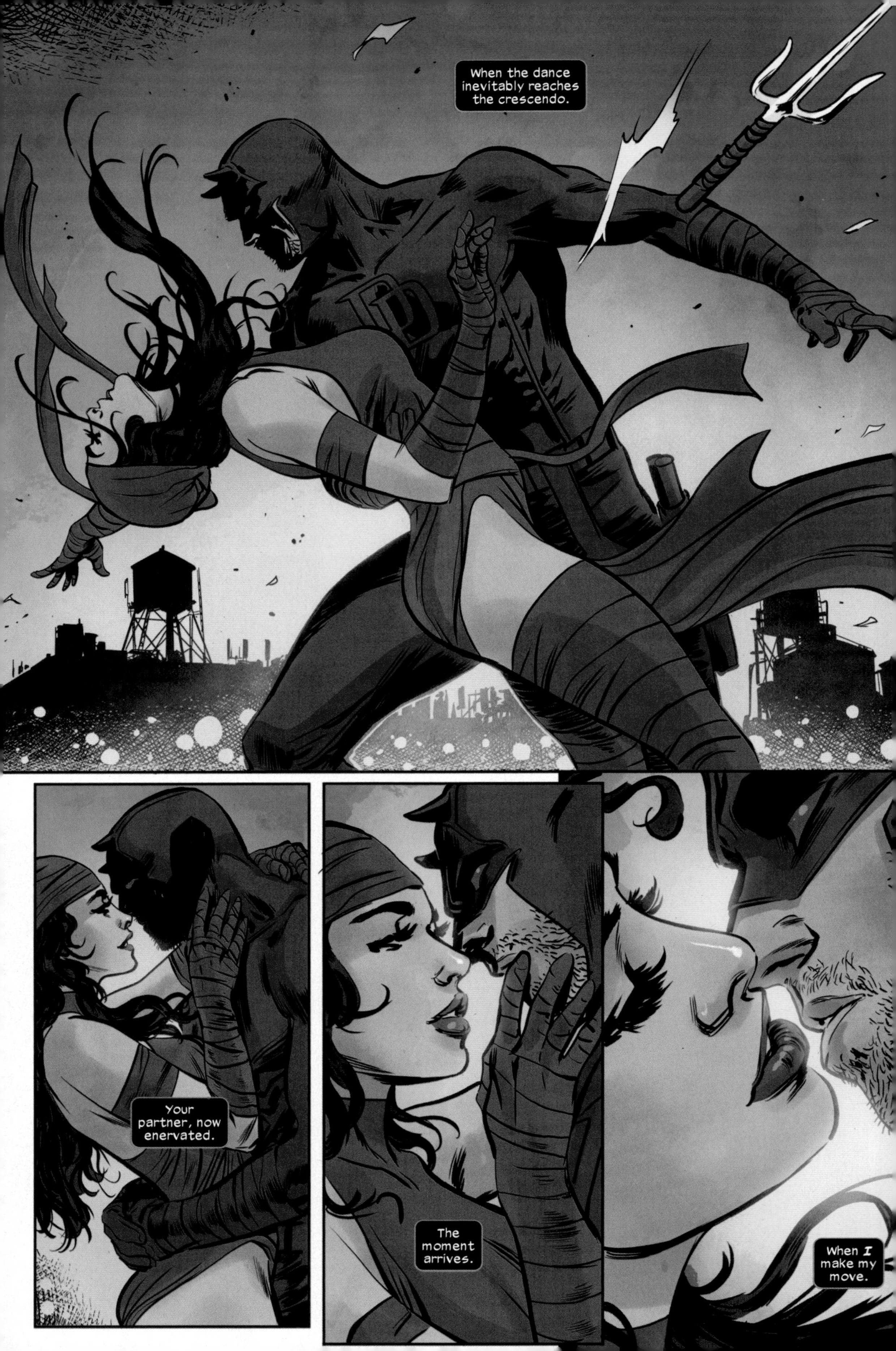
When the dance inevitably reaches the crescendo.
Your partner, now enervated.
The moment arrives.
When I make my move.

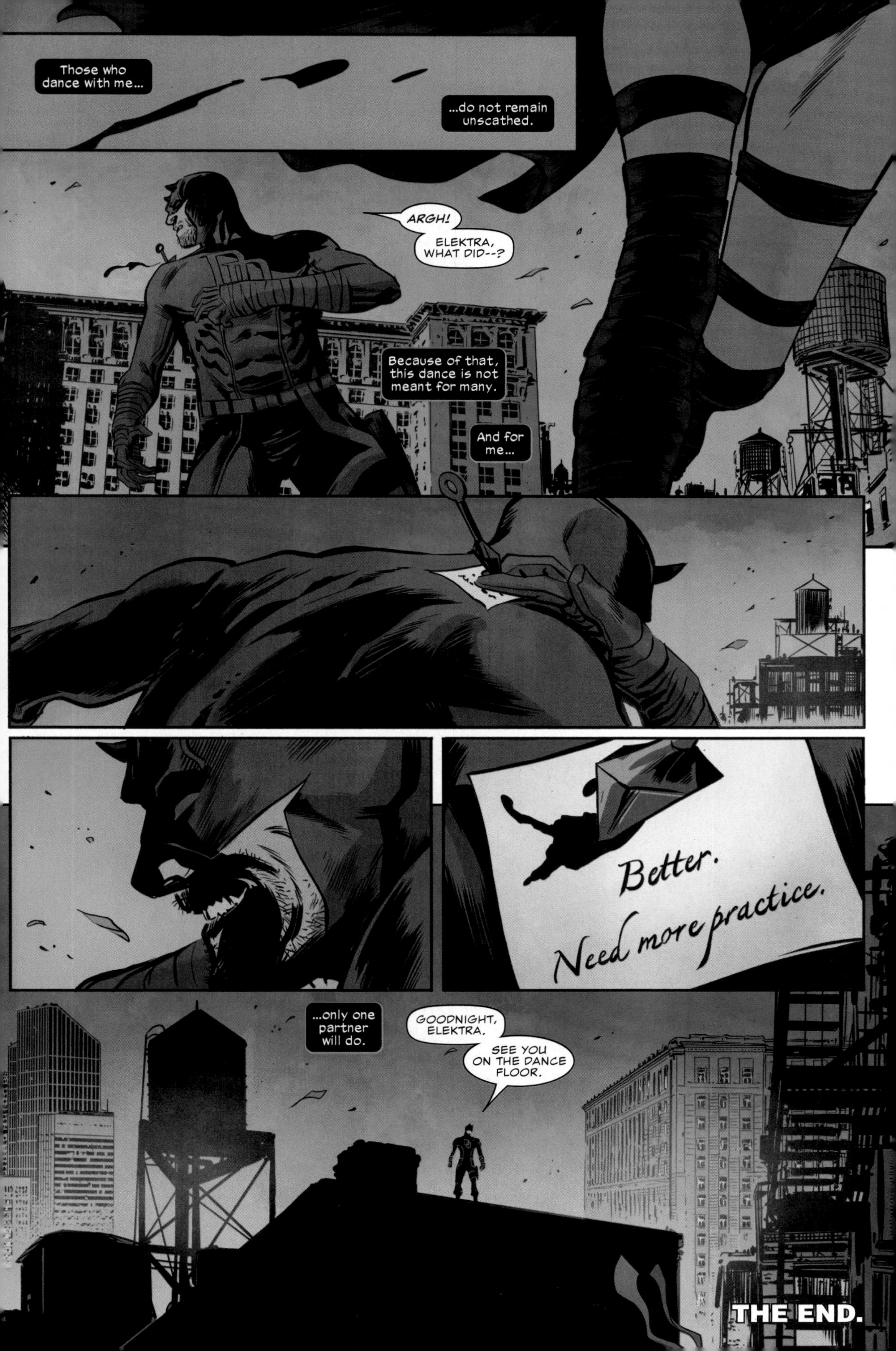
Those who dance with me...
...do not remain unscathed.
ARGH!
ELEKTRA, WHAT DID--?
Because of that, this dance is not meant for many.
And for me...
Better.
Need more practice.
...only one partner will do.
GOODNIGHT, ELEKTRA.
SEE YOU ON THE DANCE FLOOR.
THE END.

THE ELEKTRA COMPANY

PRESENTS

NiNJA
SUPER STORIES
FEATURING "FANTASTIC READER" RICHARDS

"READER" RICHARDS IS GOING TO READ US A BOOK ABOUT *NINJAS*.

NINJAS WERE MIDDLE-DYNASTY PRACTITIONERS OF THE *SHINOBI-JUTSU*.

THE *WHAT* NOW?

THAT'S A LOT OF BRAND-*NEW* WORDS, MR. RICHARDS.

I WANTED TO INCLUDE ALTERNATIVE DIALECTIC INTERPRE-TATIONS OF THE ORIGINAL *KANJI*.

OKAY, I THINK YOU'RE TALKING ABOUT READING *JAPANESE*, RIGHT?

YES, OBVIOUSLY.

WE WERE HOPING TO READ *ENGLISH* TODAY.

THAT'S LIMITING...

I WAS READING *NINE* LANGUAGES BY THE AGE OF FIVE...

OKAY.

I FOUND A BOOK ABOUT THE MOON SAYING GOOD NIGHT TO THINGS...

LET'S READ THAT!

CHAPTER ONE COVERS THE LACK OF CONTEM-PORARY ACCOUNTS OF THE SHINOBI-NO-MONO...

NEXT:

GOODNIGHT MOONKNIGHT

script and art: Ty Templeton

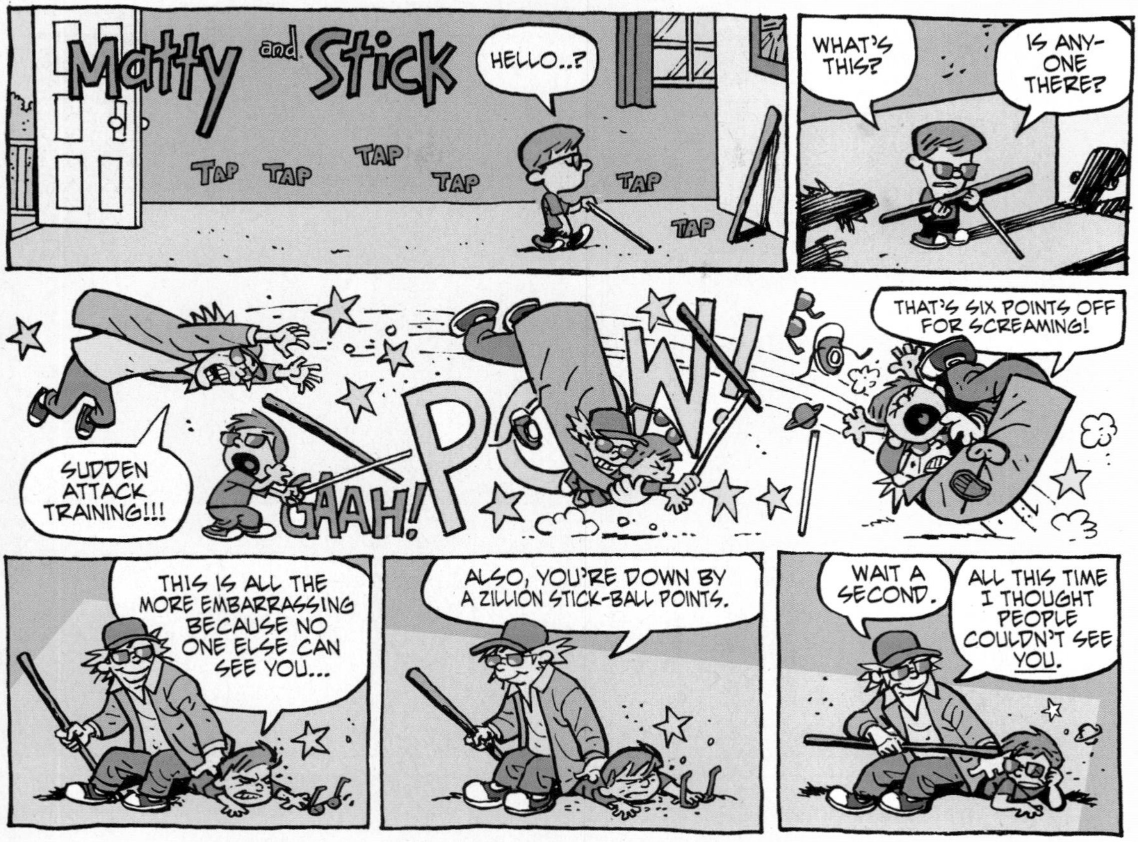
Matty and Stick
HELLO..?
TAP TAP TAP TAP TAP TAP
WHAT'S THIS?
IS ANY-ONE THERE?
SUDDEN ATTACK TRAINING!!!
GAAH!
POW!
THAT'S SIX POINTS OFF FOR SCREAMING!
THIS IS ALL THE MORE EMBARRASSING BECAUSE NO ONE ELSE CAN SEE YOU...
ALSO, YOU'RE DOWN BY A ZILLION STICK-BALL POINTS.
WAIT A SECOND.
ALL THIS TIME I THOUGHT PEOPLE COULDN'T SEE YOU.

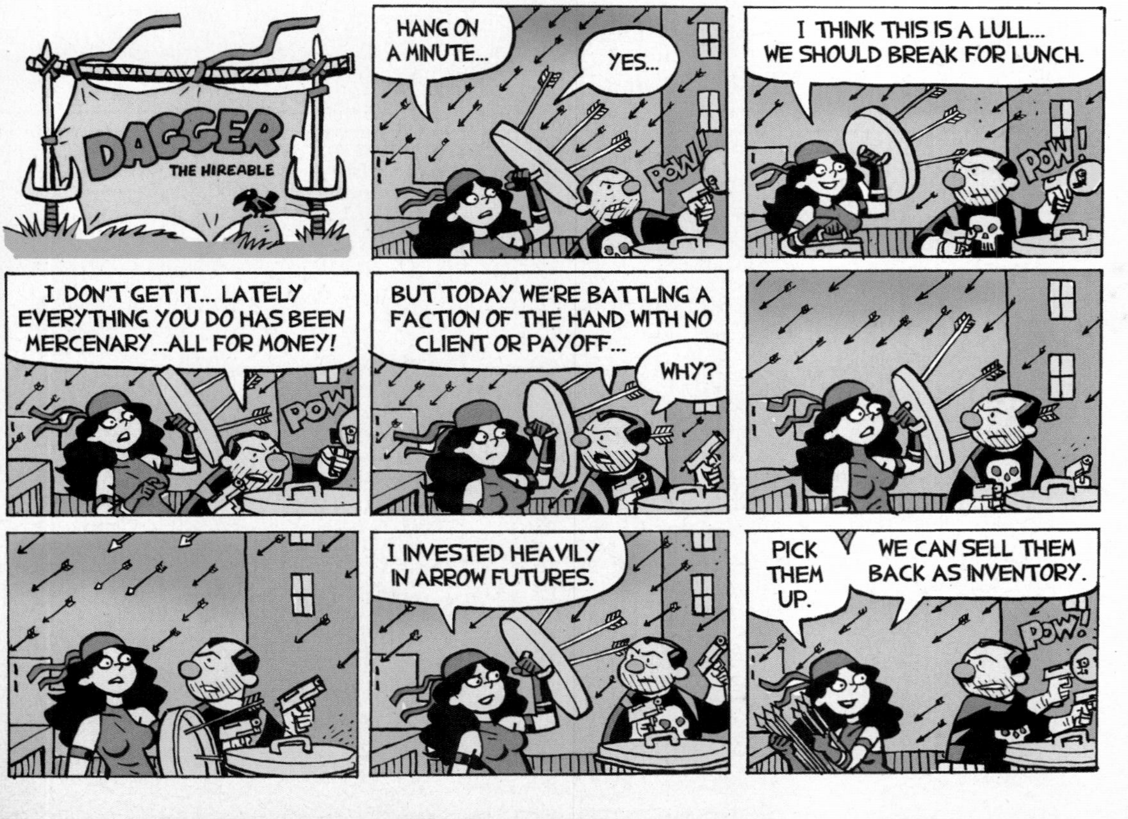
DAGGER
THE HIREABLE
HANG ON A MINUTE...
YES...
POW!
I THINK THIS IS A LULL... WE SHOULD BREAK FOR LUNCH.
POW!
I DON'T GET IT... LATELY EVERYTHING YOU DO HAS BEEN MERCENARY...ALL FOR MONEY!
POW
BUT TODAY WE'RE BATTLING A FACTION OF THE HAND WITH NO CLIENT OR PAYOFF...
WHY?
I INVESTED HEAVILY IN ARROW FUTURES.
PICK THEM UP.
WE CAN SELL THEM BACK AS INVENTORY.
POW!

MINI MARVELS

by Chris Giarrusso

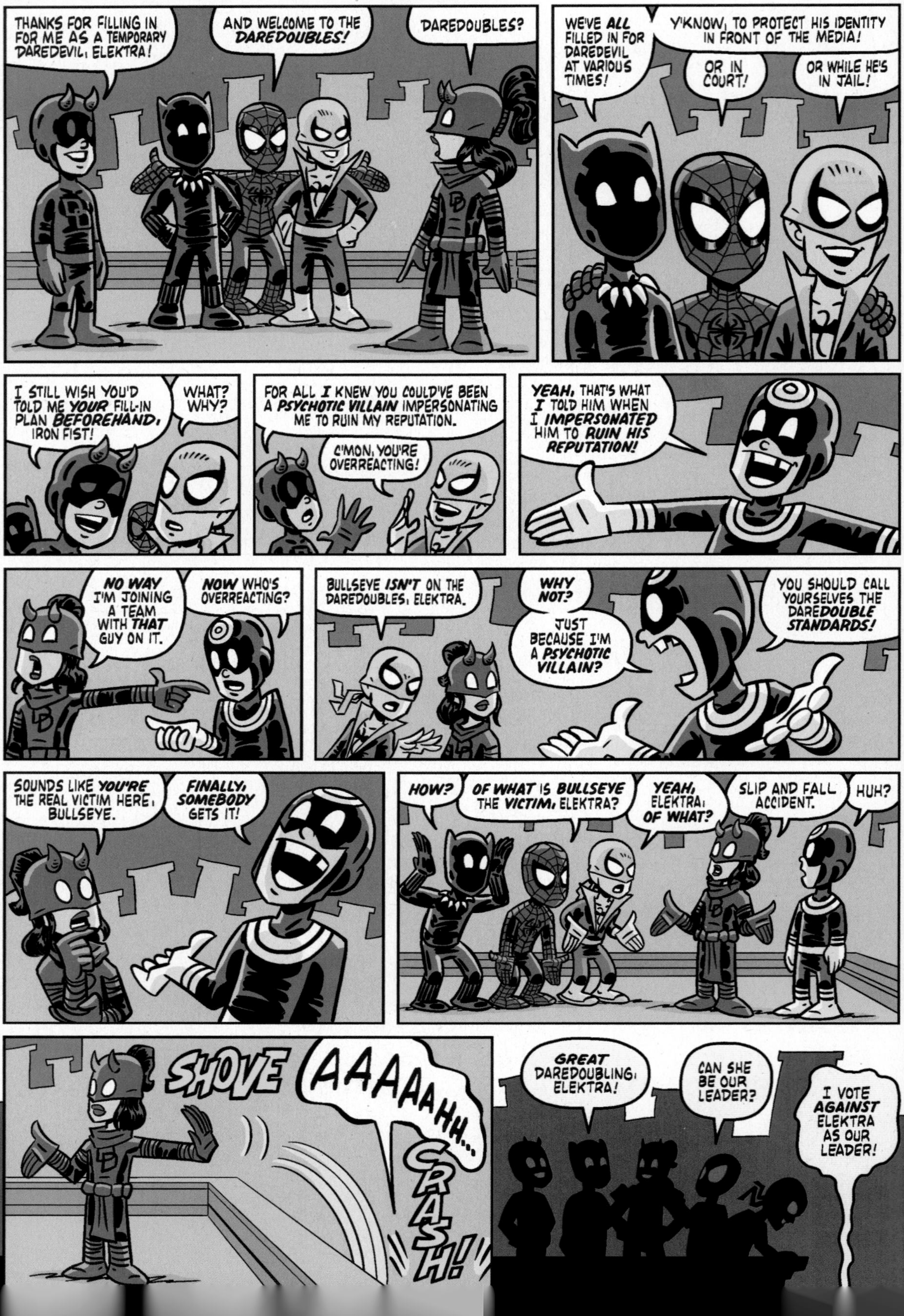
THANKS FOR FILLING IN FOR ME AS A TEMPORARY DAREDEVIL, ELEKTRA!
AND WELCOME TO THE DAREDOUBLES!
DAREDOUBLES?
WE'VE ALL FILLED IN FOR DAREDEVIL AT VARIOUS TIMES!
Y'KNOW, TO PROTECT HIS IDENTITY IN FRONT OF THE MEDIA!
OR IN COURT!
OR WHILE HE'S IN JAIL!
I STILL WISH YOU'D TOLD ME YOUR FILL-IN PLAN BEFOREHAND, IRON FIST!
WHAT? WHY?
FOR ALL I KNEW YOU COULD'VE BEEN A PSYCHOTIC VILLAIN IMPERSONATING ME TO RUIN MY REPUTATION.
C'MON, YOU'RE OVERREACTING!
YEAH, THAT'S WHAT I TOLD HIM WHEN I IMPERSONATED HIM TO RUIN HIS REPUTATION!
NO WAY I'M JOINING A TEAM WITH THAT GUY ON IT.
NOW WHO'S OVERREACTING?
BULLSEYE ISN'T ON THE DAREDOUBLES, ELEKTRA.
WHY NOT?
JUST BECAUSE I'M A PSYCHOTIC VILLAIN?
YOU SHOULD CALL YOURSELVES THE DAREDOUBLE STANDARDS!
SOUNDS LIKE YOU'RE THE REAL VICTIM HERE, BULLSEYE.
FINALLY, SOMEBODY GETS IT!
HOW?
OF WHAT IS BULLSEYE THE VICTIM, ELEKTRA?
YEAH, ELEKTRA, OF WHAT?
SLIP AND FALL ACCIDENT.
HUH?
SHOVE
AAAAAAHH...
CRASH!
GREAT DAREDOUBLING, ELEKTRA!
CAN SHE BE OUR LEADER?
I VOTE AGAINST ELEKTRA AS OUR LEADER!

ELEKTRA 100 COVER GALLERY

Face front, true believers, and behold this awesome assembly of covers starring your favorite assassin -- ELEKTRA! It's been a long and brutal road to this centennial celebration, but worth every bloody and beautiful moment! So feast your eyes on these hundred covers, and let your imaginations run wild contemplating the next 100!

- Editor

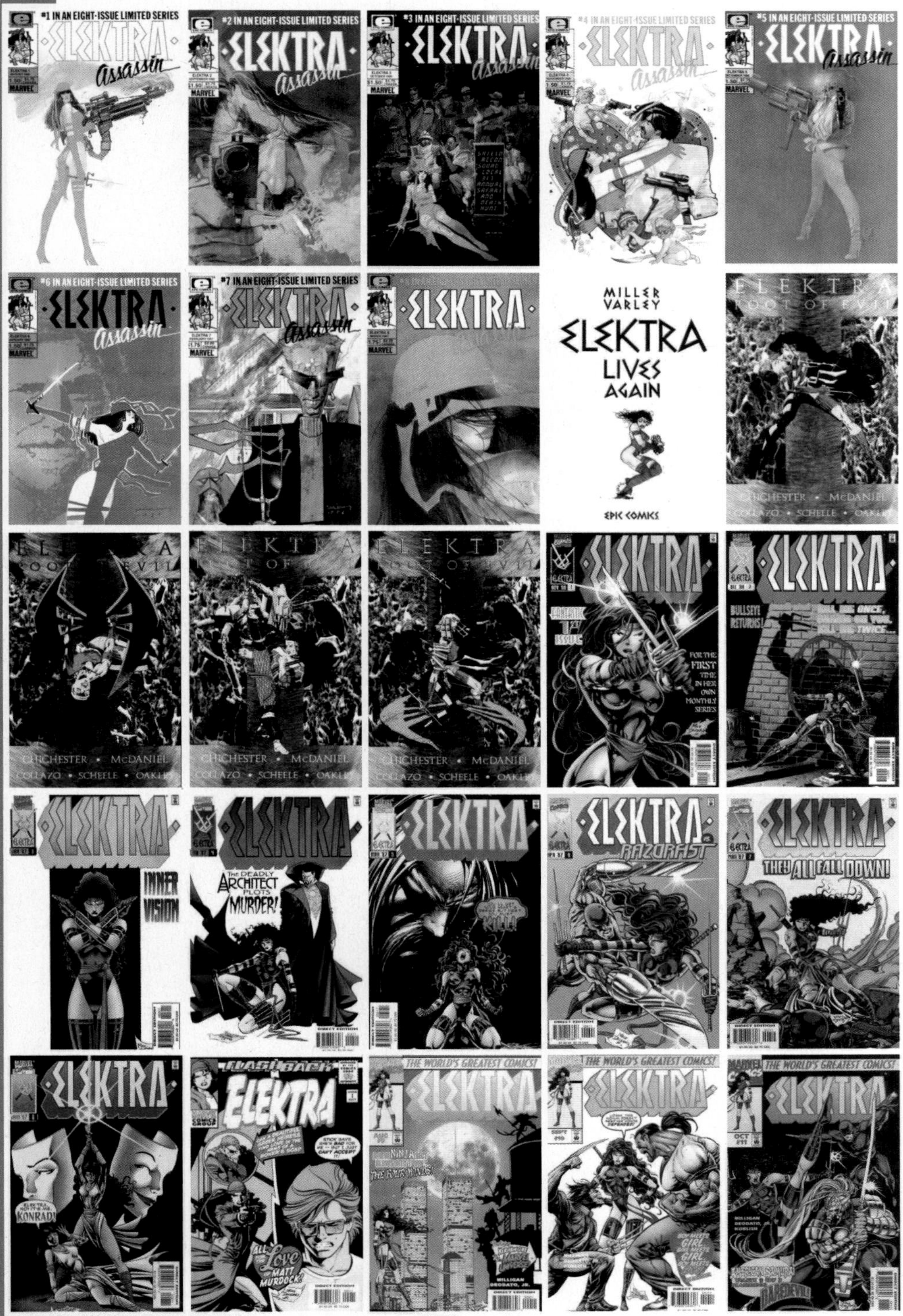

#1 IN AN EIGHT-ISSUE LIMITED SERIES
ELEKTRA Assassin
#2 IN AN EIGHT-ISSUE LIMITED SERIES
ELEKTRA Assassin
#3 IN AN EIGHT-ISSUE LIMITED SERIES
ELEKTRA Assassin
#4 IN AN EIGHT-ISSUE LIMITED SERIES
ELEKTRA Assassin
#5 IN AN EIGHT-ISSUE LIMITED SERIES
ELEKTRA Assassin
#6 IN AN EIGHT-ISSUE LIMITED SERIES
ELEKTRA Assassin
#7 IN AN EIGHT-ISSUE LIMITED SERIES
ELEKTRA Assassin
ELEKTRA
MILLER
VARLEY
ELEKTRA
LIVES
AGAIN
EPIC COMICS
ELEKTRA
ROOT OF EVIL
CHICHESTER • McDANIEL
COLLAZO • SCHEELE • OAKLEY
ELEKTRA
FOR THE FIRST TIME IN HER OWN MONTHLY SERIES
ELEKTRA
BULLSEYE RETURNS!
ELEKTRA
INNER VISION
ELEKTRA
THE DEADLY ARCHITECT PLOTS MURDER!
ELEKTRA
ELEKTRA
RAZORFAST
ELEKTRA
THEY ALL FALL DOWN!
ELEKTRA
KONRAD!
FLASHBACK
ELEKTRA
ALL in Love with MATT MURDOCK!
THE WORLD'S GREATEST COMICS!
ELEKTRA
MILLIGAN
DEODATO, JR.
THE WORLD'S GREATEST COMICS!
ELEKTRA
THE WORLD'S GREATEST COMICS!
ELEKTRA
DAREDEVIL

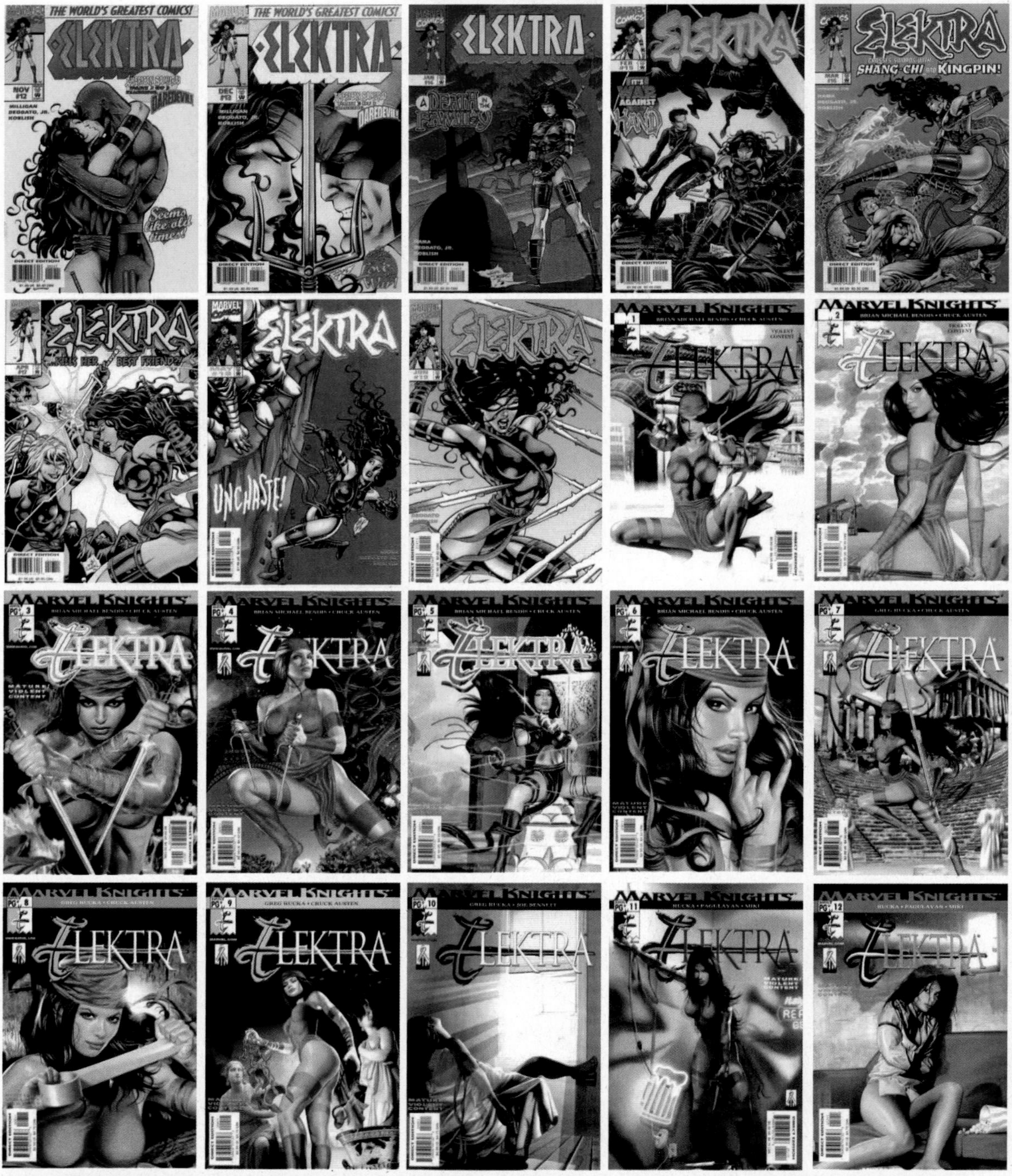
THE WORLD'S GREATEST COMICS!
ELEKTRA
NOV #12
MILLIGAN DEODATO, JR. KOBLISH
DAREDEVIL!
Seems like old times!
THE WORLD'S GREATEST COMICS!
ELEKTRA
DEC #13
MILLIGAN DEODATO, JR. KOBLISH
DAREDEVIL!
ELEKTRA
A DEATH IN THE FAMILY
ELEKTRA
IT'S WAR AGAINST THE HAND
ELEKTRA
SHANG-CHI AND KINGPIN!
ELEKTRA
ELEKTRA
UNCHASTE!
ELEKTRA
MARVEL KNIGHTS
BRIAN MICHAEL BENDIS • CHUCK AUSTEN
ELEKTRA
MARVEL KNIGHTS
BRIAN MICHAEL BENDIS • CHUCK AUSTEN
ELEKTRA
MARVEL KNIGHTS
ELEKTRA
MATURE/ VIOLENT CONTENT
MARVEL KNIGHTS
BRIAN MICHAEL BENDIS • CHUCK AUSTEN
ELEKTRA
MARVEL KNIGHTS
BRIAN MICHAEL BENDIS • CHUCK AUSTEN
ELEKTRA
MARVEL KNIGHTS
BRIAN MICHAEL BENDIS • CHUCK AUSTEN
ELEKTRA
MATURE/ VIOLENT CONTENT
MARVEL KNIGHTS
GREG RUCKA • CHUCK AUSTEN
ELEKTRA
MARVEL KNIGHTS
GREG RUCKA • CHUCK AUSTEN
ELEKTRA
MARVEL KNIGHTS
GREG RUCKA • CHUCK AUSTEN
ELEKTRA
MARVEL KNIGHTS
GREG RUCKA • JOE BENNETT
ELEKTRA
MARVEL KNIGHTS
RUCKA • PAGULAYAN • MIKI
ELEKTRA
MATURE/ VIOLENT CONTENT
MARVEL KNIGHTS
RUCKA • PAGULAYAN • MIKI
ELEKTRA
MARVEL KNIGHTS
RUCKA • PAGULAYAN • MIKI
ELEKTRA
MATURE/ VIOLENT CONTENT
MARVEL KNIGHTS
RUCKA • PAGULAYAN • MIKI
ELEKTRA
MATURE/ VIOLENT CONTENT
MARVEL KNIGHTS
RUCKA • PAGULAYAN • MIKI
ELEKTRA
MATURE/ VIOLENT CONTENT
MARVEL KNIGHTS
RUCKA • BENNETT • MIKI
ELEKTRA
MATURE/ VIOLENT CONTENT
MARVEL KNIGHTS
GREG RUCKA • JOE BENNETT
ELEKTRA

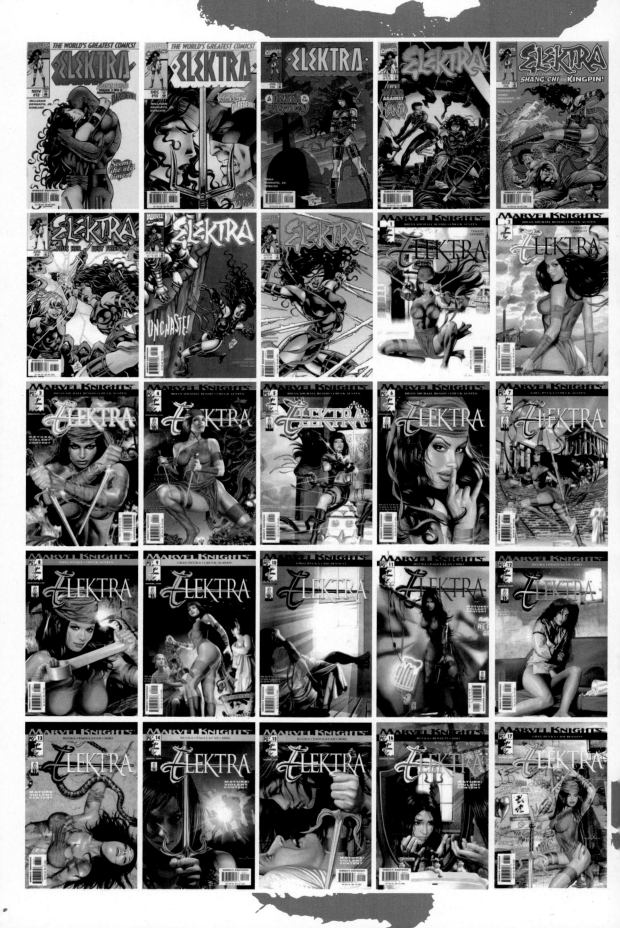

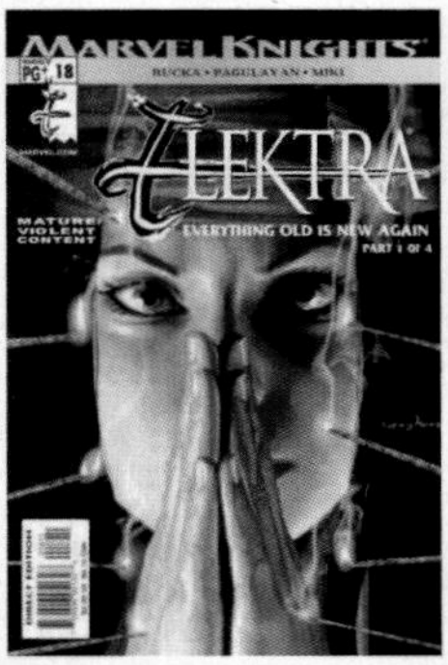
MARVEL KNIGHTS
18
RUCKA • PAGULAYAN • MIKI
ELEKTRA
MATURE/ VIOLENT CONTENT
EVERYTHING OLD IS NEW AGAIN
PART 1 OF 4
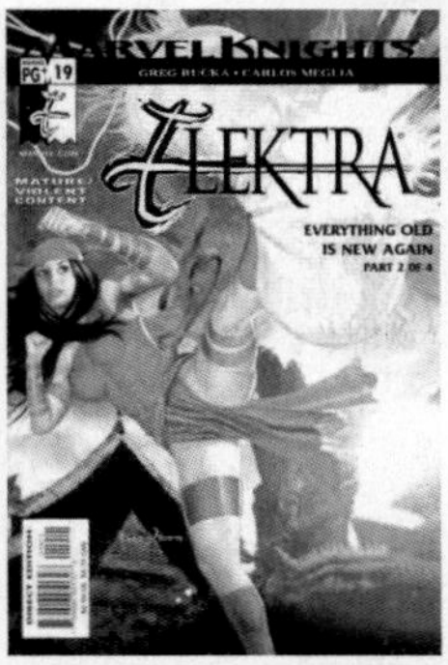
MARVEL KNIGHTS
19
GREG RUCKA • CARLOS MEGLIA
ELEKTRA
MATURE/ VIOLENT CONTENT
EVERYTHING OLD IS NEW AGAIN
PART 2 OF 4
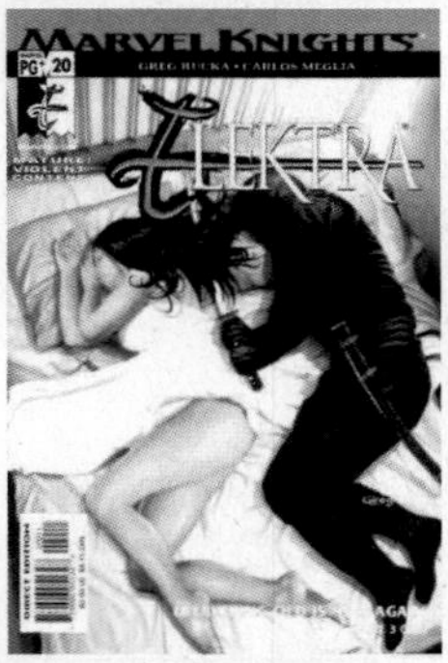
MARVEL KNIGHTS
20
GREG RUCKA • CARLOS MEGLIA
ELEKTRA
MATURE/ VIOLENT CONTENT
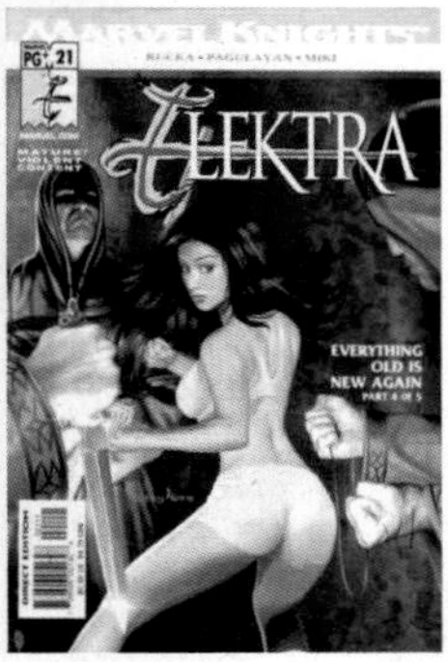
MARVEL KNIGHTS
21
RUCKA • PAGULAYAN • MIKI
ELEKTRA
MATURE/ VIOLENT CONTENT
EVERYTHING OLD IS NEW AGAIN
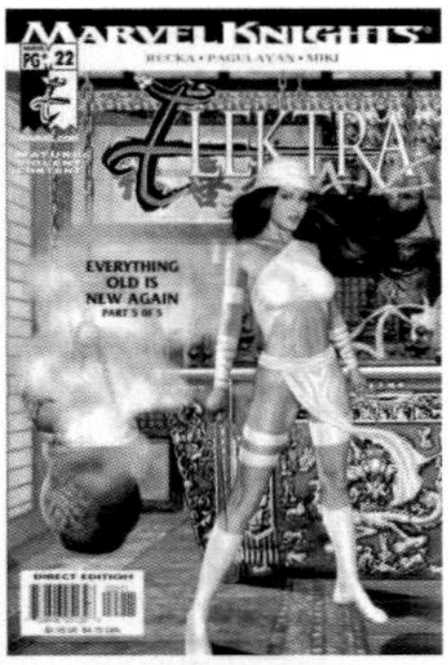
MARVEL KNIGHTS
22
RUCKA • PAGULAYAN • MIKI
ELEKTRA
EVERYTHING OLD IS NEW AGAIN
DIRECT EDITION
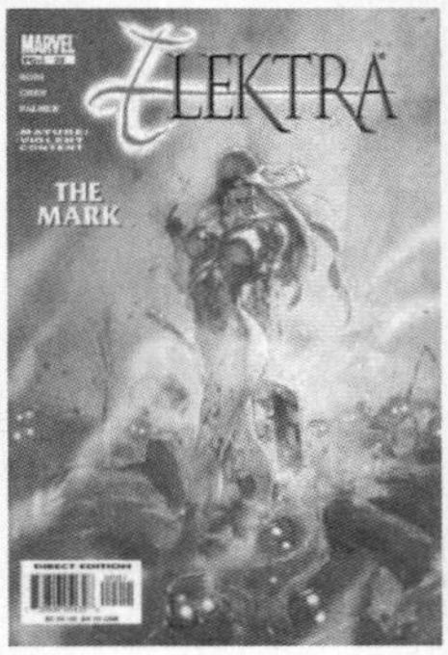
MARVEL
ELEKTRA
RODI
CHEN
PALMER
MATURE/ VIOLENT CONTENT
THE MARK
DIRECT EDITION
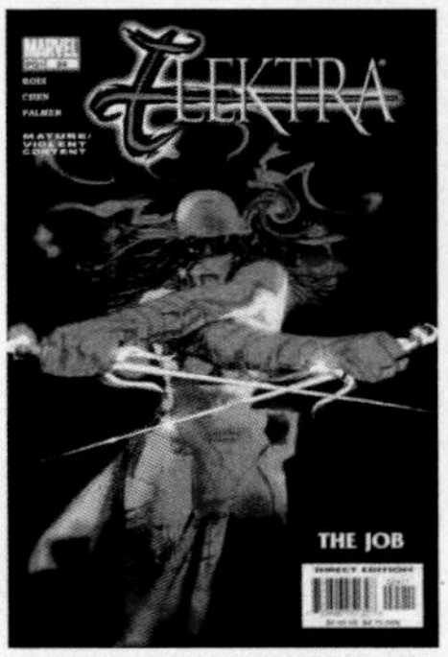
MARVEL
ELEKTRA
RODI
CHEN
PALMER
MATURE/ VIOLENT CONTENT
THE JOB
DIRECT EDITION
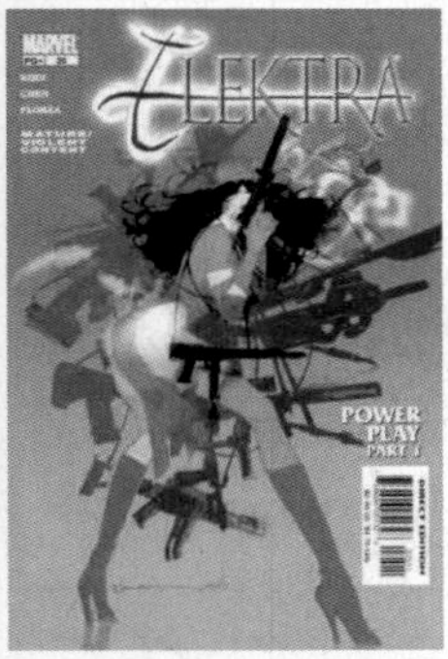
MARVEL
ELEKTRA
RODI
CHEN
FLOREA
MATURE/ VIOLENT CONTENT
POWER PLAY
PART 1
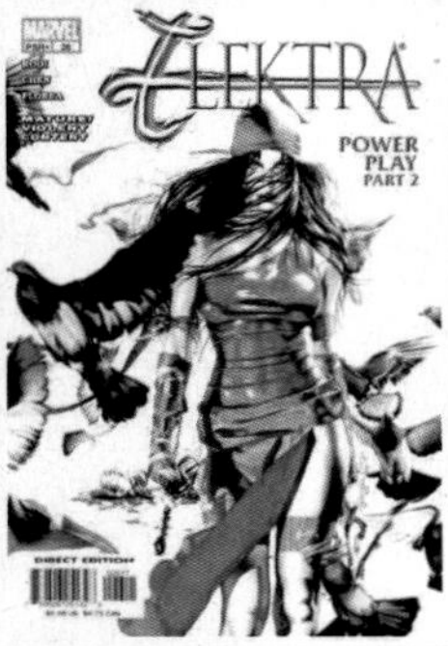
MARVEL
ELEKTRA
MATURE/ VIOLENT CONTENT
POWER PLAY
PART 2
DIRECT EDITION
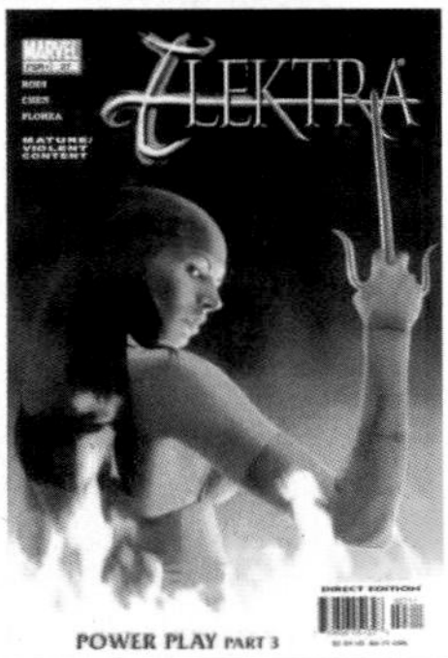
MARVEL
ELEKTRA
RODI
CHEN
FLOREA
MATURE/ VIOLENT CONTENT
DIRECT EDITION
POWER PLAY PART 3
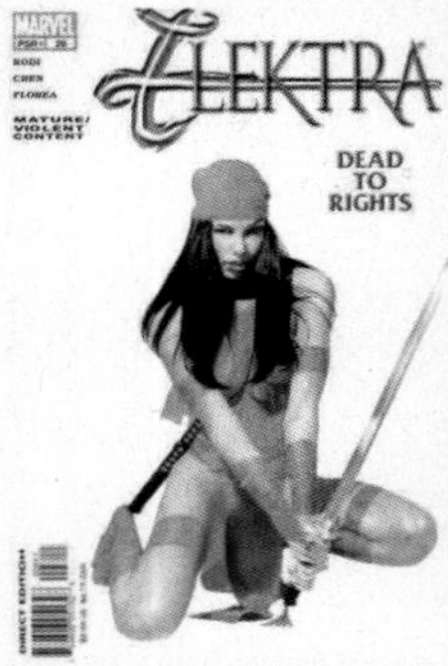
MARVEL
ELEKTRA
RODI
CHEN
FLOREA
MATURE/ VIOLENT CONTENT
DEAD TO RIGHTS
DIRECT EDITION
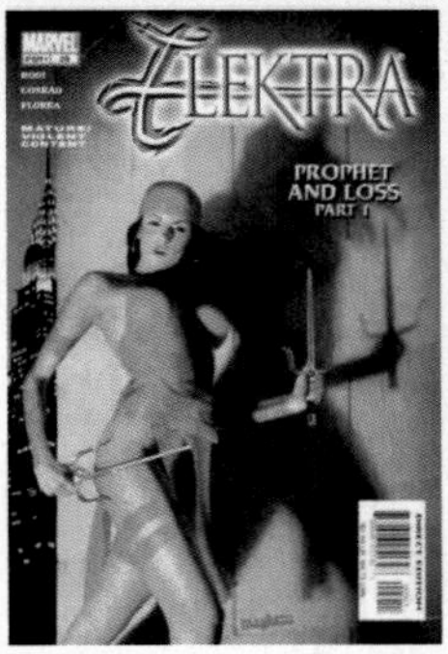
MARVEL
ELEKTRA
RODI
CONRAD
MATURE/ VIOLENT CONTENT
PROPHET AND LOSS
PART 1
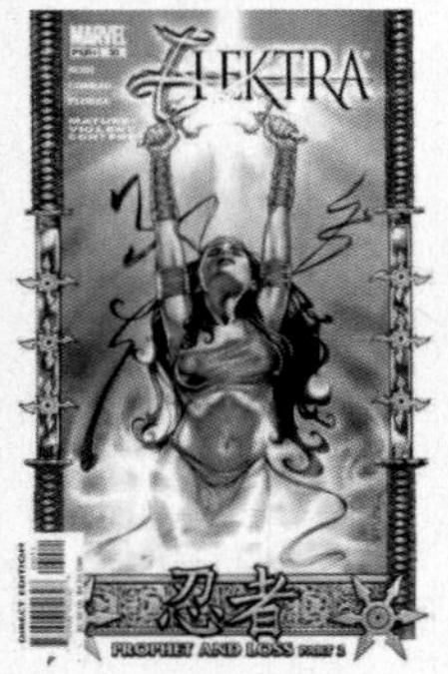
MARVEL
ELEKTRA
MATURE/ VIOLENT CONTENT
忍者
PROPHET AND LOSS PART 2
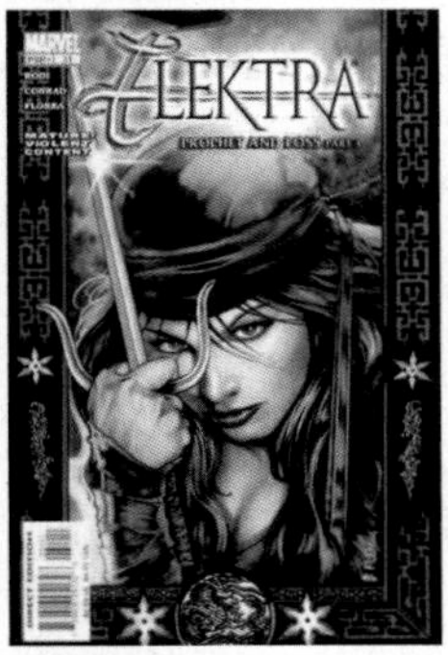
MARVEL
ELEKTRA
RODI
FLOREA
MATURE/ VIOLENT CONTENT
DIRECT EDITION
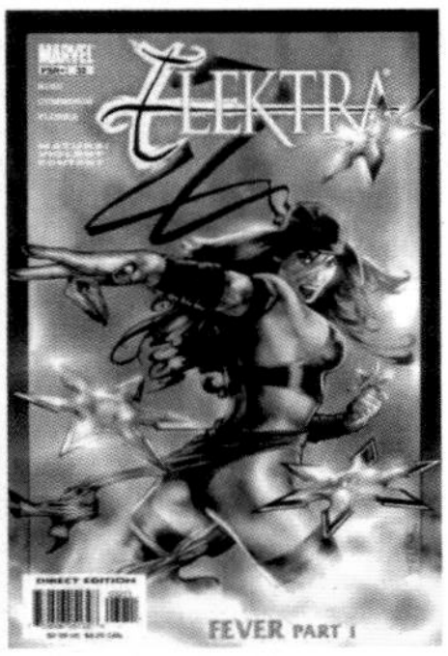
MARVEL
ELEKTRA
RODI
CUMMINGS
FLOREA
MATURE/ VIOLENT CONTENT
DIRECT EDITION
FEVER PART 1
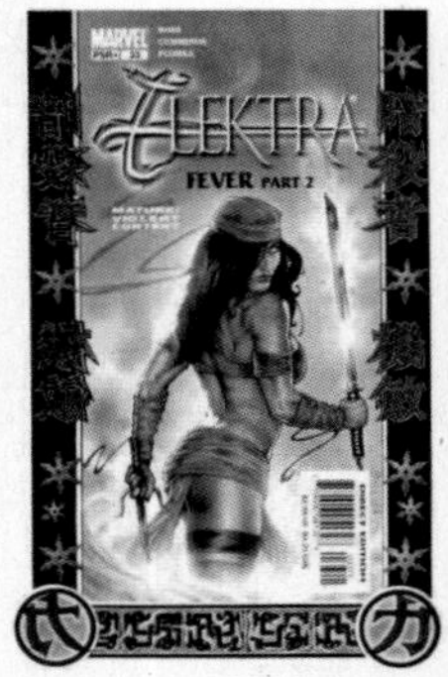
MARVEL
RODI
CUMMINGS
FLOREA
ELEKTRA
FEVER PART 2
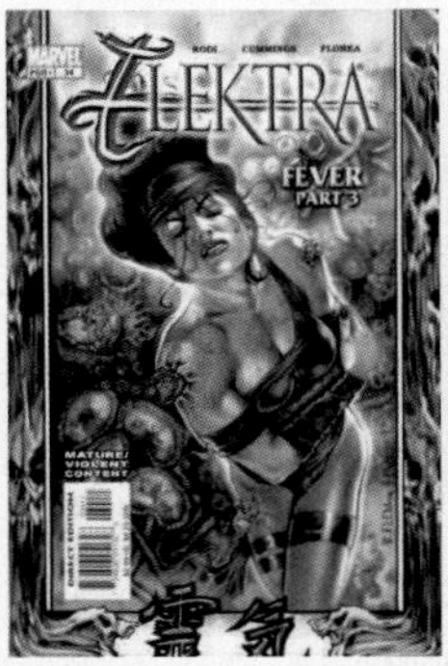
MARVEL
RODI
CUMMINGS
FLOREA
ELEKTRA
FEVER
PART 3
MATURE/ VIOLENT CONTENT
DIRECT EDITION
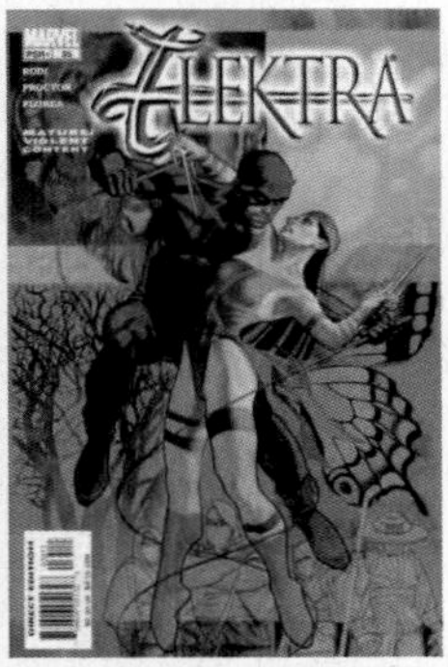
MARVEL
RODI
PROCTOR
FLOREA
ELEKTRA
MATURE/ VIOLENT CONTENT
DIRECT EDITION
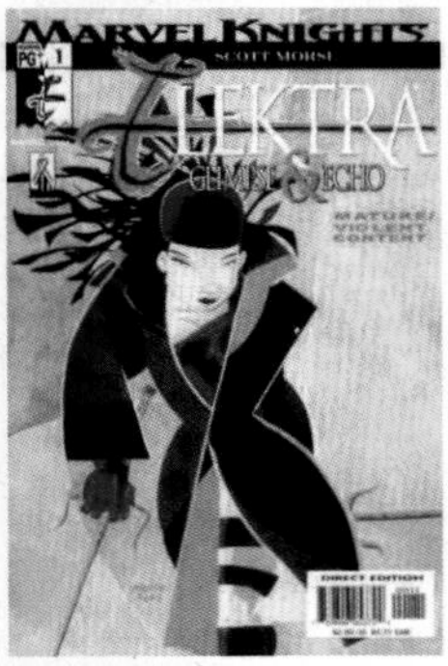
MARVEL KNIGHTS
1
SCOTT MORSE
ELEKTRA
GLIMPSE & ECHO
MATURE/ VIOLENT CONTENT
DIRECT EDITION
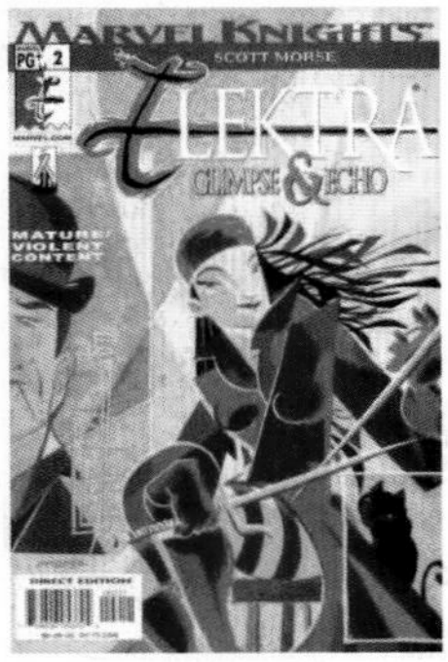
MARVEL KNIGHTS
2
SCOTT MORSE
ELEKTRA
GLIMPSE & ECHO
MATURE/ VIOLENT CONTENT
DIRECT EDITION
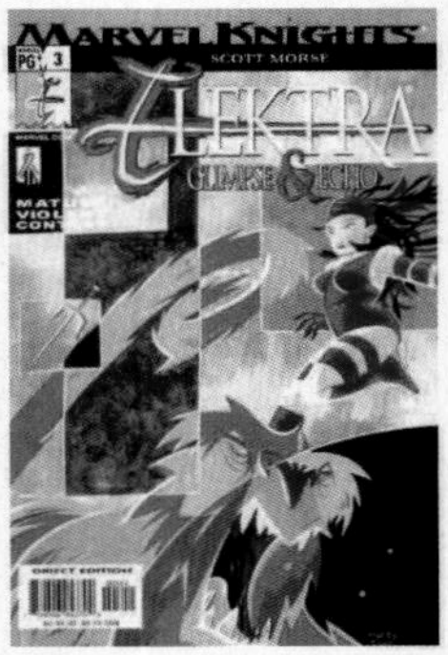
MARVEL KNIGHTS
3
SCOTT MORSE
ELEKTRA
GLIMPSE & ECHO
MATURE/ VIOLENT CONTENT
DIRECT EDITION
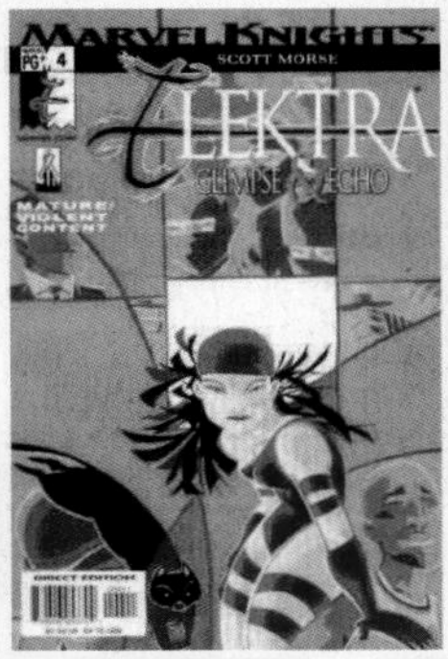
MARVEL KNIGHTS
4
SCOTT MORSE
ELEKTRA
GLIMPSE & ECHO
MATURE/ VIOLENT CONTENT
DIRECT EDITION
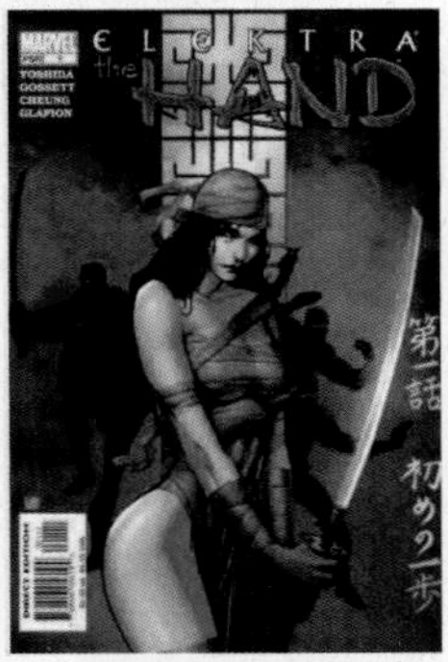
MARVEL
E L E K T R A
the HAND
YOSHIDA
GOSSETT
CHEUNG
GLAPION
第一話
初めの一歩
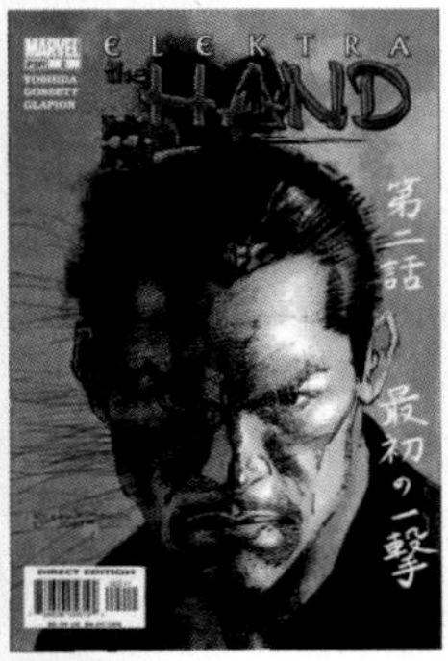
MARVEL
E L E K T R A
the HAND
YOSHIDA
GOSSETT
GLAPION
第二話
最初の一撃
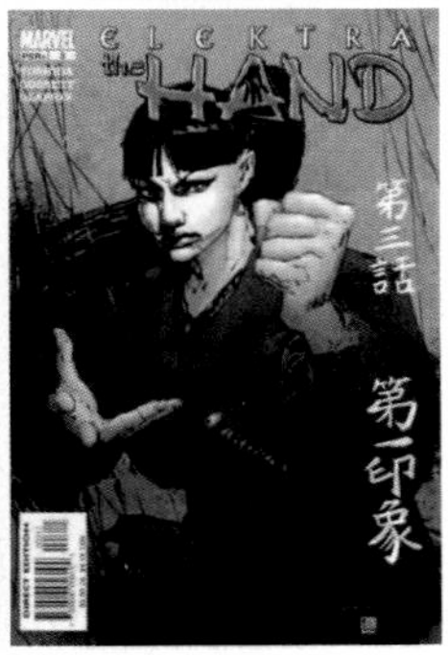
MARVEL
E L E K T R A
the HAND
YOSHIDA
GOSSETT
第三話
第一印象

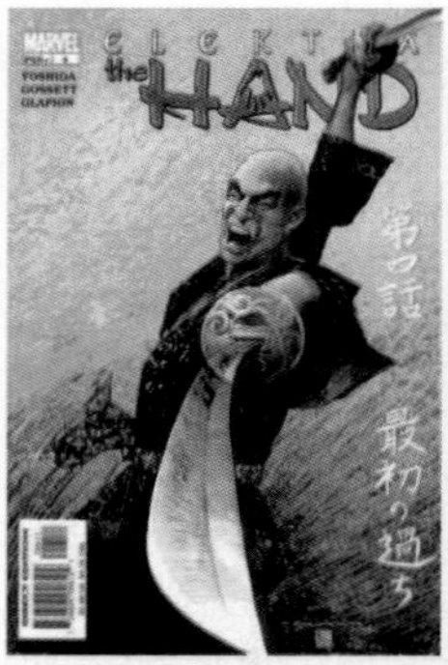
ELEKTRA
the HAND
YOSHIDA
GOSSETT
GLAPION
第四話
最初の過ち
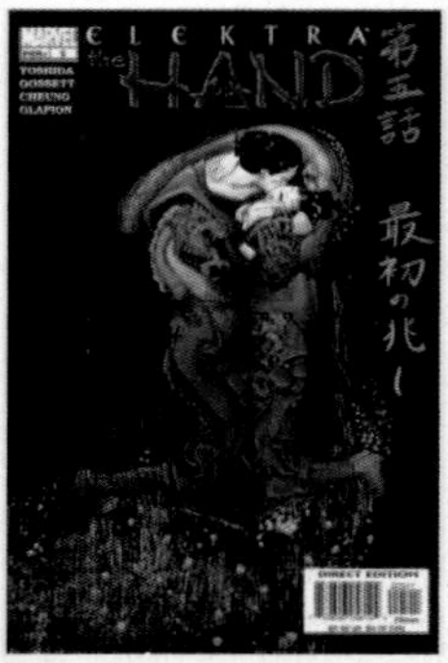
ELEKTRA
the HAND
YOSHIDA
GOSSETT
CHEUNG
GLAPION
第五話
最初の兆し
DIRECT EDITION
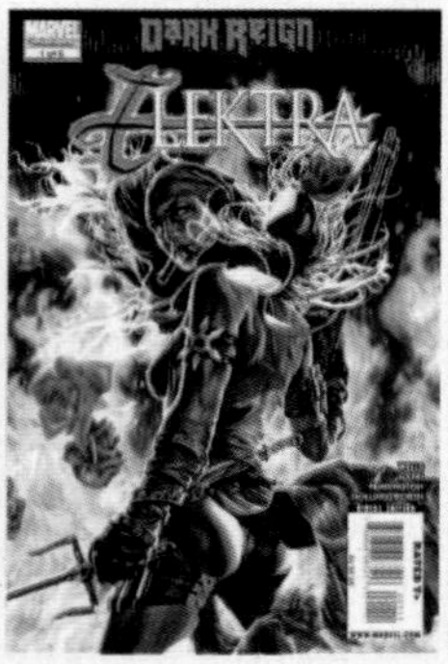
DARK REIGN
ELEKTRA
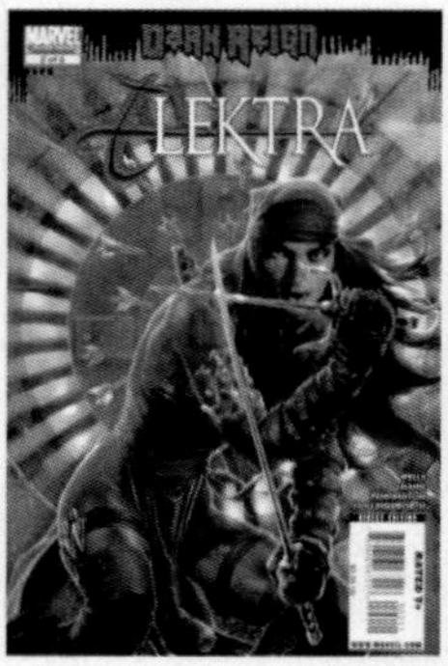
DARK REIGN
ELEKTRA
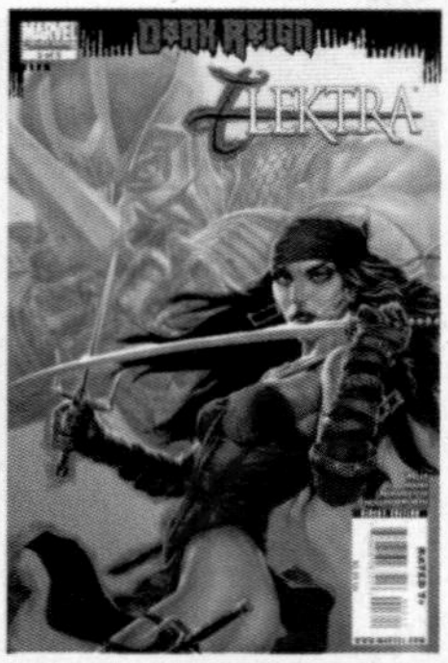
DARK REIGN
ELEKTRA
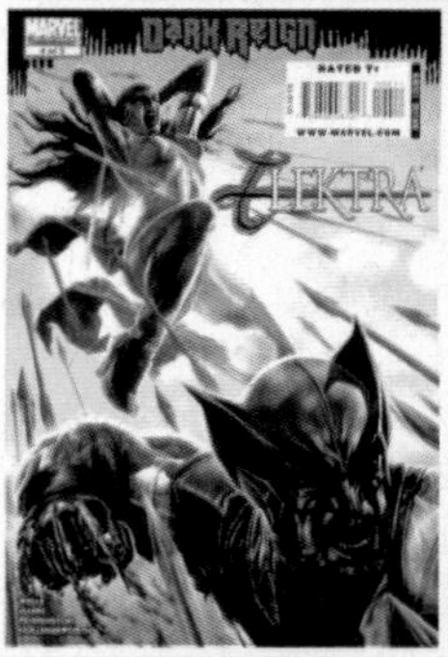
DARK REIGN
RATED T+
WWW.MARVEL.COM
ELEKTRA
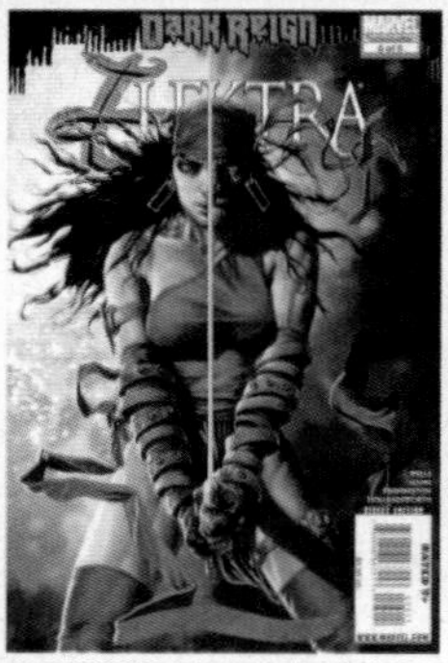
DARK REIGN
ELEKTRA
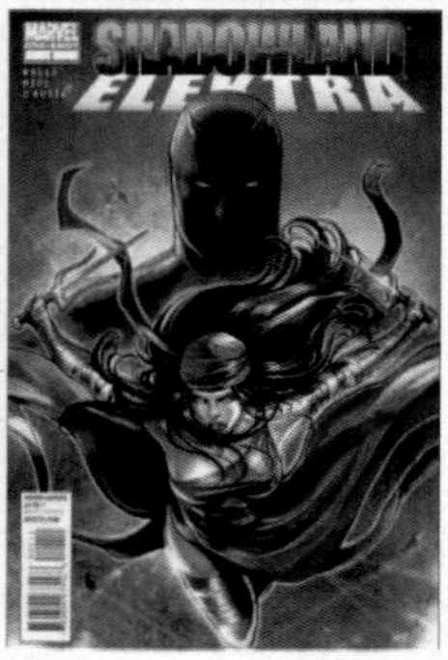
SHADOWLAND
ELEKTRA
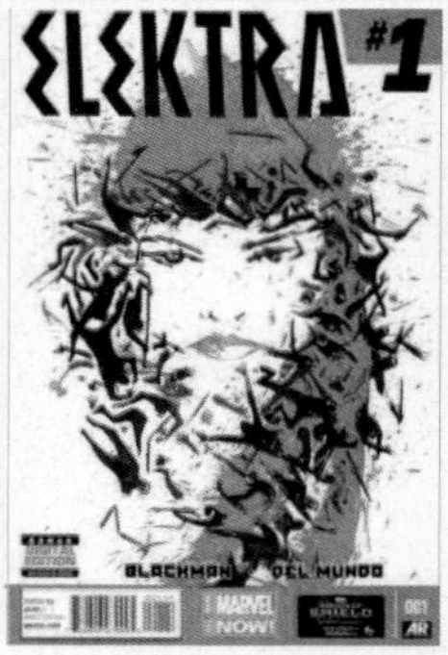
ELEKTRA #1
BLACKMAN DEL MUNDO
001
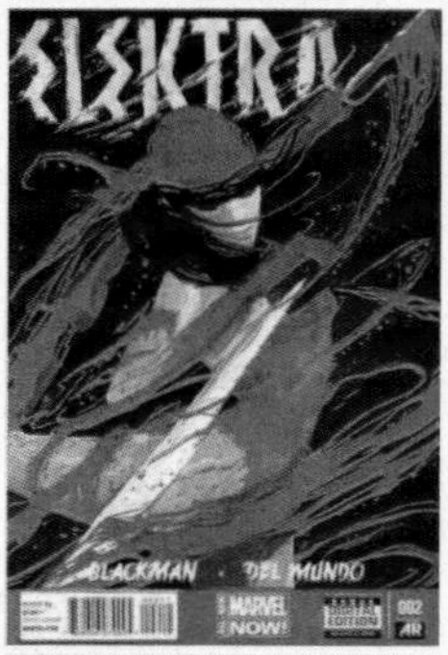
ELEKTRA
BLACKMAN DEL MUNDO
002
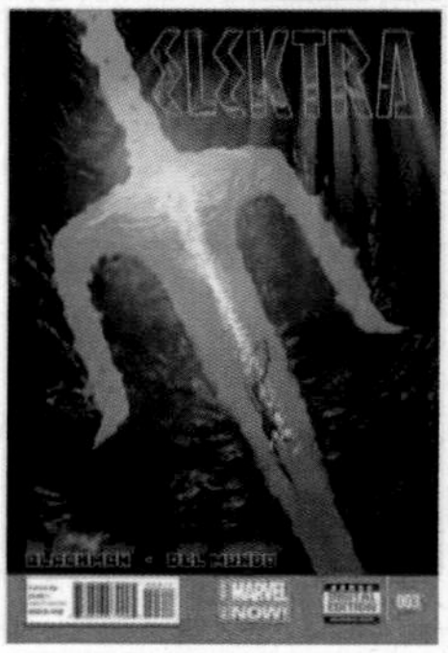
ELEKTRA
BLACKMAN DEL MUNDO
003
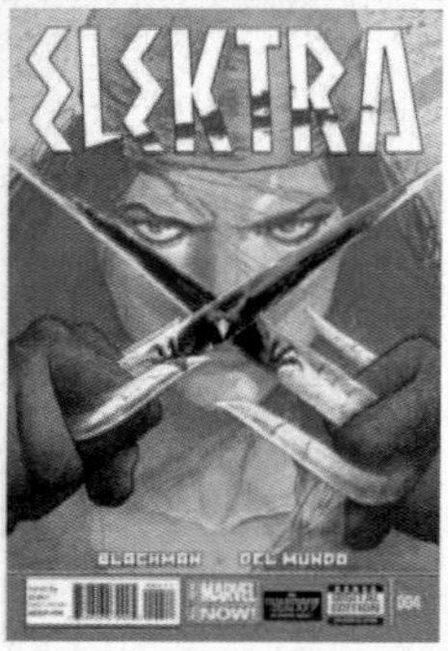
ELEKTRA
BLACKMAN DEL MUNDO
004
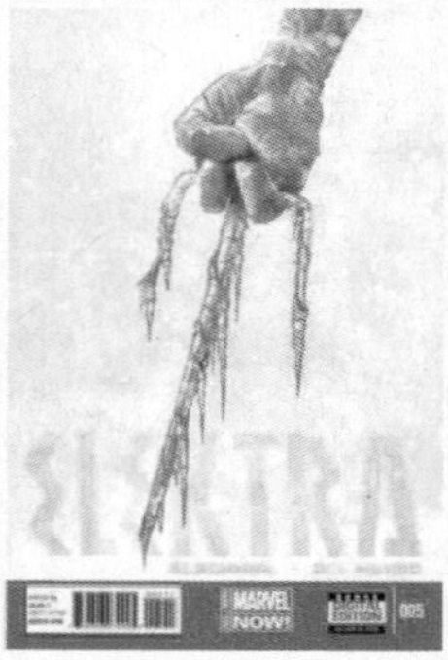
ELEKTRA
005
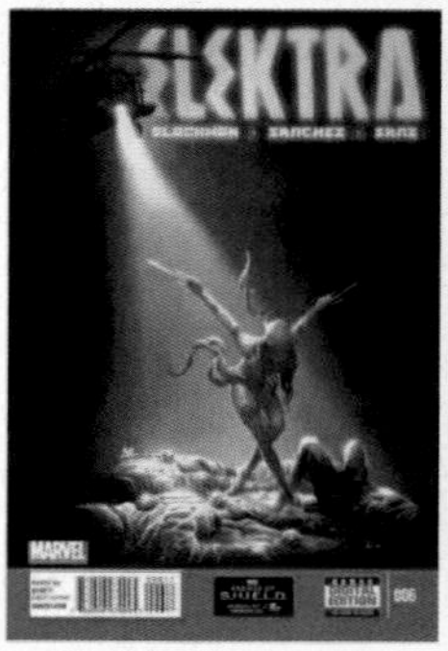
ELEKTRA
BLACKMAN SANCHEZ SANZ
006
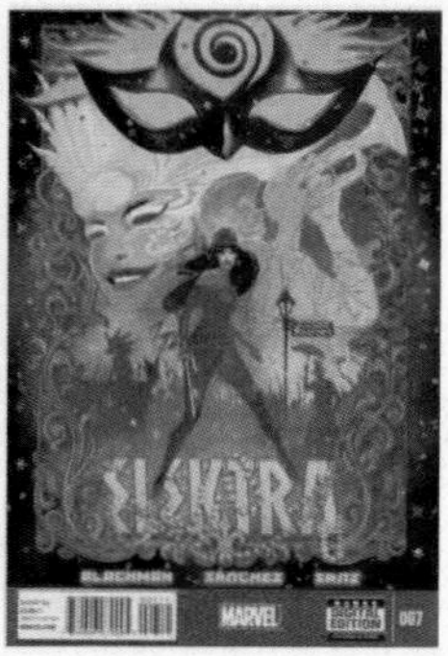
ELEKTRA
BLACKMAN SANCHEZ SANZ
007
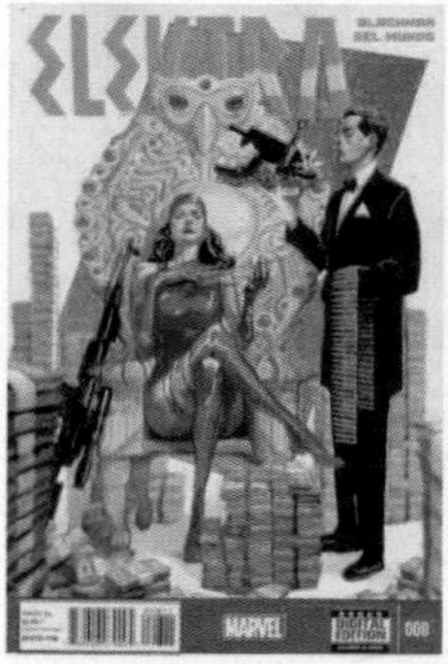
ELEKTRA
BLACKMAN
DEL MUNDO
008
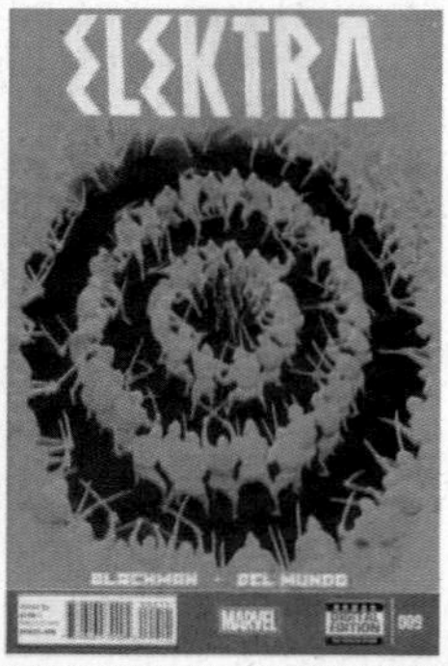
ELEKTRA
BLACKMAN DEL MUNDO
009
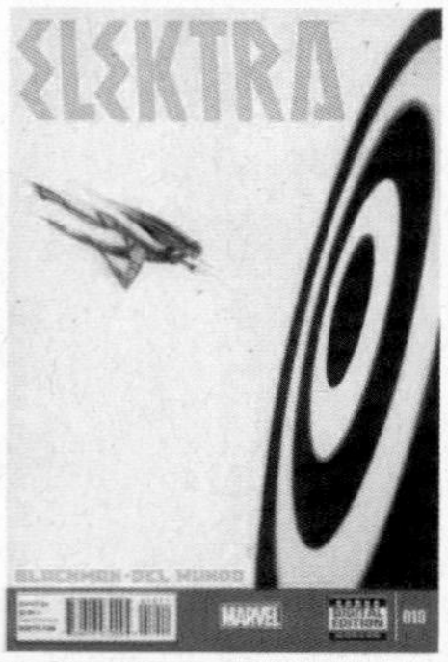
ELEKTRA
BLACKMAN DEL MUNDO
010
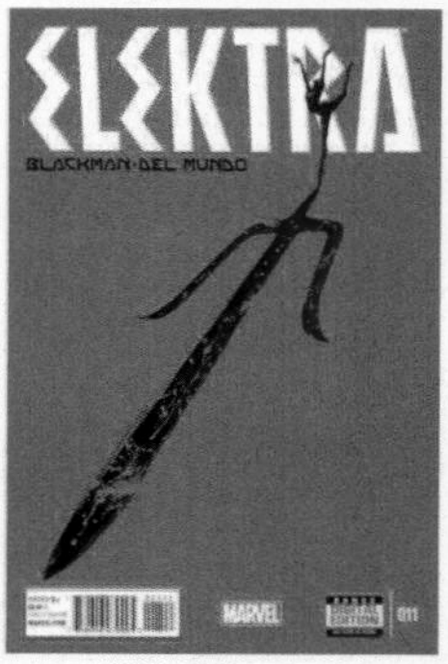
ELEKTRA
BLACKMAN DEL MUNDO
011
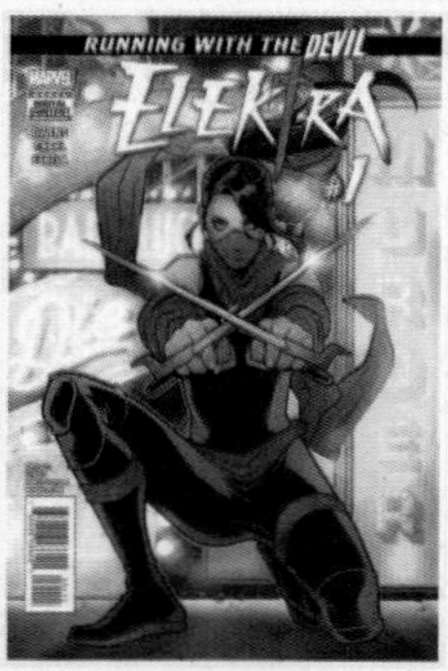
RUNNING WITH THE DEVIL
ELEKTRA
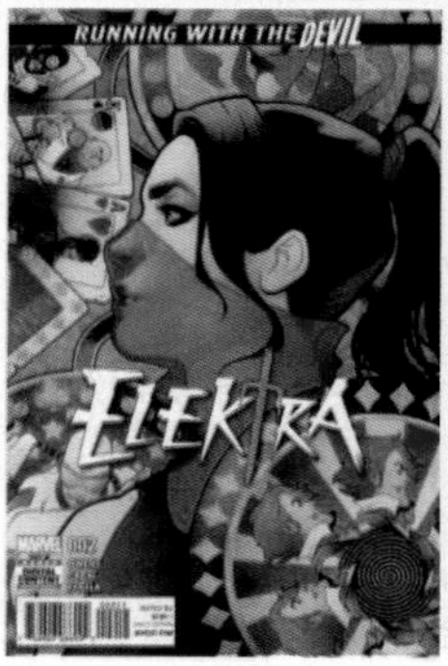
RUNNING WITH THE DEVIL
ELEKTRA
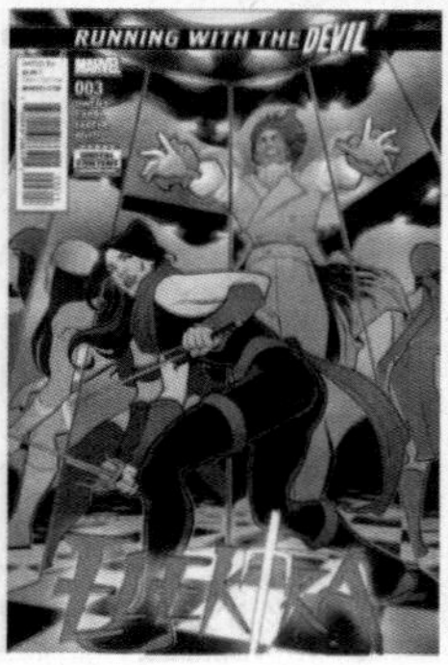
RUNNING WITH THE DEVIL
003
ELEKTRA
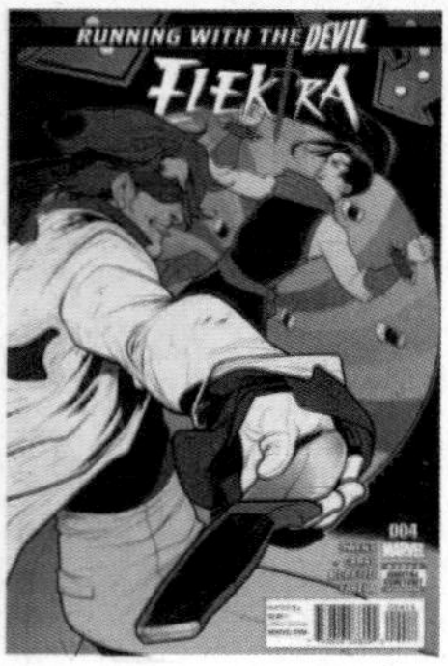
RUNNING WITH THE DEVIL
ELEKTRA
004
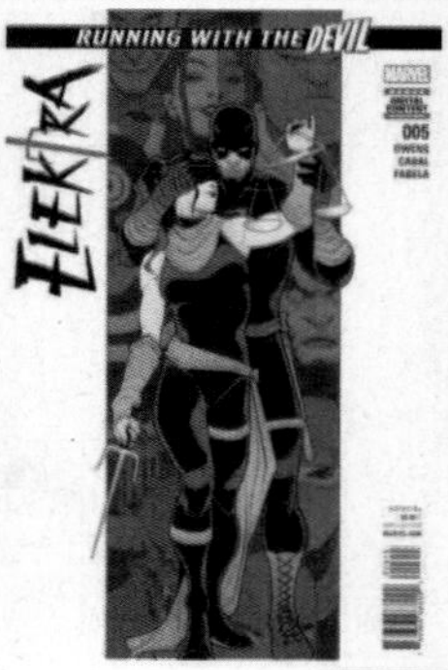
RUNNING WITH THE DEVIL
ELEKTRA
005
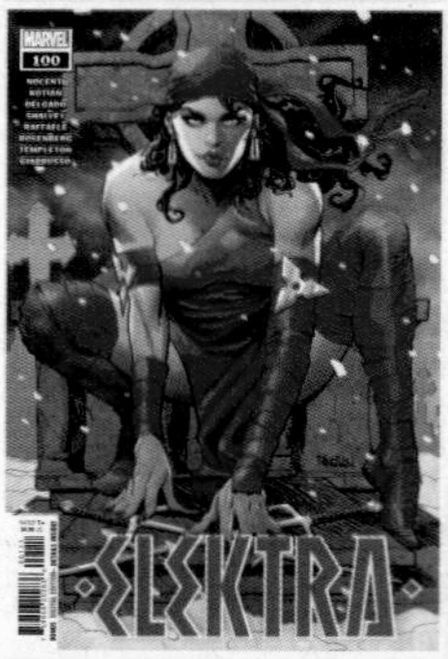
100
ELEKTRA

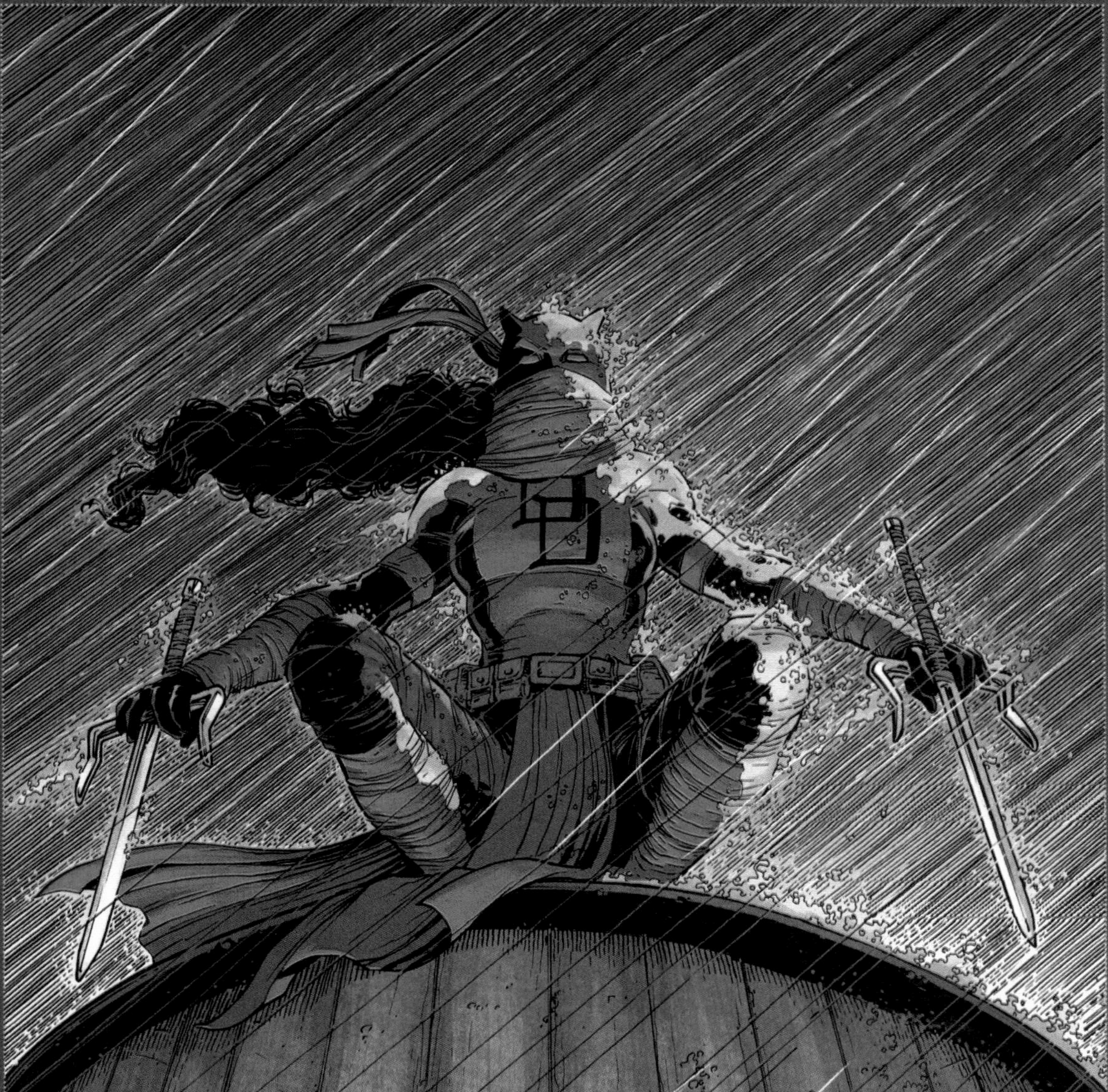

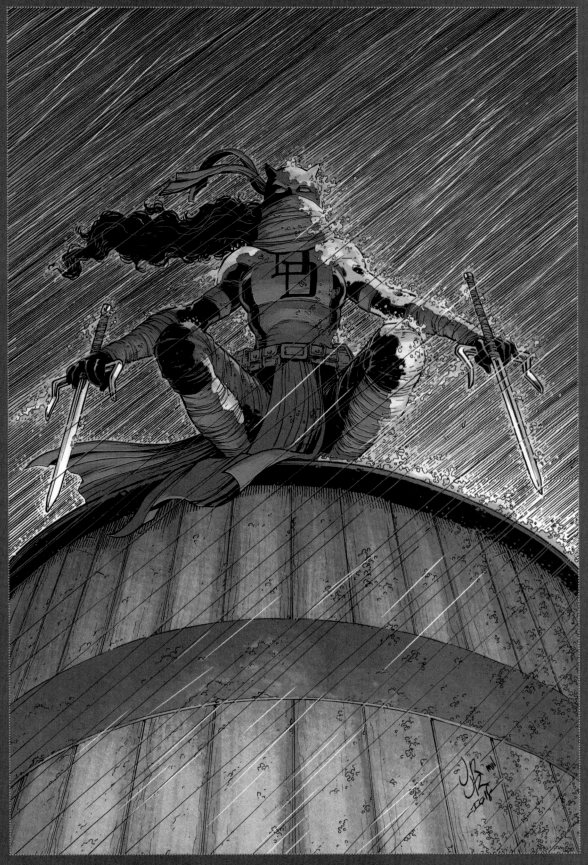

John Romita Jr., John Dell & Matthew Wilson

#1 VARIANT

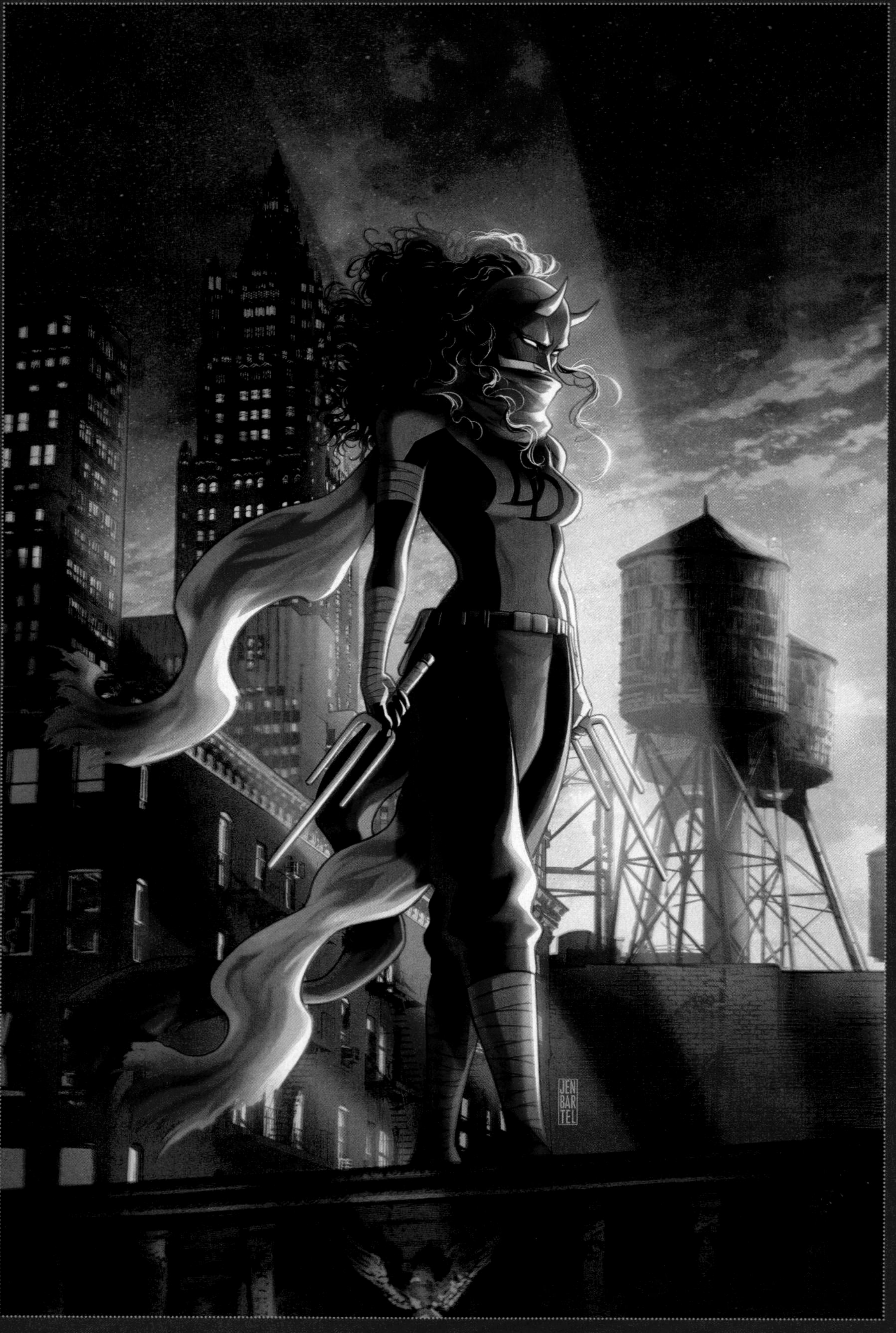
JEN
BAR
TEL

Jen Bartel

#1 VARIANT

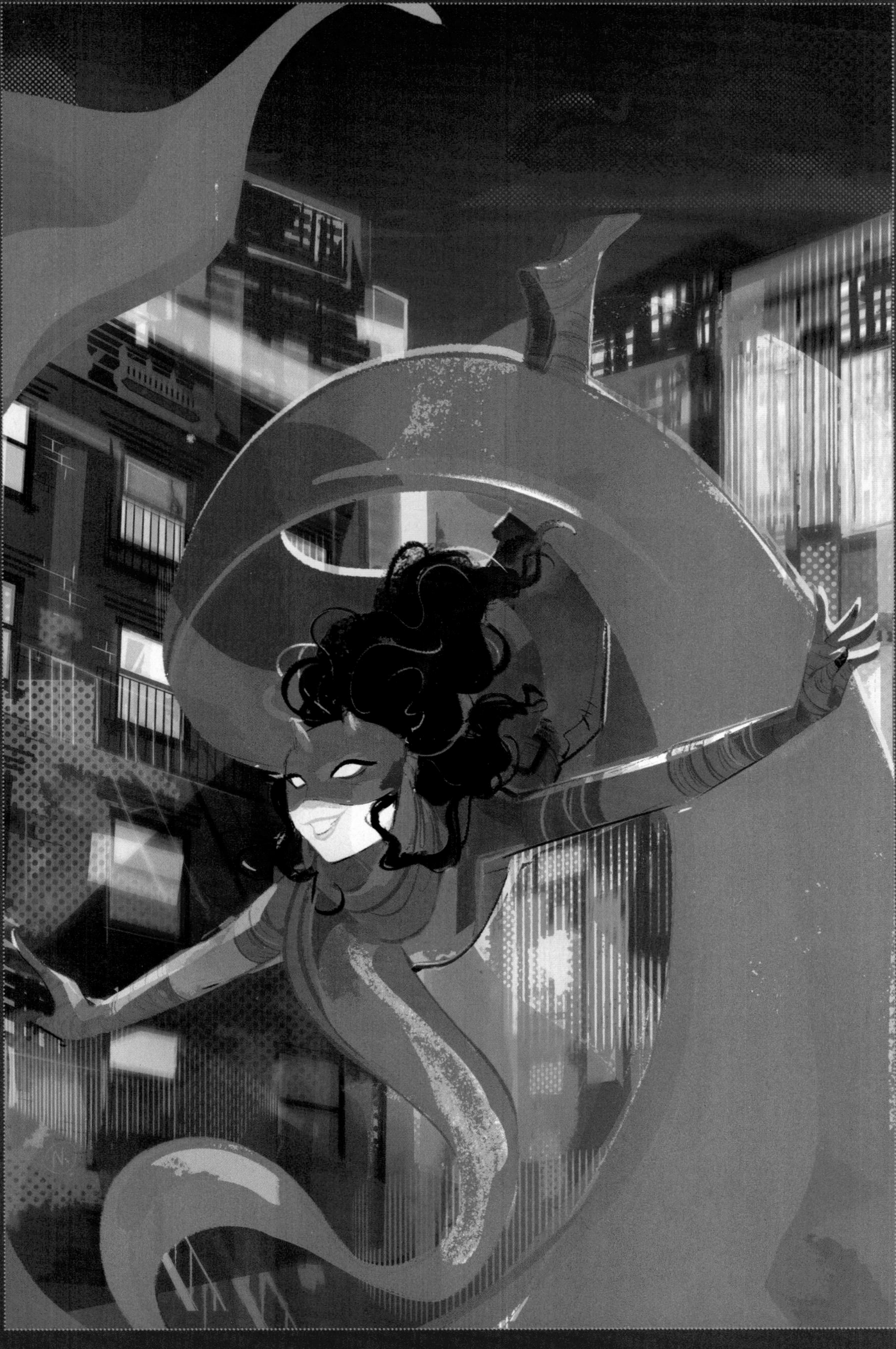

Nicoletta Baldari

#1 VARIANT

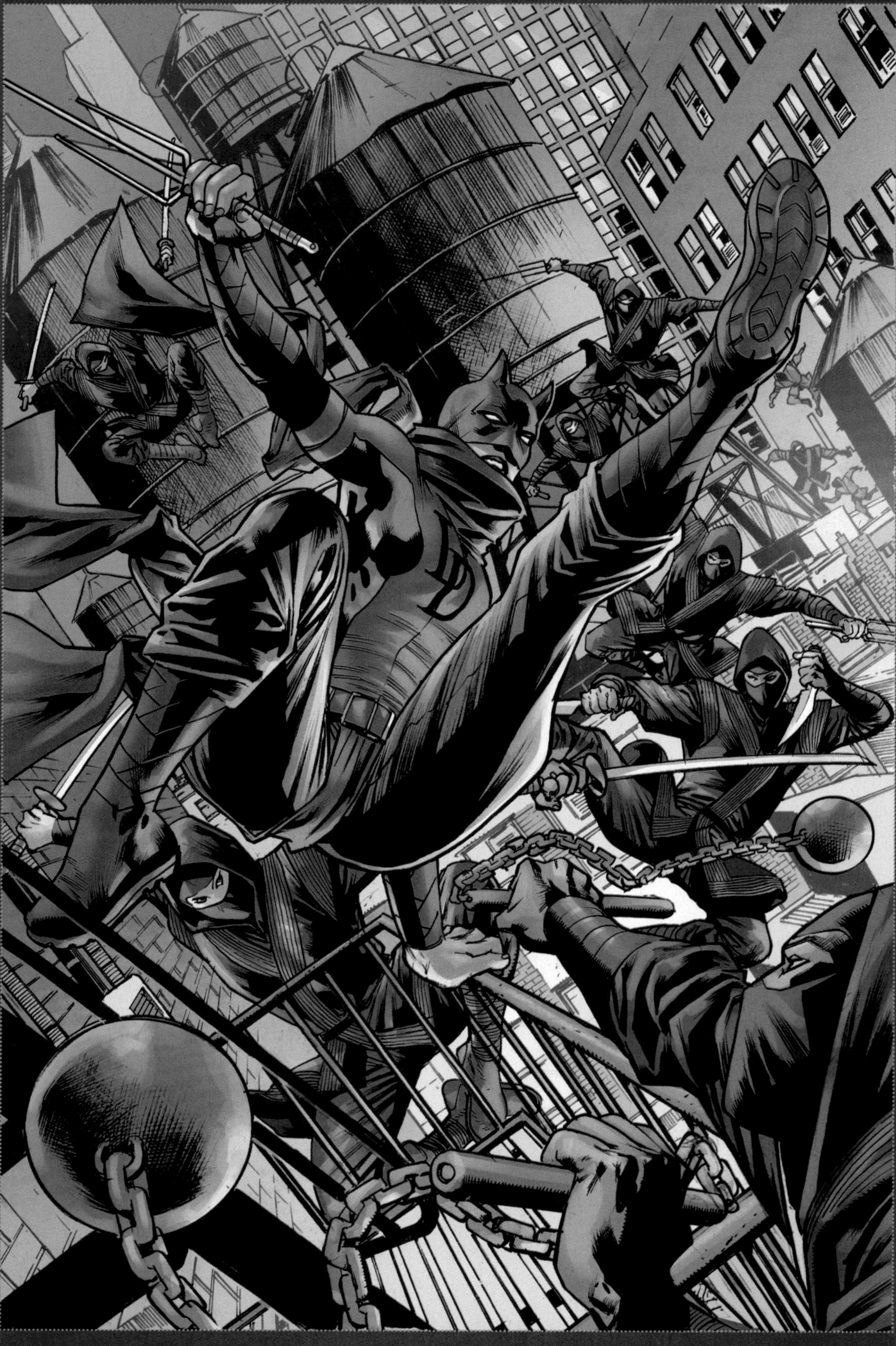

Bryan Hitch & Alex Sinclair

#1 VARIANT

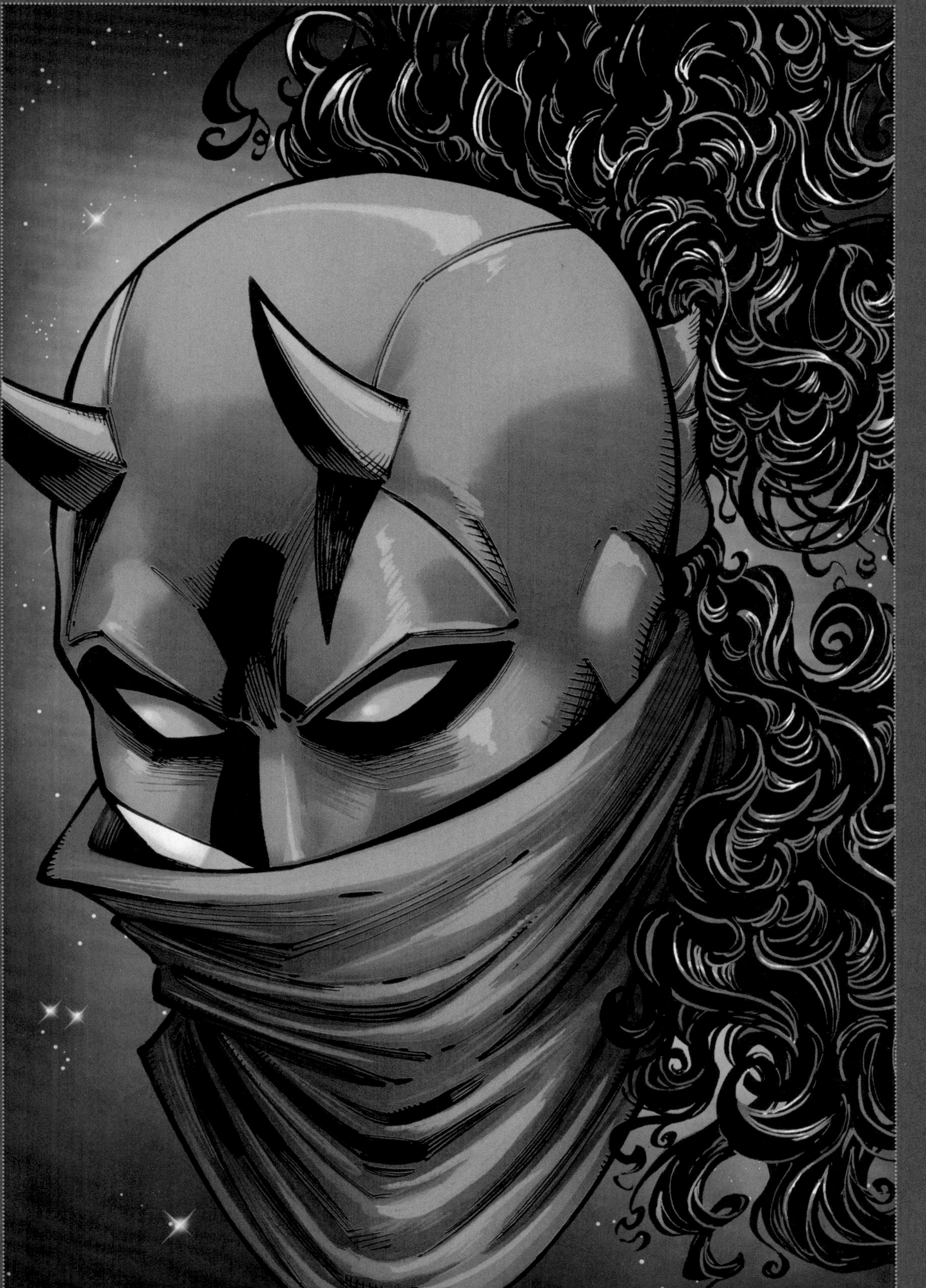

Todd Nauck & Rachelle Rosenberg

#1 HEADSHOT VARIANT

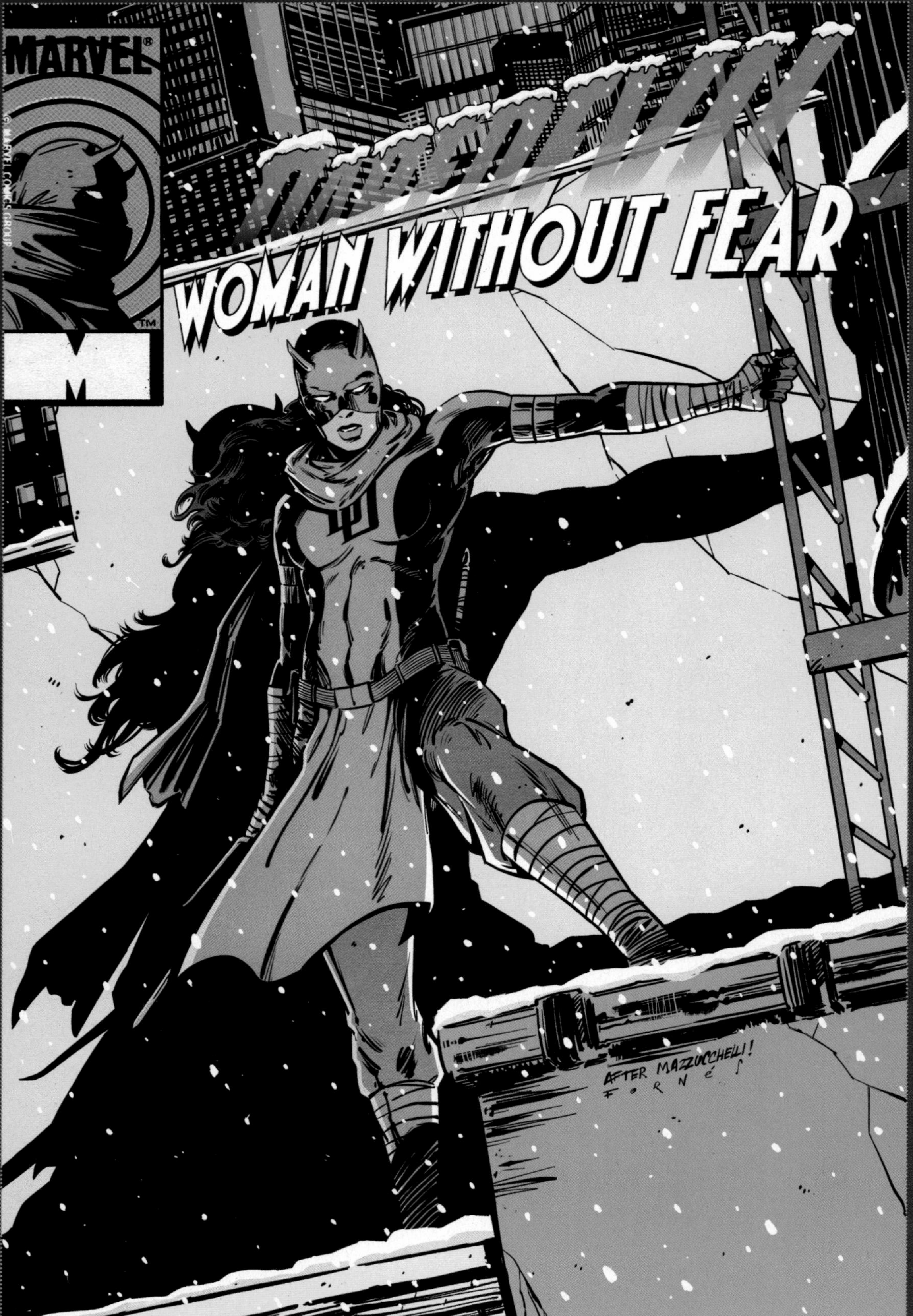
MARVEL
© MARVEL COMICS GROUP
WOMAN WITHOUT FEAR
AFTER MAZZUCCHELLI!
FORNÉS

Jorge Fornés

#2 VARIANT

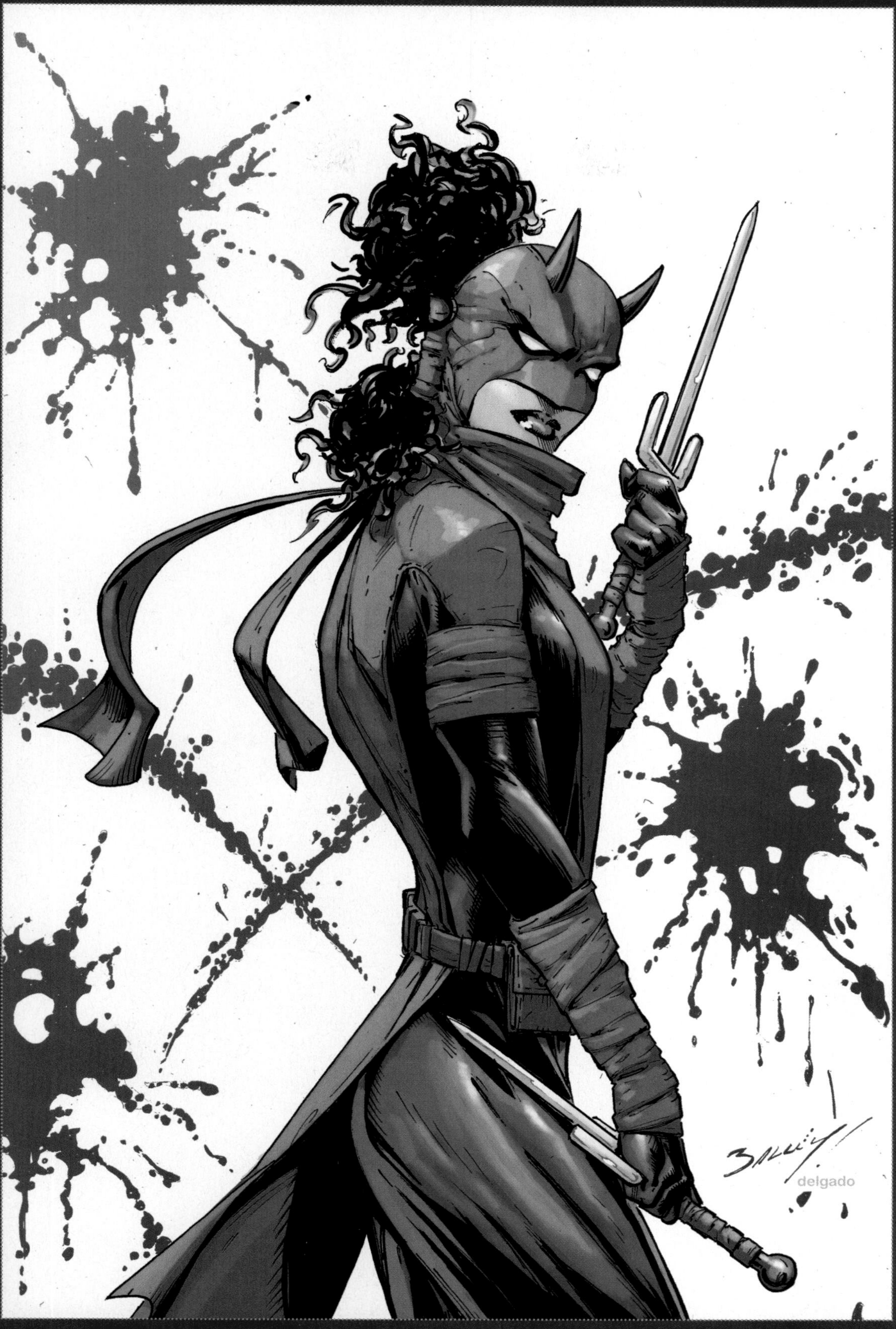
BAGLEY
delgado

Mark Bagley & Edgar Delgado

#2 VARIANT

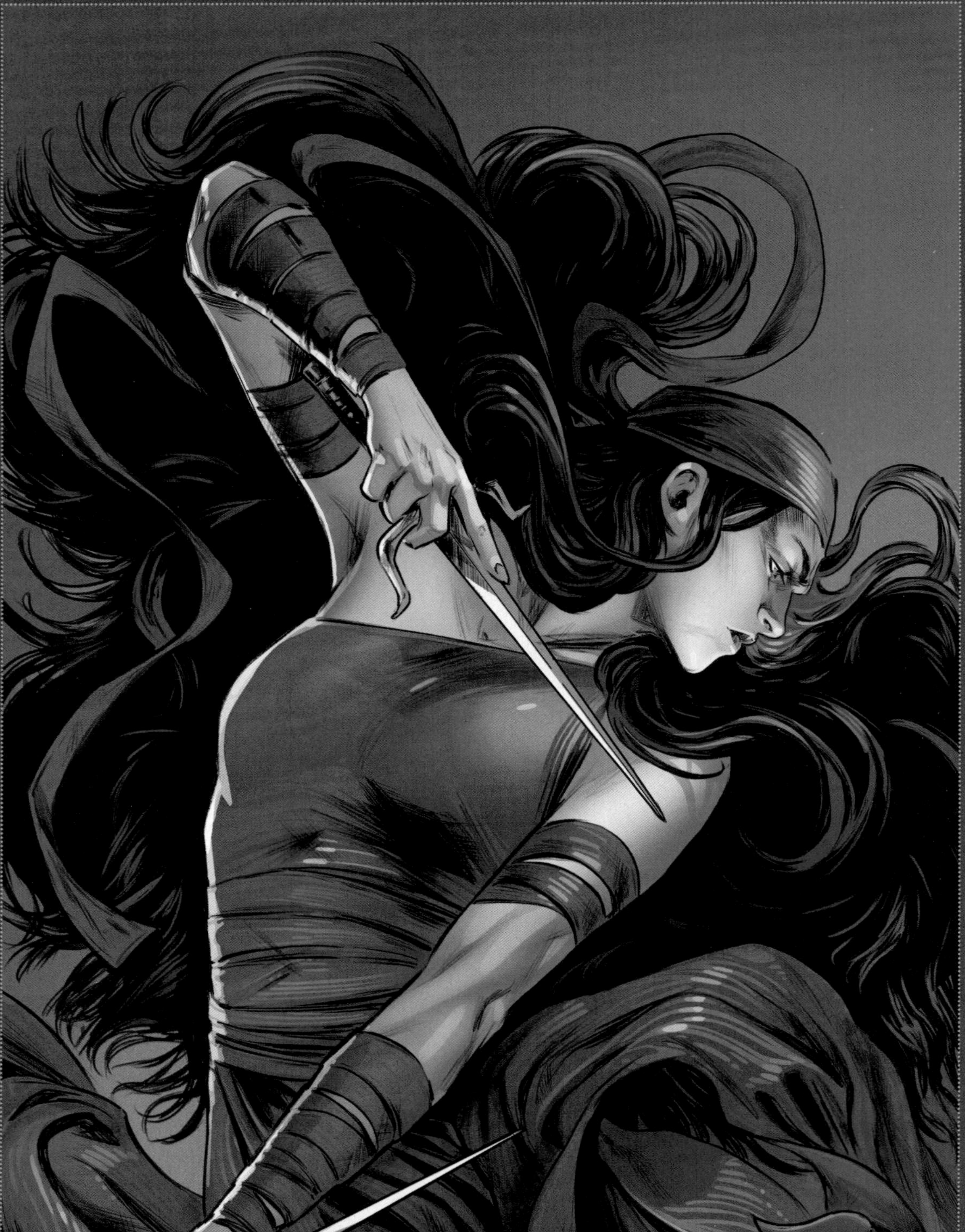

Carmen Carnero

#3 STORMBREAKERS VARIANT

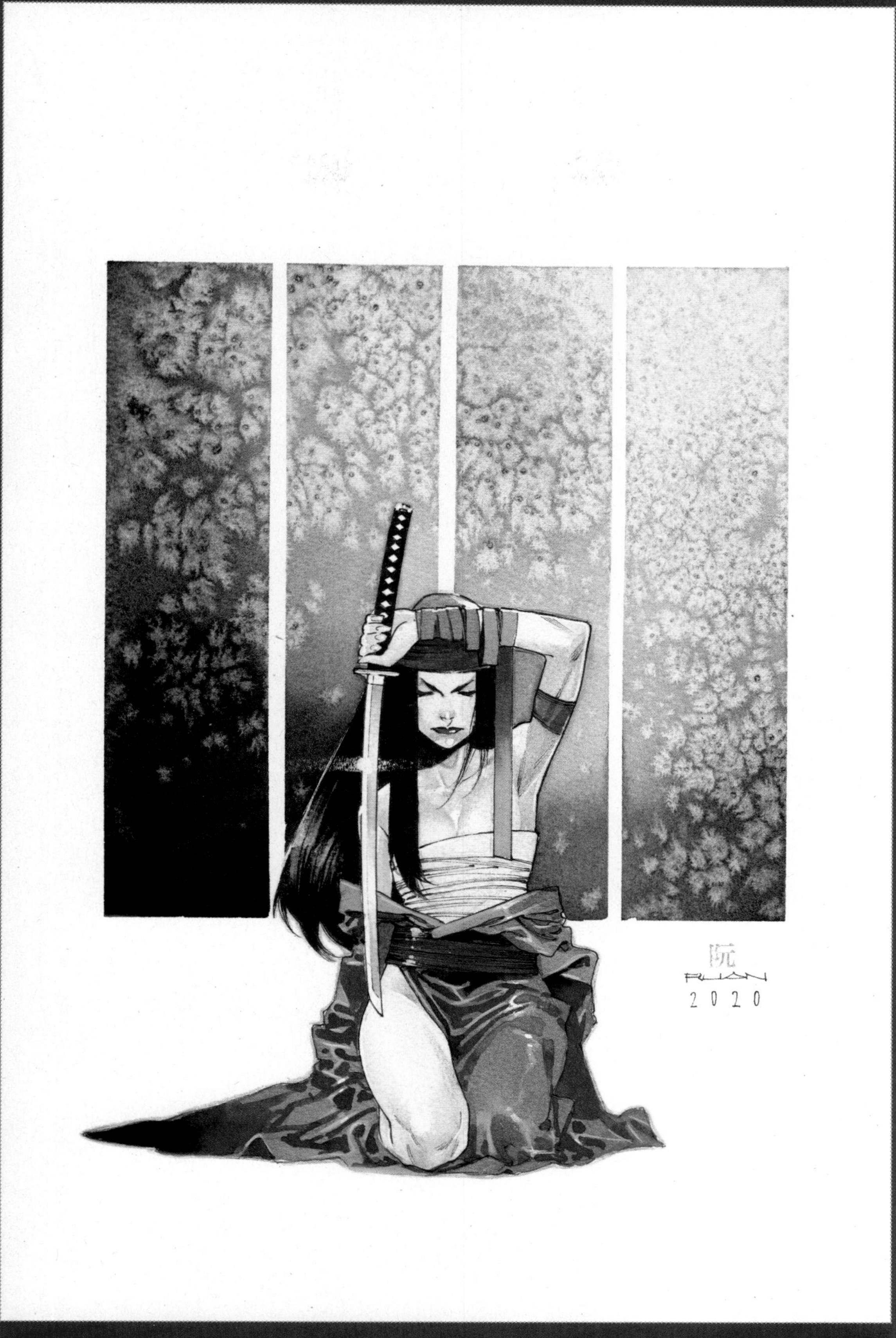
阮
RUAN
2020

Dike Ruan

#100 VARIANT

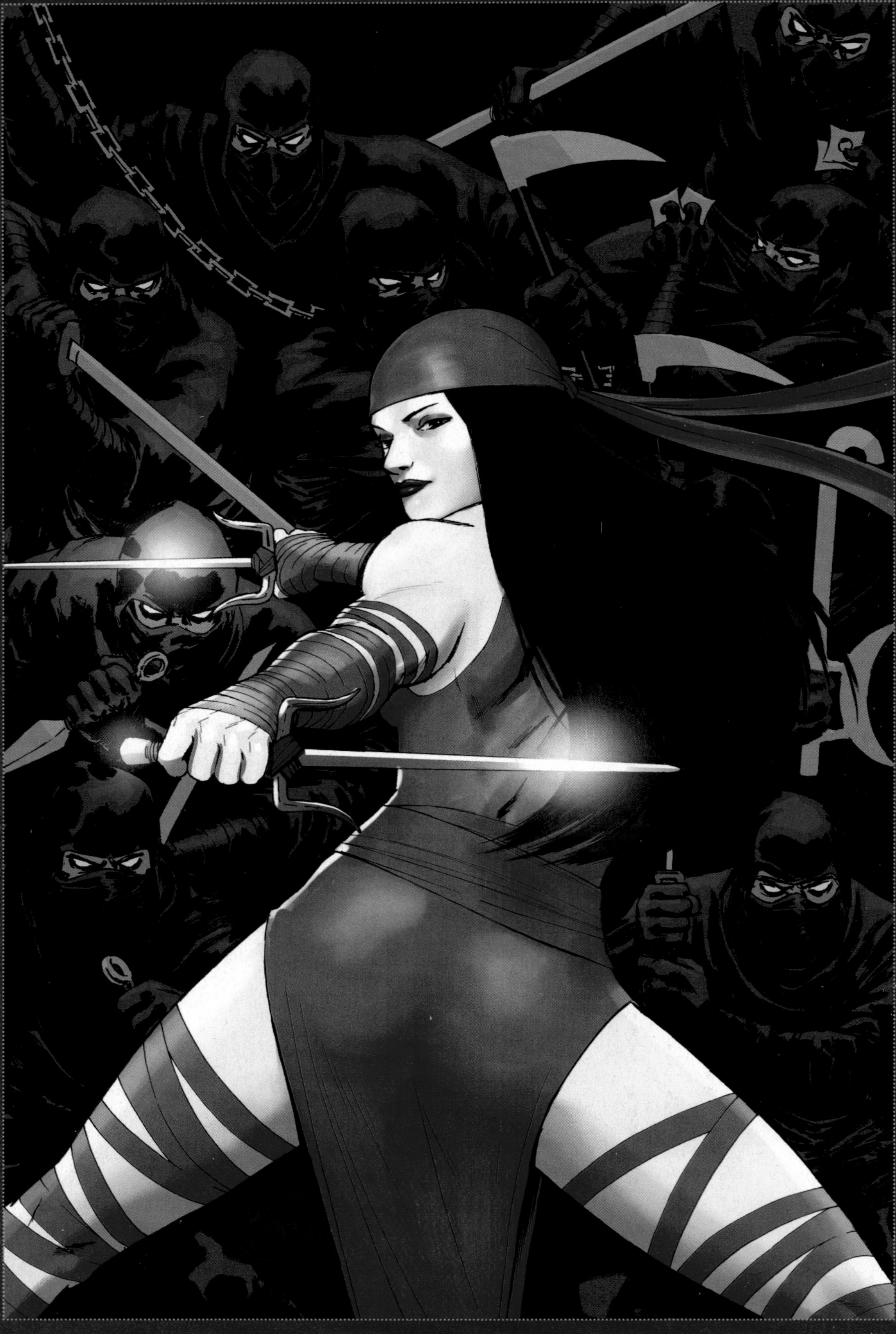

David Lopez

#100 VARIANT